Europe and Nuclear Disarmament

*Debates and Political Attitudes
in 16 European Countries*

EUROPEAN INTERUNIVERSITY PRESS
Brussels
1998

Harald MÜLLER (ed.)

Europe and Nuclear Disarmament

*Debates and Political Attitudes
in 16 European Countries*

Series *"European Policy"*
No.14

OLIN
KZ
5745
E 97
1998
c.2

© Presses Interuniversitaires Européennes – PIE
European Interuniversity Press – EIP, Brussels, 1998
Fax: +32(0)2 640 98 79
E-mail: pie@skynet.be
Website: http://www.pie-eip.com

Cover: Interligne s.a., Brussels

ISBN 90-5201-702-6
D/1998/5678/02

Table of Contents

PREFACE

PRIF's non-proliferation programme is now in its twelfth year. What started as a one-man show has diversified into a research group of nine and an international network comprising colleagues from 16 countries.

What we want is for the Europeans to do a better job as Europeans in this important area of policy – in other words, to act in greater concert and commonality. And we want them to pursue more effective strategies and policies both on non-proliferation and on nuclear disarmament. These are the objectives behind the project – over and above the goals of academic thoroughness and the provision of reliable information.

This is the eighth book that I have had the pleasure to edit or co-edit in the course of the project's twelve years of existence[1]. Once again, I should like to thank all my colleagues for their diligence and co-operation. Katja Frank, Sylvia Meier, and Simone Wisotzki assisted in the research for my own and Alexander Kelle's contributions. Gerard Holden, Margaret Clarke, and Birgit Menigat brought invaluable

---

[1] Harald MÜLLER (ed.), **A Survey of European Nuclear Policy, 1985-87**, Macmillan, London, 1989; Harald MÜLLER & Peter LOMAS (eds), **Western Europe and the Future of the Nuclear Non-Proliferation Treaty**, CEPS in collaboration with PRIF, Brussels, 1989; Harald MÜLLER (ed.), **How Western European Nuclear Policy is Made: Deciding on the Atom,** Macmillan, London, 1991; Harald MÜLLER (ed.), **European Non-proliferation Policy, 1988-1992,** European Interuniversity Press, Brussels, 1993; Harald MÜLLER (ed.), **Nuclear Export Controls in Europe,** European Interuniversity Press, Brussels, 1995; Harald MÜLLER & Janusz PRYSTROM (eds), **Central European Countries and Non-proliferation Regimes,** Polish Foundation for International Affairs, Warsaw, 1996; Harald MÜLLER (ed.), **European Non-proliferation Policy 1993-1995,** European Interuniversity Press, Brussels, 1996.

language-editing skills to bear on the individual chapters. Gudrun Weidner, as usual, guided the enterprise through all its various stages and pulled it all together: without her, the programme could never have been as productive as it has been.

This particular phase of the work was supported by a Volkswagen Foundation grant for research into options for nuclear disarmament. Support was also received from the W. Alton Jones Foundation, the John Merck Fund, the Rockefeller Brothers Fund, and the Plough-shares Fund. Our thanks go to all these sponsors.

The debate about nuclear non-proliferation and disarmament is still dominated to a very large extent by what is happening on the US scene. But it is crucial that the European voice be heard, and our aim is to help ensure this.

Harald Müller
September 1997

INTRODUCTION

Harald Müller

This chapter begins by outlining the evolution of the nuclear weapons issue in Europe from the time of the Cold War to the present and follows this with a summary of the findings of the sixteen country-studies contained in this volume.

1. Nuclear Weapons in Europe during the Cold War

Nuclear weapons have dominated the security system in Europe for forty-five years. In the eyes of the security élites and many others, it was the precarious balance of terror which kept the two blocs from starting another great war on the Continent, and even extended an invisible umbrella over the Western-oriented, though officially neutral, states outside the two alliances[1]. Both sides maintained nuclear arsenals for purposes other than simply deterring nuclear attack by the other party. In the case of NATO, such weapons were also meant to deter conventional attack by what was seen as a vastly superior WTO force. The thousands of tactical nuclear weapons owned by NATO were intended – in the West European view – not only to correct the balance on the battlefield, but also to link the European theatre to the US strategic arsenal, thereby creating a "seamless web" of deterrence, from the first shot at the border to an intercontinental

---

[1] John Lewis Gaddis, **The Long Peace**, New York, 1987; John J. Mearsheimer, *"Back to the Future: Instability in Europe after the Cold War"*, in: **International Security**, Vol.15 No.1, 1990, pp.5-56.

exchange. The United States, in contrast, viewed tactical nuclear weapons as providing a firebreak that could be used to bring hostilities to an end **before** nuclear war touched the American continent. This difference of interpretation was a source of continuous tension in the alliance, but was never grave enough to lead to an existential crisis[2].

In the case of the Soviet Union, nuclear weapons were seen as a means of achieving early superiority in a war triggered by NATO. The mass use of tactical nuclear weapons would disable NATO's defence forces – notably command and communications, airfields, and nuclear-weapons storage sites. The preconditions would then be created for a well-planned and rapid advance of victorious WTO tank and mechanized forces that would breach whatever resistance remained; meanwhile, Soviet strategic nuclear forces would deter the United States from escalating the conflict to the intercontinental level. The Soviet no-first-use doctrine was purely a propaganda ploy, not backed by any actual war plans – as is clear from documents found after the fall of the Wall: the Soviet leadership believed that the only kind of war that was winnable was a short, decisive one, and that such a war would prevent cracks forming within the WTO and spare the Soviet Union more of the kind of devastation it had experienced in two world wars.

Nuclear weapons were thus firmly embedded in the defence postures, doctrines, and strategic cultures of both sides. As long as the East-West conflict continued, this could not be otherwise. Nuclear arms control was undoubtedly able to contain the risks posed by unstable postures and the dangers of escalation associated with these; but it could not bring the nuclear confrontation itself to an end, nor enable the partners in rivalry to embark on a credible and effective path to nuclear disarmament. Sudden advances in nuclear arms control would cause consternation amongst America's European allies, and at least some sections of their élites would become concerned that the nuclear umbrella might be withdrawn. Conversely, tough talking and policies of increased armament on the part of Washington would engender similarly strong feelings, this time along the lines that American "cowboys" might draw their hapless partners into a devastating nuclear showdown. This basic dilemma in the alliance's nuclear policy

---

[2] David N. SCHWARTZ, **NATO's Nuclear Dilemmas**, Brookings, Washington, 1983.

was never really resolved, though it was quite successfully papered-over until the disappearance of the enemy who was its *raison d'être*[3].

2. The Changes since 1989

All that was in the past. The *annus mirabilis* of 1989 changed everything. The WTO collapsed, Eastern Europe turned to democracy, Soviet troops withdrew beyond the Bug, and finally the Soviet Union itself dissolved into its constituent republics. Russia, the largest product of this fission and the heir to the major portion of the former Soviet Union's military assets – including all its nuclear arms – turned out to be far too weak to present any serious threat. Anyone inclined to see Russia as an identical replacement of the USSR in terms of military threat must have been brought to their senses by the Russian performance in Chechnia. Since then, the state of the Russian armed forces has, if anything, further deteriorated, as a result of the financial crisis. To put it baldly: there is no longer any conventional military threat against which a nuclear insurance would be necessary[4].

On the contrary, the Western alliance is now the vastly superior force on the Old Continent, both quantitatively and – to an even greater extent – qualitatively. Enlargement can only enhance its ascendancy, at least in quantitative terms. Even with some modifications to the CFE Treaty, the combined forces entering the alliance during the first wave of accessions will be equivalent in size to the German Bundeswehr – a fact that can only aggravate what the Russian military leadership sees as a serious threat to its country's national security. Thus, in a curious shift of positions, Russia has adopted a stance corresponding to NATO's old policy of flexible response, or indeed to the even older doctrine of massive retaliation, in which nuclear weapons – not least the tactical versions – appeared to be the only means by which a superior conventional assault could be countered, and thus also deterred. The shift that occurred in 1993, away from a (spurious) no-first-use to

---

[3] This dilemma has been subjected to close scrutiny by Glenn SNYDER in *"The Security Dilemma in Alliance Politics"*, in: **World Politics**, Vol.36 No.4, 1984, pp.461-95.

[4] Stephen M. MEYER, *"The Devolution of Russian Military Power"*, in: **Current History**, 94/594, Oct. 1995, pp.322-8.

a first-use doctrine, is today firmly enshrined in Russian risk-assessment[5]. This is one more reason why we should be sceptical in regard to suggestions that we should leap into a non-nuclear world in a single bound. A change in the present Russian attachment to nuclear deterrence will require a major alteration in Russia's perception of its security situation; this in turn will only come after the European security order has been altered in such a way as to convince the Russian élite that the West, rather than being a threat to its huge Eurasian counterpart, is in fact a well-disposed partner. Needless to say, such a change will take time.

Russia's stance notwithstanding, there is no reason why NATO itself should stick to the old thinking on nuclear weapons. Given its position of conventional superiority, the strategic need for first use has disappeared. So has the rationale for forward deployment. Since the nuclear guarantee was thought to secure the European allies against all forms of aggression, not just the nuclear kind, it seemed necessary, both as a practical mechanism and for symbolic purposes, to have an intermeshing of conventional and nuclear forces and of American and European ground and air forces (with nuclear roles for the latter). Today, all these perceived necessities (contested even then) have obviously disappeared. Tactical nuclear weapons could be withdrawn to the United States, and European armed forces could lose their nuclear roles, with no detriment to European security. Anyone who currently believes that the cohesion of the Atlantic alliance hinges on the continued symbolism of yesteryear holds alliance cohesion in very low regard indeed.

Given the rapid development of conventional weapons technology – notably, the achievement of near-perfect precision and of high levels of efficiency, as well as the incorporation of stealth-related features – it seems reasonable to assume that convincing conventional options will ultimately be available to counter the threat of use, or, if it comes to it, the actual use, of other weapons of mass destruction. The assumption that the new mission for nuclear arms is to deter the use of chemical and biological weapons – a mission that just happened to emerge as the "evil empire" went into decline – thus appears to be

---

[5] Yuri FYODOROV, *"Prospects and Conflicts of Russian Nuclear Deterrence"*, in: **Yaderni Kontrol**, No.1, Spring 1996, pp.12-15.

mistaken. As a consequence, NATO's insistence on a first-use option – however remote and "last resort" it may be – conveys a stark message to the rest of the world that nuclear weapons are indispensable whatever the circumstances. Since NATO is the strongest military alliance in the world, with the best-developed conventional technology and a more than favourable geostrategic environment, how can any hapless government ruling a country in a far less favourable security region – and one in which the use of chemical and biological weapons is a real possibility – be expected to comprehend that it ought to forgo nuclear weapons?

The whole fabric of traditional thinking on nuclear weapons is thus justifiably under siege. In contrast with this intellectual questioning, practical nuclear weapons policy is still astonishingly conservative. It is true that unprecedented reductions have been achieved, and that more are likely to come; it is also true that, step by step, nuclear-weapon states are moving towards a degree of transparency greater than one could ever have dreamt of even five years ago – albeit with clear misgivings on the part of certain groups in these countries. And yet a revolution in thinking on nuclear weapons of a kind that would correspond to the revolution in the security situation has not yet happened. It is largely left to creative NGO projects to explore the possibilities that the new world situation has opened up for nuclear disarmament. Political officialdom apparently feels much more secure sticking to the traditional ways[6].

3. The Aims of the Study

This comparative study is part of a PRIF project on European non-proliferation policy that has now been running for ten years. The project

---

[6] Joseph ROTBLAT *et al.* (eds), **A Nuclear-Weapons Free World: Desirable? Feasible?**, Westview, Boulder, 1993; Regina COWEN KARP, **Security without Nuclear Weapons? Different Perspectives in Nonnuclear Security**, Oxford University Press, Oxford, 1992; The Henry L. Stimson Center, *Beyond the Nuclear Peril: The Year in Review and Years Ahead*, Report of the Steering Committee, Project on Eliminating Weapons of Mass Destruction, Report No.15, Washington D.C., Jan. 1995; The Henry L. Stimson Center, *An Evolving US Nuclear Posture*, Second Report of the Steering Committee, Project on Eliminating Weapons of Mass Destruction, Report No.19, Washington D.C., Dec. 1995. A good overview of the debate can be found in the **Washington Quarterly**, No.20/3, Summer 1997.

has two academic and two practical aims. Academically, it seeks, first, to give as precise an account as possible of a specific area of European Common Foreign and Security Policy: most accounts of CFSP, and of its predecessor, European Political Co-operation (EPC), only scratch the surface of documented policy – in other words, the papers put out by the Council, Commission, and European Parliament. But these are merely the visible 10 per cent of the iceberg: the bulk of the work on CFSP is conducted in committee and very rarely in public. Hence, one of the particular merits of this project is that it gives a continuous account of what is happening in this subfield of CFSP[7]. The second academic purpose is that of elucidating and comparing the national policies of member states and associated countries keen to accede to the EU at the earliest possible date, and of discovering how these national policies relate to the joint policies being pursued under the CFSP umbrella. With regard to the two practical purposes, these are: first, to help develop a more distinctively European approach to non-proliferation and disarmament, as opposed to a variety of national ones; and, secondly, to help elaborate more effective and promising strategies both for non-proliferation and for disarmament.

The project works on the assumption that non-proliferation and disarmament are closely linked. This link was strongly reaffirmed in the "Principles and Objectives" adopted by the 1995 NPT Review and Extension Conference as part of the decision to extend the treaty indefinitely. In these, the parties laid great stress on nuclear disarmament and defined the complete elimination of nuclear weapons as their unequivocal and overriding objective.

As might be expected, nuclear disarmament is a field of policy where there have traditionally been considerable gaps between the

---

[7] For a summary of the results of this work, see Harald MÜLLER, *"West European Cooperation on Nuclear Proliferation"*, in: Reinhart RUMMEL (ed.), **Toward Political Union: Planning a Common Foreign and Security Policy in the European Community**, Nomos, Baden-Baden, 1992, pp.191-210 (in the series *"Aktuelle Materialien zur Internationalen Politik"* pub. by Stiftung Wissenschaft und Politik); Alain MICHEL & Harald MÜLLER, *"The European Union"*, in: Harald MÜLLER (ed.), **European Non-proliferation Policy 1993-1995**, European Interuniversity Press, Brussels, 1996, pp.25-46; Harald MÜLLER & Lars VAN DASSEN, *"From Cacophony to Joint Action: Successes and Shortcomings of European Nuclear Non-proliferation Policy"*, in: Martin HOLLAND (ed.), **Common Foreign and Security Policy: The Record and Reforms**, Pinter, London/Washington, 1997, pp.52-72.

positions of the various European countries. There have been major differences of interest between: nuclear-weapon states, non-nuclear-weapon members of NATO, and non-nuclear non-members of NATO; NATO members with particular worries about the former Soviet threat and geographically more distant or relaxed members; and, finally, those with nuclear weapons on their soil and those that were nuclear-free. Pursuing a common foreign policy was thus a difficult task; and this was clearly revealed in the deep differences that emerged over Article VI of the NPT during the review part of the 1995 Review and Extension Conference[8].

The purpose of our study was therefore to examine thinking in the member states, and in certain associated prospective member states, of the EU, with a view to discovering how nuclear disarmament was regarded by the governments, élites, and populations in those countries. Of course, nuclear disarmament is not just some lofty abstract goal: it is related to thinking on national security, alliance interests, and the threats a country is facing. Moreover, it will probably proceed via numerous steps, and responses to these steps may reflect deeper-seated attitudes towards nuclear disarmament as such[9].

For these reasons, our country researchers were asked to analyse the respective security situations, threats, role of nuclear weapons in security policy, and relation of national security to alliance policies. They were also asked to examine attitudes to the immediate tasks relating to nuclear arms control and disarmament – in other words, measures such as the CTBT, a cut-off convention on the production of fissile materials for weapons purposes, and START II and III. They were also to look into views on more exotic proposals, such as a nuclear-weapon-free zone in Central Europe, the option of no first use, and a ban on the deployment of nuclear weapons outside NWS territory. Finally, they were asked to gauge the view of the public and of officialdom on the

---

[8] See Harald MÜLLER, *"European Nuclear Non-proliferation after the NPT Extension: Achievements, Shortcomings and Needs"*, in: Paul CORNISH, Peter VAN HAM & Joachim KRAUSE (eds), **Europe and the Challenge of Proliferation**, WEU Institute for Security Studies, Chaillot Papers No.24, Paris, 1996, pp.33-54; also Harald MÜLLER & David FISCHER, **United Divided: The Europeans and the NPT Extension Conference**, PRIF Report No.40, Frankfurt/M., 1995.

[9] See Harald MÜLLER, *"Far-Reaching Nuclear Disarmament"*, in: **UNIDIR Newsletter**, No.31, 1995, pp.31-8.

prospects of a non-nuclear world and on various proposals for bringing this about – for example, a nuclear weapon convention. The following section presents a comparative summary of the findings.

4. The Findings

4.1. Whence Danger to Europe?
Threat Assessment in the Post-Cold-War Period

The positions adopted towards nuclear disarmament are part and parcel of national security policy. They are related to the role nuclear weapons continue, or do not continue, to play in deterrence in an alliance-based or (as in the case of France and Britain) a national context. This role, in turn, relates to the threats the countries perceive themselves as facing. After the end of the East-West conflict, the dissolution of the Soviet Union, and the retreat of Russian troops behind national borders, all the governments concerned feel that their security has been enhanced; but the extent of this feeling of reassurance varies greatly.

The gain in security is felt most keenly in countries in the west of Europe. In Germany, Belgium, and the Netherlands, "uncertainty" was cited as the main security concern. Since this is a basic human condition, one may conclude that these countries are as secure as it is possible to be. In the Netherlands, the risk of a rogue state acquiring weapons of mass destruction was mentioned. This risk looms much larger for the southern countries – Italy and Spain – and France and Britain also share this concern, but add to it the residual risks arising from Russia's vast remaining nuclear arsenal. The marked concern about regional crises and the possibility of a confrontation with a rogue state armed with weapons of mass destruction reflects the broader security perspective taken by these former colonial powers and current permanent members of the UN Security Council.

The countries on NATO's northern and southern flanks – Norway, Greece, and Turkey – still keep a watchful eye on Russia. They concede that it currently presents no direct threat, but its potential strength – and, needless to say, its nuclear weaponry – still cause some nervousness, even though the countries concerned all hasten to add that of course Russia is not an enemy. Greece and Turkey also point to the risks arising from the situation in the Middle East, and Turkey keeps a close watch on the course of the conflicts in the Caucasus. Curiously but not unexpectedly, Greece ranks high on Turkey's list of security concerns, and Turkey on Greece's.

In the four former WTO members, and in neutral Austria, the official view, again, is that Russia presents no threat; but all worry that there could be a reversal of a kind that might give Russian revisionism greater prominence.

4.2. The Role of Nuclear Deterrence

One might have supposed that the drastically changed security situation would lead to a fundamental re-evaluation of the role of nuclear weapons. But this has not been the case. In all the countries that are either current or prospective members of NATO, nuclear weapons are seen as providing a vague, generalized, residual, minimum form of deterrence against undefined risks. Some interviewees also mentioned the ultimate assurance such weapons provide against renewed Russian ascendancy. Others pointed more to the south, claiming that nuclear weapons could help provide security against those who already possess or are seeking to acquire weapons of mass destruction. That said, there is some doubt (for example, in Belgium and Greece) that there can be any effective form of deterrence against irrational leaders, and that nuclear weapons can be of any use at all against the new threats that now exist. There does, however, appear, in principle, to be a vague consensus that, for the time being at least, it is no bad thing to have a few nuclear weapons around. There is little difference of attitude between established and prospective NATO members, and the latter tend to follow alliance leadership unhesitatingly.

Not surprisingly, the feeling of a need for residual deterrence is strongest in the two nuclear-weapon states. Although both have trimmed their nuclear arsenals and put greater emphasis on conventional forces, they insist on the continued usefulness of the deterrent – even against an as yet unidentified enemy. France sticks to the old distinction between a "final warning" and the devastation of a full strategic strike visited on any aggressor who refuses to be warned. Interestingly, both France and the UK reject the idea of nuclear counterproliferation, in the sense of a pre-emptive use of nuclear weapons against another state's reserves of weapons of mass destruction.

Conversely, and equally unsurprisingly, the belief in residual deterrence is least strong in the two neutral countries. Sweden now acknowledges – or has realized – that throughout the Cold War it was covered by NATO's nuclear umbrella; yet there is no great love lost there for nuclear deterrence. It continues to be either a non-topic of conversation or, to many, a dirty word. In Austria, there is some controversy between diplomats and defence people over the use of deterrence. Given the deep-seated aversion of the Austrian public to anything nuclear, it is unlikely that any government in Vienna could officially espouse even minimum deterrence without provoking a public outcry.

4.3. The Domestic Debate on Nuclear Deterrence

The idea that huge numbers of people could concern themselves with nuclear arms and disarmament is by no means an alien one in Europe: in the fifties, and again in the eighties, millions of people took to the streets to protest against the deployment of certain weapons in their countries. Between these bouts of activity, there were periods of relative calm. As regards the present, it is fair to say we find ourselves in a "nuclear lull". The eyes of the public and politicians are focused on other issues: the economic situation, unemployment, and reforms to the welfare state intended to revive the economy currently dominate the political debate. Foreign policy has undoubtedly lost its primacy, and violent conflicts that bring influxes of refugees and asylum-seekers loom much larger than questions of arms control and disarmament. It is safe to assume that the élites and the general public are, on the whole, agreed that nuclear arms control should continue; but this goal is not pursued with any great vigour. In the special bodies charged with looking into this issue, the situation is, of course, different; but the public, the mass media, and the general run of politicians show little interest in it.

As a consequence, there is, in most countries, an absence of serious domestic debate. In autumn 1995, there was a brief upsurge in the discussion, as a result of the French nuclear tests. There were parliamentary debates about, and government condemnations of, the French decision (or explanations as to why such condemnations were not forthcoming). Practically all the EU states engaged in this type of debate. In addition, there was a highly publicized discussion at the European level, involving the Council, the Commission, and, on several occasions, the European Parliament. In some cases, this was followed by a short period of demonstrations and boycotts of French products such as cheese and champagne. Significantly, much of the protest was motivated by a concern not with disarmament, but with the environment, echoing the initial motives for the late-fifties popular opposition to atmospheric testing, which ultimately led to the conclusion of the Partial Test Ban Treaty. After the last French test, attention waned.

In fact, civilian nuclear issues are debated much more earnestly and vigorously than disarmament. Whether it be the Austrian opposition to the Bohunice and Temelin nuclear power plants in the Czech Republic, or the Greek (and Bulgarian) concerns about the Kozlodui power plant in Bulgaria (rated by many experts as the least safe reactor in Europe), or the German anti-nuclear demonstrations against the transport of Castor radwaste containers, the opponents of nuclear energy have been much more successful in mobilizing mass opinion than have the campaigners for nuclear disarmament: the latter's attempts to direct the public's attention to the few hundred US bombs left in Western Europe aroused virtually no response.

Substantive debate has thus remained confined to:

- Defence ministries and arms control departments; but these were concerned either to maintain the alliance line, or, in the case of newly acceding states, to secure entry to NATO. This preoccupation precluded almost all in-depth treatment of the issues involved in nuclear disarmament.
- Non-governmental abolitionists, who want the new security situation to be exploited to secure far-reaching nuclear disarmament, eventually leading to a nuclear-weapon-free world. But those who hold this view are few, and are by and large not taken seriously by governments. Nor do they exert any tangible influence on public opinion.

Sweden constitutes something of an exception. A low-key disarmament discourse has been taking place there between NGO disarmament groups (which are quite influential), the parliamentary standing committee on foreign affairs, and the specialized disarmament sections in the foreign ministry. In parliament at large, however, and amongst the wider public, the situation was not markedly different from that observed in most of the other countries.

4.4. The Role of the Atlantic Alliance

Relationship to the Atlantic alliance is the defining perspective from which security issues in general and the nuclear question in particular are viewed by the countries concerned. This is true even of those which, by tradition and by virtue of their legal position, have maintained a degree of distance from NATO: in Sweden and Austria, for example, a discussion has begun about the viability of neutral status after the end of the Cold War – and indeed, deciding between what parties neutrality is now supposed to obtain is problematic. The obvious solution for both countries would be to join NATO. This option is still felt to run counter to the tradition of neutrality, but the taboo has been considerably weakened. As a consequence, both countries are entertaining some of the more exotic notions for nuclear disarmament (see below) with more flexibility and interest than most of the other states, but there is not much readiness to confront alliance positions head-on or with any great vigour. Typically, Sweden's initial opposition to Baltic membership of NATO has given way to measured support for its neighbours' aspirations.

For those countries wishing to accede to NATO – Poland, Hungary, the Czech Republic, and Bulgaria – NATO positions virtually dictate national policy, and NATO membership is seen as the precondition for future national security. As a consequence, these countries try their best to avoid stances that could alienate the alliance or its major members, and this severely restricts their readiness to assume a high national profile on nuclear disarmament.

NATO members who had taken up special positions in the past have now moved closer to the mainstream. Spain is actively considering full reintegration into the military structure, and it is only the

Gibraltar issue that stands in the way of a final decision on this. France has also moved closer to military integration, but this development has been halted by the dispute over the Naples command and by the more markedly anti-American stance of the new government. That said, in nuclear matters, France is not too unhappy about the control that NATO exerts over its potentially more maverick members. Finally, Greece, which under Andreas Papandreou was NATO's odd-man-out, now has renounced its previous, almost hostile attitude towards the alliance and is much more trying to keep in line with alliance politics.

For all European members of NATO, membership of the alliance has an undoubted bearing on their position in regard to disarmament. None wishes to deviate too far from the NATO line, or from a line compatible with the policies of the latter or of its major members – notably the United States. The kinds of policy initiatives that can be expected from the European countries are thus severely circumscribed. EU membership produces a similar effect of solidarity, though to a lesser degree: the reactions of Spain, Greece, Germany, and Belgium to French testing, for example, were more low-key than one might have expected. The perceived need to avoid too sharp a critique of a fellow EU member was one of the major motives here.

4.5. NATO Enlargement and the Nuclear Issue

The whole nuclear issue is being largely overshadowed by NATO expansion. This emerges very clearly from the reactions to the proposed creation of a nuclear-weapon-free zone in Central and Eastern Europe. The idea for such a zone dates back to the fifties, when it was known as the "Rapacki Plan", after the then Polish minister of foreign affairs. The purpose of the plan was, of course, to prevent the deployment of tactical nuclear weapons in Western Europe, and particularly in Germany, thereby perpetuating the conventional superiority of Soviet and WTO forces in this region. For this reason, it was ruled out by NATO and its member states. Today, however, the situation is very different, with NATO fielding by far the strongest conventional forces and enjoying unchallenged superiority. Despite this, there was no reconsideration of the merits of this proposal when it was put forward by Belarus, evidently with Russian consent, during the 1995 NPT Review and Extension Conference. Instead, it was summarily rejected.

Prospective NATO members are willing to accept nuclear weapons on their territory if this will secure them admission to the alliance. But by and large, there is little enthusiasm for such a prospect, and most of the population in the countries concerned appear to be opposed to it. In fact, had the alliance not decided on the three "nos" – no reason, no intention, and no plan to change the present nuclear posture – the growing debate about deployment could well have turned the public in several, or indeed all, prospective member states against NATO membership. However, the political élites are not willing to set a binding legal seal on the non-deployment position, because they fear this might result in their countries' being accorded a diminished status, or being turned once more into a "buffer" between the major powers – a prospect they abhor. A small number even hold the erroneous belief – obviously through lack of information – that without nuclear deployment, the security guarantee contained in the Washington Treaty would not apply with the same force.

NATO's established members, for their part, argue that they are in a difficult position, because prospective members want tangible nuclear guarantees without reduced membership. They therefore believe it is impossible to agree to the Belorussian proposal for negotiations on a nuclear-weapon-free zone, as such an arrangement would confer a special status on the new members, setting them apart from their alliance partners against their own will. We thus have the curious situation of prospective members being opposed to such a zone because they believe established members would then deal with them in a discriminatory, second-class way, while established members are unwilling to agree to the zone on the grounds that prospective members reject this option. In the study, a distinct position was adopted by members of the Italian, Turkish, and Belgian élites, who argued that, as new members would be entitled to a full share in the guarantees, they should also fully share the risks by at least allowing the option of deployment. Curiously, while many political leaders in prospective member states view a legal non-nuclear status as a serious disadvantage, respondents in these countries regard it as an undeserved privilege!

The declared willingness of future members to accommodate nuclear weapons is not without risk as far as popular sympathy for NATO is concerned. Public opinion polls in the prospective member states show that approval of NATO membership plummets if such membership entails an obligation to deploy nuclear weapons at home. Even more dramatically: if Russia responded with deployments of its own, it is not unlikely that this renewed nuclear confrontation would reawaken opposition in some West European countries not only to nuclear weapons, but the Western alliance as such. The three "nos" were therefore not just a NATO favour to Russia: this position was adopted very much in NATO's own interest.

Despite all this, it is by no means clear that the creation of a nuclear-weapon-free zone in Central Eastern Europe would be to the strategic disadvantage of either NATO or its new members. Whether or not it would depends very much on the size of the zone and the specific provisions of the treaty enshrining it. If, for example, the zone encompassed Sweden, Finland, the Baltic states, Belarus, the Ukraine, Poland, Hungary, eastern Germany (already rendered nuclear-weapon-free by the "Two plus Four" treaty), the Czech Republic, Slovakia, Bulgaria, Romania, the Kaliningrad Oblast, and a strip extending, say, 200 km east of Russia's western border, this would preclude the Russian Federation's deploying nuclear weapons in the immediate neighbourhood of potential new NATO members, thereby avoiding the kind of situation that was obtained during the Cold War, when both alliances had tactical nuclear weapons deployed literally within sight of each other. If, in addition, the validity of such a treaty were made contingent on the observance of other accords – such as the CFE Treaty, the Vienna documents, and the Paris Charter – then NATO would be authorized to bring nuclear weapons forward when a threat arose: in order for the necessary concentration of forces to be assembled in forward areas for an attack, these various agreements would have to be breached. It is reasonable to assume that the security of all, not just of Russia, would be well served by such a web of agreements. However, NATO has opted to make unilateral concessions on nuclear deployment – in the form of the three "nos" mentioned above – without any input from Russia, because it prefers politically binding rather than legally binding agreements. Everyone must judge for themselves the wisdom of such a policy.

The NATO-Russian Founding Act has clearly laid this issue to rest for a while. It now appears that nuclear deployment, at least, will not place added strains on Western-Russian relations, on top of the tensions created by NATO enlargement as such. However, the great preoccupation with enlargement and its consequences has actually pushed nuclear disarmament onto the sidelines of the European security debate. The initial finding of the present study – namely, that there is virtually no debate on its central theme, nuclear disarmament – can be traced back directly to this preoccupation, which has made nuclear disarmament into a non-issue.

4.6. The Priority and Urgency of Nuclear Disarmament

There is no sense of urgency in regard to nuclear disarmament: the drama which surrounded nuclear weapons in the early eighties has almost completely disappeared – a perverse effect of arms control success. Reports about the chaotic situation in the nuclear world, and about the illegal trading that goes on in it, have not aroused the same kind of public concern as did the previous perception of an immediate threat of nuclear war.

Given the absence of any public debate or sense of urgency on the part of the political leadership, the bureaucracies dealing with foreign affairs are basically left to their own devices. Not surprisingly, they adhere closely to traditional priorities. In Belgium, Spain, Hungary, Italy, Bulgaria, the Czech Republic, Poland, Austria, and Turkey, nuclear arms control and disarmament are given low priority, and there are no national initiatives on these issues – although they are seen in a positive light and are considered part of routine national security policy. Uncontroversial proposals therefore receive general support. Germany, the Netherlands, Norway, and Sweden are inclined to be more active. In addition to its traditional commitment to arms control, Norway, for example, faces the special problem of the situation in the Barents Sea, with its combination of safety and security concerns. But it is clear that even these – traditionally more active – countries are not pursuing these issues with the same degree of energy as in the eighties.

Ironically but understandably, it is the two nuclear-weapon states, France and Britain, which give nuclear disarmament most prominence, perceiving it to be linked to core national interests. The demand for nuclear disarmament is a demand directed at them (not a demand they can choose to raise if they so wish, as is the case for the non-nuclear-weapon states). Moreover, the combination of tight budgets and the absence of any tangible threat forces them into difficult decisions and trade-offs regarding both the structure of their entire armed forces and the place of nuclear weapons in their overall defence postures. As a consequence, the two inevitably have to pay more attention to the issue than their partners.

4.7. Agreement on "Next Steps"

Given the divergences of interest, it may come as a surprise that the study did find one significant area of consensus – namely, the next steps to be taken in the disarmament process. There is unanimous support for the Test Ban, with all countries according a high priority to its entry into force. The clear split that emerged in the very last phase of the Test Ban negotiations, when the UK was the only member of the Western Group to side with Russia and China in adopting a hardline position on entry into force (i.e. insisting on Indian ratification as a condition) appears not to play a role at present.

All parties likewise strongly support the immediate start of negotiations on a convention to prohibit the production of fissile material for weapons purposes ("cut-off" or "FMCT"). It is generally agreed – in line with the "Principles and Objectives" adopted by the 1995 NPT Review and Extension Conference – that a cut-off should be the next step in multilateral disarmament, following the Test Ban; but there are some significant variations in national positions. Germany wants an "irreversibility clause" to be included – that is to say, a clause prohibiting the military reuse of fissile material resulting from nuclear disarmament and/or not presently in military use. Sweden, taking this a step further, is looking favourably on the request by several non-aligned states that existing stocks of fissile material should be included in the negotiations – a position vigorously opposed by the nuclear-weapon states. There now appears to be a strong tendency on the part of European non-nuclear-weapon states to think that the nuclear-weapon states could somehow be more amenable to the non-aligned request for an *ad hoc* committee on nuclear disarmament to be set up at the CD – though they would not go so far as to ask the nuclear-weapon states to allow the creation of a committee with a negotiating mandate. As far as they are concerned, a deliberative body would suffice.

There is also unequivocal support for the START process: all countries want to see the Russian Duma ratify the START II treaty as soon as possible, thereby paving the way for its entry into force; and all would like the START III negotiations to begin soon, leading to deeper cuts in the nuclear arsenals of the superpowers. This, again, is the point at which differences start. The two neutral countries, Sweden and Austria, would like the three smaller nuclear-weapon states to be involved in START III. This is something about which France and Britain appear – at least for the present – not too enthusiastic; but there is some support for this view in Belgium, Spain, Greece, and Italy. In other words, a sizeable number of EU countries believe that the time has come for the two European nuclear-weapon states to do more than just unilaterally cut their nuclear forces to a size more appropriate to the post-Cold War strategic environment, and to make legally binding commitments in the context of a negotiated disarmament process. However, as long as this is not the clearly articulated view of a significant majority, it is unlikely that much pressure will be put on France and Britain to accede to this demand.

4.8. Sympathetic Scepticism in regard to More "Exotic" Proposals

Whereas there is substantial agreement on the "mainstream" nuclear disarmament measures, the same is not true for the more "exotic" proposals that are being discussed, chiefly in the international NGO community. Only the two Scandinavian countries under review here have put forward these kinds of measures for consideration in the near future. Norway supports the idea of imposing limits on tactical nuclear weapons and of undertaking to close down the nuclear test sites in the nuclear-weapon states once and for all. Sweden agrees with its neighbour that the imposition of legal constraints on tactical nuclear weapons should be pursued as a matter of urgency. In addition, it accords a high priority to the drafting of an international legal instrument dealing with negative security assurances – that is, guarantees by the nuclear-weapon states not to use, or to threaten to use, nuclear weapons against non-nuclear-weapon states. The possibility of such a convention was raised in the 1995 "Principles and Objectives".

Here again, policy preferences are dictated to an astonishing degree by alliance solidarity: what we have seen in the debate on NATO enlargement, the nuclear issue, and the proposals for a nuclear-weapon-free zone also applies to the demand that NATO shift to a policy of "no first use". The changed strategic situation undoubtedly poses a challenge to NATO's traditional doctrine, whereby it reserves the option to use nuclear weapons first. Yet the suggestion of a change was met with a resounding "No!" from the interviewees in all the NATO member states under review here. Sympathy for it, if any exists, comes from opposition parties. If there is any on the government side, it is evidently subordinated to consciously exercised alliance discipline. Only in the two neutral states, Sweden and Austria, is there any support for the shift – and the Austrian endorsement is conditional on the continued validity and full implementation of the CFE Treaty.

A very non-committal and vague kind of sympathy for the more exotic disarmament proposals is displayed by the non-nuclear-weapon states. Some (e.g. Hungary, Bulgaria) simply do not give any thought to such far-reaching proposals; others (Norway, Sweden) would support a treaty limiting or prohibiting tactical nuclear weapons. Germany is a lone supporter of a nuclear arms register as a means to greater transparency[10]. But none of these countries presses any of these issues. Meanwhile, France, the UK, and Turkey seek to stall far-reaching measures such as these, feeling that their national postures and security interests could be compromised.

One area in which a large group of non-nuclear-weapon states appear to share a greater desire for practical measures is that of the imposition of safeguards on fissile material and, more generally, the extension of safeguards in nuclear-weapon states. Not only would this enhance transparency and, as a corollary, act as an incentive to bureaucracies in

---

[10] See Harald Müller & Katja Frank, *"A Nuclear Weapons Register: Concepts, Issues and Opportunities"*, in: Malcolm Chalmers, Mitsuro Donowaki & Owen Green, **Developing Arms Transparency: The Future of the UN Register**, University of Bradford Arms Register Studies, No.7, Bradford, 1997, pp.233-55; Harald Müller, **A Nuclear Weapons Register: A Good Idea Whose Time Has Come,** PRIF Reports, Frankfurt/M., 1998.

nuclear-weapon states to observe the strictest standards of accountancy and physical security – an aspect of particular importance for Russia; it would also work to reduce the discrimination built into the unequal obligations of nuclear-weapon and non-nuclear-weapon states under the NPT. Approval for these kinds of measures was expressed in Germany, Belgium, the Netherlands, Spain, the Czech Republic, Greece, Sweden, and Austria – in other words, the majority of the non-nuclear-weapons states under review.

4.9. Not Much Hope for a Nuclear-Weapon-Free World

In terms of their attitudes to comprehensive nuclear disarmament, the countries considered in this study fell into four distinct groups. The first was somewhat sympathetic to the idea, this sympathy being strongest in Scandinavia (Norway and Sweden); but even here, the idea of tackling the problem in a single step – through a nuclear weapons convention – was not seen as a realistic option. The same general acceptance was expressed in Austria and Greece, but only in Greece was any support articulated for the "convention option" – and then only with the qualification that this was definitely not something that could be realized in the near future.

In the second group, general support for the idea of comprehensive nuclear disarmament as such was combined with strong qualifications that reveal a deep scepticism in regard to the chances of this idea being realized and to the time-scale within which it could seriously be considered. Belgium fell into this group, and a similar non-committal scepticism was found in Bulgaria, Hungary, the Czech Republic, and Poland, where the notion of a nuclear-arms-free world appears to be of very little political interest.

The third group consists of non-nuclear-weapon NATO members who, while endorsing nuclear disarmament in principle, prefer for the time being to rely on residual nuclear deterrence. It was this view which prompted Italy, the Netherlands, and Germany to intervene in the International Court of Justice's proceedings on the illegality of nuclear weapons and ask it to abstain from giving advice. Turkey also asserts that it seeks the ultimate goal of nuclear disarmament, but, because of its proximity to the Russian Federation and its location within a ring of three zones of turmoil – the Balkans, the Caucasus, and the Middle East – it relies on the continuing existence of the nuclear umbrella for its national security.

The final group is, of course, made up of the two nuclear-weapon states. These have in theory undertaken to reduce their arsenals to zero within an unspecified period, but are keen to preserve their nuclear status for the foreseeable future.

4.10. The Prevailing Attitude of Passivity

At government level, the prevailing attitude is one of passivity. In the absence of perceived political urgency, of a serious security threat involving nuclear weapons, and of irresistible domestic pressure, there is no political will to pursue a disarmament agenda. The countries most immediately concerned by the nuclear question, France and the UK, obviously have no incentive to press the issue. For the rest, taking bold initiatives would inevitably embroil them in a quarrel with their nuclear-armed partners and would not pay off either domestically or among their peers. In this situation, supporting a middle-of-the-road, common-sense, "next step" agenda, or, even more convenient, passively following the lead of those who are prepared to make a move, is quite rational behaviour. Of course, this could change, if one of five things happened. First, the deteriorating state of command and control systems, the poor maintenance of nuclear weapons, and the declining morale of Russian armed personnel, including the Strategic Rocket Forces, could once again make nuclear weapons into a tangible threat, though in a different way than in the past. Second, a definite anti-Western turn in Russian defence policy after NATO enlargement could give nuclear weapons new prominence, this time in a very similar way to the past. This could then stimulate public concern again, and promote nuclear arms control to a higher position on the national security agenda. Third, tensions, in East Asia that would set the USA and China against each other might trigger a new nuclear arms race that could have repercussions in Europe – though it is doubtful that this would really change the prevailing attitudes. Fourth, a dramatic case of nuclear proliferation could open up a new debate. Or, fifth and finally, the present US discussion about the nuclear future could force the Europeans to rethink the issue. If none of these scenarios materializes, the situation is not very likely to change.

4.11. Deviations from the General Passivity

Some countries deviate from this pattern of passivity in one way or another. Three groups are discernible here.

France and the UK are forced to take a position on disarmament issues by virtue of the fact that they are nuclear-weapon states. The pressure here emanates from two quarters. First, it is impossible for these countries simply to ignore the persistent demands of non-aligned states that they should make good their promises on disarmament. They have to respond in two ways: by finding good arguments as to why the more radical requests can reasonably and legitimately be refused, and by offering to undertake meaningful arms control and disarmament measures that go some way to mollifying non-aligned wrath whilst leaving some nuclear arsenals safely in their own hands. The second source of pressure is these countries' own force-planning, which is having to be made in a period of fiscal constraint. This pushes them in the direction of reductions and operational changes but makes it more and more difficult to maintain a viable deterrent into a boundless future. Changes in numbers and operational practices, in their turn, have to be presented in the perspective of nuclear disarmament – which forces Paris and London to think virtually permanently in these terms.

The second exception is the neutral countries, Sweden and Austria, where interest in taking moderate steps in a multilateral context appears to be stronger than elsewhere. Sweden in particular is traditionally very active at the CD and tries to enrich the debate there by bringing its own proposals to it. The Netherlands, though quite alliance-minded and conservative in defence matters – and thus clearly distinct from the two neutral countries – has a very active corps of disarmament diplomats and, like Sweden, has acquired a rather high profile in this area.

Finally, there is Germany, the pivotal economic power in the EU, with one of the strongest armies on the Continent but without nuclear weapons or plans to develop these. Germany has traditionally had a great interest in reducing the NPT "discrimination gap", most tangibly expressed in the asymmetry between verification measures in nuclear-weapon and non-nuclear-weapon states. Driven by this concern, Germany has become the champion of enhanced transparency and expanded safeguards in nuclear-weapon states. Worries about the physical security of fissile material in Russia reinforce this attitude. There is a strong consensus on this issue in the country, and nuclear-weapon states would be ill-advised to ignore this concern or put it to one side, as they tended to do during the early phase of the "93 + 2" negotiations.

5. Conclusion

In stark contrast to the situation in the United States, nuclear disarmament is almost a non-issue in Europe. Where nuclear matters are discussed at all – that is, mainly in the specialist departments of defence and foreign ministries – a good deal of conservatism and passivity prevails. Security élites are quite content to have a degree of residual deterrence, even though they are unable to identify any obvious threat worth deterring. Consensus exists on mainstream proposals for nuclear disarmament – in other words, the next steps to be taken. When it comes to more far-reaching suggestions, however, national opinions, where they exist at all, tend to be divided.

It is NATO that pulls the strings on the nuclear issue: it gives clear direction to the non-nuclear-weapon states, both members and would-be members, and provides a convenient cover for the status of the two nuclear-weapon states. The neutral countries are in no mood to challenge the dominant security organization in Europe; and NATO itself is a body where the innate conservatism of national bureaucracies is fully reflected. Pressure from the USA is probably the only thing that will change this entrenched pattern.

This innate conservatism also makes most security élites somewhat unenthusiastic about the idea of a European nuclear deterrent – Eurodeterrent – as considered by France. Interest in this proposal, though not entirely non-existent, is very muted. The desire to hold at bay the potential risk to NATO and to the US commitment to European security prevails, and the issue is thus explored only with the greatest caution.

For those who advocate comprehensive nuclear disarmament, this is disappointing. It is almost impossible to exaggerate just how much hard work is needed to convince the Europeans – even those supposedly well disposed towards arms control and disarmament – that serious steps have to be taken in this direction. This is clearly an important task: nuclear conservatives in the USA use the allied reticence to highlight the dangers of proliferation associated with too bold an American disarmament policy. Some European allies, they say, could panic and have recourse to a nuclear deterrent of their own. Germany, despite the absence of any indications of such a move on its part, is, as usual, cast as the suspect. To get the US debate under way may therefore require some move on the European side, but to shift the European blockage, some US initiative is indispensable. In the NATO nuclear game, it seems, we have a catch-22 situation.

There are inherent risks associated with NATO enlargement and the possible Russian reaction to it. For the moment, the nuclear issue appears to have been laid to rest by the three "nos". However, since NATO has refused to give this commitment a binding form, no concessions have been wrought from Russia, and nuclear arms now occupy a fairly prominent place in the latter's overall national defence posture. As long as there is no treaty imposing limits on tactical nuclear forces or regional deployments (as a nuclear-weapon-free zone would do), the risk of a return to nuclear confrontation will persist. NATO is running this risk needlessly, out of an attitude of conservatism.

European countries – be they nuclear-weapon or non-nuclear-weapon states – have not come to grips with their own commitment to promote nuclear disarmament. They are largely ignoring the landmark advice given by the International Court of Justice in summer 1996. And they are disregarding the substantial debate going on in the United States. The first, modest task is therefore simply to get a nuclear debate started in Europe.

FRANCE

Camille GRAND

1. Introduction

French security policy has undergone a veritable revolution since the election of President Jacques Chirac in May 1995. It is widely agreed that the changes have been as crucial as those of the early 1960's when de Gaulle ended the Algerian war, set up an independent nuclear force and withdrew France from NATO's integrated military structures. Some even argue that nothing comparable has been since 1945.

The process of reform was in France delayed after the end of the Cold War, mainly for political reasons. From 1993 to 1995, France passed through a period of *"cohabitation"* with a gaullist Prime Minister, Edouard Balladur, and a socialist President, François Mitterrand. In February 1994, the Ministry of Defence released a new *Livre Blanc sur la Défense*[1]. The new *Livre Blanc* was commissioned by Edouard Balladur and his conservative Defence Minister François Léotard. During the *"cohabitation"* period, however, the President retained most decision-making power on defence policy. Given these political contingencies, the *Livre Blanc* did not proceed to a major strategic reassessment on the lines of the US "Bottom-up review" and "Nuclear Posture Review", or other similar post-Cold War reforms in Europe. This is all the more true as regards the nuclear posture. The Defence White Pa-

---

[1] *Livre Blanc sur la Défense* 1994, La Documentation française, Collection des rapports officiels, Paris, 1994 (also available in English and in German). It was the first White Paper on Defence since 1972.

per and a Procurement Law[2] were released by the Balladur government, and these two documents are very interesting, but they were the product of a compromise between president, government and parliament and reflected the traditional consensus on defence rather than a true attempt to reform French security policy[3].

After his election in 1995, Jacques Chirac engaged a genuine "revolution in the founding principles of [French] defence policy" as Minister of Defence Charles Millon has written[4]. This major reappraisal was possible since Chirac was a newly elected president and also because he is a gaullist, which his two predecessors, Giscard d'Estaing and Mitterrand, had not been. This enabled Chirac to proceed to break some taboos, for instance about NATO, in areas where non-gaullists had to be more careful and respect gaullist dogmas.

Most of these decisions were announced after the end of the nuclear testing controversy. In 1996, every part of French defence policy saw drastic changes:
- compulsory military service is to be abolished; by 2002 France will have a professional army;
- a major downsizing of the Army, Navy and Air Force has been announced;
- the entire defence industry is to be reorganised;
- a new Procurement Law is being prepared;
- the deterrence posture is being reviewed;
- the relationship to NATO has been changed.

Most of these changes were announced by President Chirac in a television interview on February 22, 1996[5], and detailed in a speech to the *Ecole militaire* on February 23, 1996[6]. Of course nuclear issues were not forgotten by the President and the government. They were not at the heart

---

[2] See as well the *Loi de programmation militaire 1995-2000*.

[3] On the nuclear diplomacy itself, see Camille GRAND, *"La diplomatie nucléaire du président Chirac"*, in a special issue *"La politique étrangère de Jacques Chirac"* of **Relations internationales et stratégiques**, No.25, Spring 1997.

[4] Charles MILLON, *"Vers une défense nouvelle"*, in: **Le Monde**, 27 February 1996.

[5] See the transcript in Ministère des Affaires étrangères, *Politique étrangère de la France*, January-February 1996, La Documentation Française, Paris, 1996, pp.216-225.

[6] See the full text and an official presentation of the reforms in Ministère de la Défense, *1997-2015 Une Défense nouvelle*, SIRPA, Paris, 1996.

of the announcements, since a lot had been said during the 1995-6 series of nuclear tests. Nuclear policy nevertheless remains a key issue in French security policy, and Chirac has also taken various decisions on French deterrence strategy and arms control policy. However, these were announced over a longer period as the resumption of nuclear testing obliged the administration to put forward new initiatives as a way of responding to the international pressure on France.

In this context, the study of French policy can make use for perhaps the first time of a large number of official documents. For over 20 years, political scientists have worked on and quoted the unique White Paper of 1972 and half a dozen important speeches[7], but they now have to take note of a large number of documents and a rapidly evolving defence policy. This is obviously the case almost everywhere after the Cold War, but it is all the more notable in France as the changes were announced over a very short period of time after decades without any change in defence policy.

2. Perception of the Security Situation after the End of the Cold War

2.1. French Defence and Nuclear Policy during the Cold War

During the Cold War, French strategy was designed to meet a wide variety of potential threats, ranging from an all-out attack by the Soviet and Warsaw Pact forces in West Germany to low intensity conflicts in sub-Saharan Africa. The theatres of action covered were the so-called "three circles":

- national territory, covered by deterrence and territorial defence;
- the European theatre, in which the First Army and later the Rapid Action Force (FAR) were to meet French commitments to the Western Alliance, as part of a wider deterrent posture;
- out of area action, mainly in Africa and the Middle East.

---

[7] For a good collection of these documents, see Dominique DAVID (ed.), **La politique de défense de la France, textes et documents**, FEDN/La Documentation française, 1989.

There were some affirmations that French strategy should be multi-directional, namely the famous paper by General Ailleret in 1967 that proposed a *tous azimuts* concept[8]. Aside from these rather abstruse strategic debates, French nuclear strategy was primarily designed to deal with an immediate and massive threat: the Soviet Union. The latter, however, was explicitly named as the enemy in official documents only in 1983 and in the 1984-1988 Procurement Law prepared by the socialist government, which stated: "One may fear that it is indeed the policy of the Soviet Union to challenge the security, and thus the independence, of our continent." Accordingly, the French nuclear arsenal and strategy were designed and developed to ensure the credibility vis-à-vis the Soviet Union of a "weak to the strong" posture[9].

In the early 1990s, the decline of the "designated" enemy led to a new debate on the role of nuclear weapons. On the one hand, some argued that no changes were needed, since a nuclear posture that deterred the Soviet Union (or at least was perceived or misperceived as fulfilling this function) could deter any other country. This was more or less the view of President Mitterrand. On the other hand, other experts in the political, military and academic communities advocated a major strategic reappraisal. They suggested a modification of the French strategic concept from a "weak to the strong" deterrent posture to a so-called "strong to the weak" or "strong to the crazy" war-fighting strategy[10]. The Gulf War started this debate, which now seems to have been settled, since François Mitterrand, and his successor, Jacques Chirac, have on several occasions re-stated the traditional deterrent posture.

---

[8] See Charles AILLERET, *"Défense dirigée ou défense tous azimuts"*, in: **Revue de défense nationale**, décembre 1967, pp.1923-1932. *"Tous azimuts"* indicated that French strategic nuclear forces might be targeted in **all** directions.

[9] For a comprehensive overview of French deterrence policy during the Cold War, see David YOST, *"France's Deterrent Posture and Security in Europe"*, in: **Adelphi Papers**, Nos 184 & 185, IISS, London, Winter 1984/85.

[10] On the debate on the revision of the French deterrence concept, see Pascal BONIFACE, **Contre le révisionnisme nucléaire**, Ellipses, Paris, 1994.

2.2. The Threat Assessment of the 1994 *Livre Blanc sur la défense* Remains Valid

In addition to being the first defence white paper for 22 years, the 1994 *Livre Blanc* produced the longest official report on the threats and risks to French security after the Cold War. If most of the presentation of defence policy has been changed by President Chirac, the threat assessment remains. In the first pages of the White Paper, one finds the following statement describing France's international situation: "For the first time in its history, France does not face a direct military threat near its borders. However, new risks can affect its security and its defence. (...) No one denies that the main and global threat – direct, concrete and measurable – that threatened our vital interest has vanished today and probably for a long time.[11]" The White Paper admits that French defence policy and its nuclear component face a "crisis of its funding principles" as a leading analyst, General Poirier, has written[12].

The White Paper then puts forward the following threat assessment:

"1) The global Soviet threat has disappeared. Nevertheless, in Europe, Russia will remain a strong military power, which must be treated as such in our strategic evaluation. Moreover, local or regional crises, which might degenerate into conventional wars, may challenge the shift of the continent toward a new equilibrium.

More broadly, the main risk to security now lies in regional conflicts which could challenge the search for international stability (...).

2) The military power of a number of regional powers is likely to increase not only in the field of conventional weapons but also, given proliferation, in the field of weapons of mass destruction, including nuclear weapons, by the beginning of next century.[13]"

---

[11] *Livre Blanc sur la Défense* 1994, p.17.

[12] See Lucien POIRIER, *"La crise des fondements"*, in: **Stratégique**, No.53, 1/1992, pp.117-152, reproduced and expanded in Lucien POIRIER, **La crise des fondements**, Economica, Paris, 1994, 188 p.

[13] *Livre Blanc sur la Défense* 1994, p.35.

As far as responses to these threats are concerned, the White Paper places a new emphasis on conventional forces and clearly tends to reduce the role of nuclear weapons in French strategy. Nevertheless, the concept of deterrence is clearly reaffirmed; according to the White Paper, "the nuclear forces must permanently be capable of fulfilling two functions: to inflict a blow causing unacceptable damage and liable to be repeated; to proceed to a limited strike against military targets as a way of issuing a ultimate warning.[14]"

The White Paper lists six scenarios, two of which clearly involve nuclear weapons:

1. Regional conflict which does not involve French "vital interests": no role for nuclear weapons.
2. **Regional conflicts that may involve French "vital interests"** in Europe or "in a longer time-frame, in the Mediterranean and in the Near and Middle East". In this case, according to the White Paper, "a deterrent manoeuvre, adapted to this particular context, might be necessary to accompany our decision to intervene".
3. Attacks on the territorial integrity of French territories overseas (French West Indies, Guyana, Indian Ocean and South Pacific islands): these territories are covered by deterrence according to the White Paper, with no further elaboration.
4. "Implementation of bilateral defence treaties" (primarily with African countries): no role for nuclear weapons.
5. "Operations in favour of peace and international law": no role for nuclear weapons unless the peace mission evolves into a n°2 scenario.
6. **"Resurgence of a major threat against Western Europe"**: the role of deterrence is certainly central in this scenario, yet, even though it is considered as "hardly plausible today", this scenario, if it occurred, would be considered "a deadly risk" for France.

Despite the numerous reforms announced by the Chirac administration, the threat assessment made in the 1994 *Livre Blanc* remains valid. Chirac has slightly modified the responses to these threats, which are now based on four main "functions":

---

[14] *Ibid.*, p.82 (Official translation).

- nuclear deterrence;
- crisis prevention with the help of intelligence and pre-position forces;
- force projection;
- safety and protection of national territory vis-à-vis new types of threats (terrorism, drugs, etc.)[15].

Behind this wording, one finds a reassessment of budgetary priorities from nuclear weapons and territorial defence to intelligence and force projection, and more specifically a justification for moving to a professional army.

3. The Role of Nuclear Weapons in French Security Policy

3.1. An Unchallenged Deterrence Policy

The *Livre Blanc* rejected any evolution from a purely deterrent posture to a war-fighting strategy. It was greatly concerned about the specific issue of nuclear proliferation, a threat mentioned in chapter 1 ("Evolution of risks and threats"). "Arms control, disarmament and non-proliferation agreements" are quoted in chapter 3 ("Reference framework of our defence policy"). The n°2 scenario is of course the most interesting example of this new interest. Nevertheless, it cannot be seen as the basis of a French counter-proliferation doctrine in the American sense, in spite of efforts by some politicians and military analysts, to interpret it in this way.

So-called "conventional deterrence" theories are described as "dangerous mistakes". In spite of the above mentioned efforts to shift from a deterrent posture to a first strike strategy in the South, these ideas were abandoned as the discussions on the White Paper proceeded. Not only does the word "counter-proliferation" remain taboo in French official language, but the concept itself, after an interested first look, was not imported into France. Firstly, because the defenders of traditional

---

[15] See Ministère de la Défense, *1997-2015 Une défense nouvelle*, SIRPA, Paris, 1996, pp.18-19.

deterrence (President Mitterrand in the first place) retained a key role in the decision-making process that led to the White Paper. Secondly, because "American" counter-proliferation was very quickly criticised in France as inefficient and undermining deterrence. It was (sometimes improperly) almost exclusively associated with a pre-emptive nuclear strike strategy, and was thus dismissed as inconsistent with the French deterrence posture. Under these circumstances, France did not develop a actual military counter-proliferation doctrine. Nevertheless, scenario 2 (regional conflicts that may involve French "vital interests") could provide the basis for such an evolution if interpreted differently. The "deterrent manoeuvre, adapted to this particular context" could indeed evolve towards a military counter-proliferation posture if the President so decided. But neither Mitterrand nor Chirac has interpreted the scenario in this way. On the whole, the new concern over proliferation has not lead to a French counter-proliferation doctrine. Proliferation remains primarily a problem to be dealt with by means of the classic tools of non-proliferation and deterrence. However, such proposals might reappear if a consistent threat from the South was to be perceived or misperceived.

Altogether, the *Livre blanc sur la défense 1994* was an extremely consensual document. It did not challenge French defence policy, and was obviously intended to adapt the Cold War posture rather than to conceptualise a brand new strategy. It was clearly an expression of the traditional French consensus on defence. It was decided, in order to preserve this consensus in a period of *"cohabitation"*, to leave many options open and leave the hard choices to the President to be elected in May 1995. Jacques Chirac did make many of these choices. In the first place, he decided that the resumption of nuclear testing was necessary. Later, he announced several important disarmament initiatives (see below). Finally, as part of his redrafting of French defence policy, he reviewed and downsized the nuclear posture by dismantling the two ground-to-ground nuclear systems (Albion S-3 D missiles and Hadès missiles). However, he did not change the deterrence strategy. As he said on February 23rd, 1996: "this ambitious program of adaptation and modernisation of our deterrence shows the will of France to continue to guarantee its ultimate security in any circumstances. Based on deterrence, the French nuclear strategy remains, *ne variatur*, a defensive one. Nevertheless any aggressor who would attempt to strike at our vital interests must remain convinced of our capacity and resolution to preserve them.[16]"

3.2. The Future of the French Nuclear Arsenal

The Procurement Law for the next six years *(Loi de programmation militaire 1995-2000)*, voted in April 1994, completed and implemented the White Paper. It confirmed the decline in nuclear spending, which started in 1990. 129 billion francs were assigned to nuclear forces equipment, primarily to the development and purchase of two new-generation nuclear submarines (SNLE-NG) out of the four due to re-place the first generation SNLEs. In general terms, spending on nuclear forces has declined by more than a third since the end of the Cold War, falling from over 40% of the procurement budget in the sixties (1964-1969), to 30-35% in the seventies and eighties, to about 30% in the early nineties, and about 20% today.

This general tendency has been accelerated by a growing budget-ary constraint which dictates more cuts in military spending. The Minister of Defence of the Chirac administration, Charles Millon, set up in 1995 a "strategic committee" which decided on new cuts in military spending. A new Procurement Law for the upcoming six years was drafted and voted in 1996 (it replaces the one voted in 1994), and a further 18% decline in military procurement spending has been decided. 105,8 billion francs over six years are assigned to nuclear deterrence. Under these new conditions, the nuclear share goes below the 20 billion francs mark per year to about 17,6 billion. In comparison, in the last decade (1986-1995), it averaged more than 30 billion per year in 1996 francs[17]. The share of nuclear forces within the *Titre V* (procurement) of the defence budget is down to 21%, the lowest level since the birth of the French nuclear arsenal.

---

[16] Speech before the *Ecole militaire,* 23 February 1996, as quoted in Ministère de la Défense, *1997-2015 Une Défense nouvelle*, SIRPA, Paris, 1996.

[17] On these budgetary problems and on French defense policy in general, see the Chapter *"France"* in the yearbook: Pascal BONIFACE (ed.), **L'Année stratégique**, published by IRIS since 1987, and specifically the 1995, 1996 and 1997 editions.

Most important military (and especially nuclear) programs have been delayed. The final choices were made by the Chirac administration in February 1996. French deterrence will test primarily upon four new-generation SLBMs, two of which will be permanently at sea, and a new missile (M51) is under development to replace the M45 by 2010-2015. The second component will be a renewed air-to-ground capability (with both a strategic and a prestrategic role), with the *Rafale* fighter-bomber plane carrying an upgraded version of the ASMP *(Air-Sol Moyenne Portée)* missile. Chirac simultaneously announced the complete dismantling of both the Albion IRBMs and the Hadès short-range missiles (which had been in storage since 1993).

In the medium-to-long term, two points have become clear:

- France intends to retain a nuclear capability and a deterrence posture;
- the budgetary constraints combined with a set of new priorities (outer space, projection capabilities, intelligence, peacekeeping missions), will continue to reduce the role of nuclear weapons in French strategy and their share of military spending.

3.3. A "Concerted" European Deterrence?

Various projects for the Europeanization of the French nuclear arsenal have been formulated since the 1950's[18]. However, France had always been reluctant to share the core of its nuclear power. Only in January 1992 did President Mitterrand suggest an examination of the basis of a European nuclear doctrine[19]. Since this proposal, a debate has been going on in France on the ways and means of nuclear cooperation in Western Europe[20]. The *Livre Blanc sur la Défense* also considered this perspective in very general terms.

---

[18] The idea goes back as far as the Chaban-Delmas/Strauss/Taviani 1957-1958 Agreements.

[19] **Le Monde**, January 13, 1992.

[20] For the debate on concerted deterrence, see the dossier titled *"La France, la dissuasion et l'Europe"*, in: **Relations internationales et stratégiques**, No.21,

In January 1995, Alain Juppé[21] introduced the concept of *"dissuasion concertée"* (concerted deterrence)[22]. It would therefore be unfair to see these proposals as nothing more than a tactical move to counter the anti-French-tests campaign, even though this certainly played a role in the new French initiatives of summer and fall 1995. The obvious lack of interest (to say the least) expressed by the possible non-nuclear partners led France to almost drop the subject for a year. It nevertheless remains an important topic in France and is proposed in every single official paper or speech. France is more open than ever to discussions among Europeans. Yet, for the moment, cooperation is more likely to develop between the three Western nuclear powers. The participation of Germany in these discussions is also seen as desirable and necessary in Paris, and the basis for German participation has been established with the "Franco-German concept on security and defence" issued after the Nuremberg Franco-German summit of December 1996. In order to gain the support of its West European partner and for other reasons as well, France has taken several steps towards NATO designed to make these talks easier.

Spring 1996. For various perspectives on European deterrence, see among many papers: Frédéric BOZO, *"Une doctrine nucléaire européenne: pour quoi faire et comment?"*, in: **Politique étrangère**, 2/1992, pp.407-421; Roberto ZADRA, *"European Integration and Nuclear Deterrence After the Cold War"*, **Chaillot Paper**, No.5, Institute for Security Studies, WEU, November 1992; David YOST, *"Europe and Nuclear Deterrence"*, **Survival**, Autumn 1993, pp.97-120; M. DE DECKER, *Le rôle et l'avenir des armes nucléaires*, Document 1420 of WEU Assembly, May 19, 1994; Bruno TERTRAIS, *"Quelle dimension européenne pour la dissuasion nucléaire?"*, in: **Relations internationales et stratégiques**, No.18, Summer 1995, pp.165-170; Pascal BONIFACE, *"French Nuclear Strategy and European Deterrence: les Rendez-vous Manqués"*, in: **Contemporary Security Policy**, Vol.17, No.2, August 1996.

[21] Foreign Affairs Minister (1993-1995), and Prime Minister since the election of Jacques Chirac in May 1995.

[22] See Juppé's speech *"What Horizon for French Foreign Policy?"* (January 30, 1995) in: **Politique étrangère**, 1/1995, pp.245-259; for the debate on concerted deterrence, see also the dossier of the quarterly **Relations internationales et stratégiques**, No.21, Spring 1996, entitled *"La France, la dissuasion et l'Europe"*.

4. The Public Debate about Nuclear Weapons and Nuclear Disarmament

After the 1995 debate on nuclear testing, things returned to normal in France and there was no further public discussion of nuclear issues. The French nuclear consensus[23] was rebuilt on four pillars: the maintenance of nuclear deterrence, the rejection of a war-fighting strategy, the Europeanization of the French deterrent and the promotion of disarmament as long it does not lead to the complete elimination of nuclear weapons in the short term. The leading French political parties (gaullist RPR, center-right UDF and socialist PS) broadly share these principles. Moreover, a vast majority of public opinion agrees with these views. A poll commissioned by SIRPA in July 1996 showed that 61%[24] of the French thought that nuclear deterrence was necessary to French security (only 28% opposed this view).

Opposition to nuclear weapons is restricted to minority parties (the Greens and the Communists) which get only 10-15% of the votes. There are very few NGOs promoting nuclear disarmament in France and they enjoy very little popular support. For instance, during the resumption of nuclear testing, even though a majority of the French opposed the decision, anti-test demonstrations never attracted more than a few thousand people.

Altogether, disarmament is rather a non-issue in the French public debate.

---

[23] See Pascal BONIFACE & François THUAL, *"Refonder le consensus sur la dissuasion nucléaire"*, in: **Le Monde**, November 24-25, 1995.

[24] Three points more than in 1995 after the resumption of nuclear testing.

5. Developments in French Nuclear Arms Control Policy and the Attitude of the Political and Security Elites towards Nuclear Arms, Nuclear Arms Control and Disarmament

5.1. The Background of French Arms Control Policy

In the early period of nuclear arms control and disarmament, France was extremely reluctant to join arms control treaties and negotiations: it never signed the Partial Test Ban Treaty (PTBT) of 1963, it refused to join the Non-Proliferation Treaty (NPT) for more than twenty years, and it never took part in any bilateral or multilateral disarmament negotiations.

In the 1960s, this attitude was justified with the argument that most arms control negotiations were means to maintain the superpower nuclear duopoly and not true disarmament steps. France even practised an "empty chair" policy in the various disarmament fora to protest against this duopoly. It also emphasised the overwhelming difference in the size of the existing nuclear arsenals belonging to superpowers and medium powers.

During the 1970s and 80s, France followed the same principles even though it proved more open-minded. It did join the Conference on Disarmament in Geneva but was still reluctant to sign any nuclear limitation agreement. The French government did support the Strategic Arms Limitation Talks (SALT) process and the Intermediate Nuclear Forces (INF) Treaty, but never took an active part in nuclear disarmament as the French stockpile was still growing.

In 1983, President Mitterrand laid down the conditions for possible French participation in nuclear disarmament[25] ("correction of the fundamental differences" between the arsenals of the two superpowers and of the other nuclear weapons states, the end of the conventional disparity in Europe, and the end of the race in antimissile, antisubmarine and antisatellite weapons). For a long time, these conditions were still operative, as President Mitterrand made clear in May 1994 when he said:

---

[25] September 28, 1983, speech before the UN General Assembly.

"If one compares two countries which possess 20,000 nuclear devices each to a country with 500 nuclear warheads, one cannot just say, let's reduce our arsenals by 500 warheads! We shall then decide later at what time we will join the move [toward nuclear disarmament]." This policy of refusal has nevertheless undergone drastic changes since 1991. In the early 1990s, new worries about nuclear proliferation and the global changes in international security led to a major policy shift. Its main elements were announced by President Mitterrand in his June 1991 United Nations speech promoting an international disarmament plan. Besides various actions in favour of chemical and conventional disarmament, France decided to join the NPT as a nuclear power (it acceded to the treaty in August 1992). In the years 1991-1993, the socialist government announced various unilateral nuclear disarmament steps[26]: early withdrawal of several prestrategic weapons systems without any replacements (Pluton short-range missiles, AN-52 air-dropped bombs); reduction of the level of alert; and non-deployment of the *Hadès* medium range missile. In April 1992, Mitterrand also announced a moratorium on nuclear testing, which lasted for three years.

5.2. The Downsizing of the French Nuclear Arsenal

Between 1991 and 1995, according to the sub-director for disarmament (Ministry of Foreign Affairs), France completed a 15% unilateral reduction of its nuclear arsenal[27]. Further unilateral steps have been decided by President Chirac. The non-replacement of the 30 *Mirage IV-P* bombers has already been announced, the dismantling of the 18 *plateau d'Albion S-3D* IRBMs (Intermediate Range Ballistic Missiles) has been effective since September 1996 when they were taken off alert status, and the complete withdrawal and dismantling of the 30 *Hadès* missiles has also been announced. In terms of warheads deployed, this means another 10 to 15% cut in the next few years.

---

[26] **Le Monde**, March 19, 1993.

[27] Michel Duclos, *"La Conférence de prorogation du TNP et les questions de désarmement nucléaire"*, in: **Politique étrangère**, 3/1995, pp.723-729.

Even though many of these reductions were motivated by budgetary constraints and only *a posteriori* presented as disarmament measures, they nevertheless indicate a new trend in French nuclear policy. Until 1990, the French nuclear arsenal was growing in size and capacity. These decisions have thus put an end to this growth and started a true disarmament process. Finally, it is important to remember that the present French warhead stockpile remains below 5% of the arsenal of either the United States or Russia.

During the NPT Conference, France also accepted the principle of future cuts when it accepted the declaration on "Principles and Objectives for Nuclear Non-Proliferation and Disarmament". Section 4 goes beyond the traditional Article VI wording as it announces its "program of action": "The determined pursuit by the nuclear-weapon States of systematic and progressive efforts to reduce nuclear weapons globally, with the ultimate goal of eliminating those weapons, and by all States of general and complete disarmament under strict and effective international control."

It remains to be seen how this goal will be implemented, and to what extent the French administration is fully aware of the scope of this commitment, which was confirmed and emphasised by the July 1996 International Court of Justice Advisory Opinion on the legality of the threat or use of nuclear weapons[28].

In 1996, Chirac announced during a visit to South-East Asia his intention to turn France into a "champion of disarmament". Hervé de Charette explained this further in an article printed in *Le Monde* entitled *"La France, championne réaliste du désarmement*[29]*"* which promoted the CTBT and listed French commitments in favour of the implementation of the CWC, the negotiation of a cut-off convention, the updating of the CFE treaty and a review of the inhumane weapons convention.

---

[28] On the ICJ Advisory Opinion, see *Die Friedens Warte*, Band 71, Heft 3, 1996, including our paper, *"Legality of the Threat or Use of Nuclear Weapons - A French Perspective on the ICJ Advisory Opinion"*.

[29] See **Le Monde**, July 13, 1996.

5.3. French Views on Upcoming and Possible Nuclear Disarmament Steps

CTBT

As far as the CTBT is concerned, France was for decades strongly opposed to nuclear test limitation or interdiction. In view of this, the decision announced on July 4, 1993, to participate in the CTB negotiation was indeed a great step. Since then, France has been an active participant in the CD negotiations, and the French moratorium (1992-1995) contributed to progress in the CTB talks.

During the NPT Conference, the French delegation accepted the 1996 deadline for completing the CTBT negotiations, but insisted on the wording "utmost restraint" concerning the period before the entry into force of the Treaty, in preference to the prohibition of any further tests. This was obviously meant to leave the door open for a resumption of nuclear testing by the new President (elected on May 7, 1995). In August 1995, France was the first nuclear weapon state to support the "zero-yield option" in the CTBT negotiations ("prohibition of any nuclear weapon test explosion or any nuclear explosion, no matter how small") and to accept the so-called "Australian" definition of a nuclear test[30]. This decision, immediately followed by a White House statement, was clearly a breakthrough in the CTBT negotiations, since the other NWS rallied to the same position later in 1995. France was among the first signatories of the CTBT in September 1996 and has announced a further measure by definitively closing its test site[31] and signing the Rarotonga Treaty in March 1996, thus becoming one of the two nuclear powers (the other is the UK) without a national test site.

Cut-Off Agreement

France also agrees with the principle of a cut-off treaty. It supported the idea of a cut-off agreement as early as December 1993 in a UNGA vote, and also supports the "early conclusion of negotiations

---

[30] See Ambassador Errera's speech before the C.D., August 10, 1995 (confirmed by a communiqué of the *Présidence de la République*, August 16, 1995).

[31] President Chirac's TV interview, February 22, 1996.

on a non-discriminatory and universally applicable convention banning the production of fissile material for nuclear weapons or other
nuclear explosive devices" (declaration on objectives and principles,
1995). France stopped plutonium production for military purposes in
1992, and highly enriched uranium (HEU) production has also
ended – as President Chirac announced in February 1996. France's
stockpiles are nevertheless relatively large. According to the *1996
SIPRI Yearbook* estimates, there are 4.8 tons of plutonium and 25 tons
of HEU. Since President Chirac mentioned the stockpiles available
as a good reason to stop producing weapons grade fissile material,
we are unlikely to see these stocks transferred to be used for civilian
purposes, at least in large quantities.

France has also been seen to be reluctant on two further issues.
The level of intrusiveness of the cut-off treaty verification system has
raised some worries in French nuclear circles[32]. The French nuclear
establishment is obviously not yet used to the idea of IAEA inspections of its military facilities. Moreover, the suggestion made by some
arms controllers to move from a "fissban" to a plutonium ban would
lead to a strong French opposition as such a plutonium ban would
not be compatible with the French nuclear industry's projects (development of MOX fuel).

No-first Use and Security Assurances

France has also announced new security assurances, both positive
and negative. These were contained in a letter to the UN Secretary
General dated April 6, 1995, and in a statement to the CD on the same
day.

On negative security assurances, France has clarified the existing
negative assurances given in 1982[33], specifically: "France reaffirms
that it will not use nuclear weapons against non-nuclear-weapon

---

[32] According to a presentation by Tom Cochran in an NGO forum; see
Disarmament Times, May 1994.

[33] Speech of Claude Cheysson (External Relations Minister) to the UN General
Assembly, June 11, 1982: France "will not use nuclear arms against a State that
does not have them and that has pledged not to seek them, unless an act of
aggression is carried out in association or alliance with a nuclear-weapon State
against France or against a State to which France has a security commitment."

States Parties to the NPT, except in the case of an invasion or any other attack on France, its territory, its armed forces or other troops, or against its allies or a State towards which it has a security commitment, carried out or sustained by such a State in alliance or association with a nuclear-weapon State." This declaration harmonises the French position with the statements made by the USA, the United Kingdom and Russia. Its main novelty lies in the limitation to NPT Parties, which was not mentioned in the 1982 statement.

On positive security assurances, France had abstained in 1968 when resolution 255 was voted. It was therefore considered that France had never given any positive assurances. The decision announced in April 1995 gave the following assurances: "France, as a Permanent Member of the Security Council, pledges that in the event of attack with nuclear weapons or the threat of such attack against a non-nuclear-weapon State party to the NPT, France will immediately inform the Security Council and act within the Council to ensure that the latter takes immediate steps to provide, in accordance with the Charter, the necessary assistance to any State which is the victim of such an act of aggression." Following this statement, France co-sponsored resolution 984 (April 11, 1995).

The new French policy toward security assurances involves more of a change than one might at first think. Cheysson's 1982 speech had been discussed or corrected by other French officials on several occasions. It was common even recently, to hear expressions of the view that it was undermining the French deterrent posture.

It is interesting to note that uncertainties remain on the extent of the negative assurances provided by France. In a declaration before the *Sénat* commenting on the assurances given, Alain Juppé explicitly mentioned the use of "weapons of mass destruction" as potentially justifying a nuclear response[34]. This interpretation contradicts the negative security assurances granted, but juridically the international commitment should prevail over the ministerial interpretation[35].

---

[34] Quoted in Xavier DE VILLEPIN, *"La lutte contre la prolifération nucléaire"*, in: *Rapport au nom de la Commission des Affaires étrangères, de la Défense et des Forces armées du Sénat*, No.311, June 1995.

[35] As noted in Pascal BONIFACE, *"Dissuasion et non-prolifération: un équilibre difficile, nécessaire mais rompu"*, in: **Politique étrangère**, 3/1995, pp.707-721.

The issue of the appropriate response to an attack by chemical or biological weapons has not been yet resolved or discussed in detail. Broadly, the general idea in military circles is that it is unlikely in the near future but if it occurred, one could always change the policy. Accordingly a certain level of uncertainty for the potential aggressor is seen as preferable.

On no-first use itself, France remains extremely reluctant to undertake a commitment in contradiction with its deterrence strategy, which allows first use if vital interests are threatened. Some voices have been raised in favour of no-first use[36], but they remain rather isolated.

France's Attitude towards Nuclear Weapon Free Zones

France has signed and ratified both protocols of the Tlatelolco Treaty, Protocol I in 1974 and Protocol II much later in 1992. But France refused until recently to commit itself to the other existing NWFZs. This position has changed fundamentally since 1995. Not only did France support the wording of the "Declaration on Objectives and Principles" on NWFZ, it also signed two new treaties in 1996. After the last testing campaign, France signed the three protocols of the Rarotonga Treaty (March 8, 1996), together with the United States and the United Kingdom. A few days later, France signed Protocols I, II and III (as France has some territories in the African NWFZ) of the Pelindaba Treaty at the Cairo signing ceremony (April 11, 1996), France is the only NWS to have deposited its instruments of ratification, in September 1996. President Chirac also said in March 1996 that France would sign the protocol to the Bangkok Treaty establishing a South-East Asian NWFZ as soon as "some technical details with the other nuclear powers" were solved. Finally there is the Central European NWFZ, which is rather a non-issue in France. Most observers assume that France would follow NATO policy (i.e. opposition) on this issue, whatever President Chirac might say about the general principle of support for NWFZ.

---

[36] See for instance Marisol TOURAINE, *"Le facteur nucléaire après la guerre froide"*, in: **Politique étrangère**, 2/1992, pp.395-405. Touraine advocates leaving to the aggressor the decision to cross the nuclear rubicon. See also the statement by Jean-Marie GUÉHENNO (at that time head of policy planning for the Foreign Affairs minister) in *"Un nouveau débat stratégique"*, Documentation Française/ SIRPA, Paris, 1993 (1992 symposium papers).

A Nuclear Weapons Register and other Transparency Measures

This proposal is an irritant in Paris, as everyone recalls the Kinkel proposal of 1994 as a blow to both the CFSP and the Franco-German cooperation. But, putting aside this episode, one can note the new French openness in nuclear matters which makes it possible that similar proposals, which would be made necessary by a cut-off agreement, might in the future be more acceptable.

France's Participation in International Nuclear Arms Limitation and Reduction Treaties

As far as actual nuclear disarmament is concerned, France reaffirmed during the NPT Conference its commitment under article VI to pursue in good faith negotiations on nuclear disarmament as an "ultimate goal". France, with the previously described unilateral disarmament steps and the commitments entered into during the NPT renewal process and in the CD in Geneva, has clearly shifted its nuclear disarmament policy from extreme reluctance to cautious but serious participation.

As we wrote in the conclusion to our survey of French non-proliferation policy (1993-1995): "The next decade will be the occasion to test the new French commitment to more nuclear arms control and disarmament: will France implement Article VI, or will it stick to the severe logic of a renewed minimal deterrence policy? All depends on the future legitimacy of nuclear weapons. A deterrence posture and a non-proliferation policy are compatible, as are disarmament steps and continued minimal deterrence. Complete elimination of nuclear weapons is however not compatible with the French view that nuclear weapons retain a certain role in international security.[37]"

Hervé de Charette, the present Minister of Foreign Affairs, has stated France's readiness in principle to participate in a "multilateral discussion among nuclear powers" in order to accelerate progress towards nuclear disarmament[38]. However, Jacques Chirac made it

---

[37] Camille GRAND & Philippe RICHARD, *"France"*, in: Harald MÜLLER (ed.), **European Non-Proliferation Policy 1993-1995**, PRIF, European Interuniversity Press, Brussels, 1996, pp.61-84.

[38] See speech of Hervé de Charette before the *Institut des Hautes Etudes de Défense Nationale (IHEDN),* October 12, 1995.

clear that he thought the Minister of Foreign Affairs had been some-what too positive about future nuclear disarmament talks. In a June 1996 speech, the President said: "I do not, however, think that French participation in international negotiations on the reduction of nuclear weapons is a topical subject. Our deterrence posture has been defined, in our new plans, at a carefully defined level designed to ensure our security. (…) Today, other fields of disarmament should be the focus of our attention.[39]" One can argue that the conditions for French par-ticipation laid down in 1983 by President Mitterrand are still opera-tive. To a certain extent, France is waiting to see whether the START treaties are implemented before it gets involved in any future nego-tiations.

In this context, any initiatives aimed at undermining the legitimacy of nuclear weapons in international security after the Cold War and at promoting nuclear disarmament are still viewed with anxiety in France. These include the ICJ procedure on the legality of the threat or use of nuclear weapons, the Canberra Commission Report released in August 1996, the resolutions voted year after year by the United Nations General Assembly, the 1995 award of the Nobel Peace Prize to the Pugwash movement, and the attempts made by non-aligned countries to promote the elimination of nuclear weapons in the Ge-neva Conference on Disarmament.

France seems to be ready to accept future international negotia-tions on further limitations to nuclear forces, but it is for the moment highly unlikely that France will support any initiative that would threaten its ability to remain a nuclear power in the medium-to-long term. Therefore, a treaty banning the development of new warheads or a convention on the elimination of nuclear weapons would not at present find support in Paris.

---

[39] Jacques CHIRAC, *"La politique de défense de la France"*, in: **Défense nationale**, August-September 1996, pp.7-18 (speech before the *IHEDN*, June 8, 1996).

6. Conclusion

It is extremely important to note that the French political and security elites are not fully aware of nuclear arms control and disarmament proposals made abroad. For most people in the elites, the NWS are confronted with the usual NGO and non-aligned hostility to nuclear weapons, which is nothing new. It seems that for most decision-makers this it not an important or immediate issue. If the Chirac administration has decided at the highest level to be an active participant in disarmament, it will put the emphasis on non-nuclear issues in the near future and does not think that the existence of nuclear weapons themselves will be at stake in the short-to-medium term. The victory of the socialist-communist-green coalition in the spring 1997 parliamentary election is as well unlikely to generate major changes, on the contrary one could argue that it has opened the way to a wider consensus by integrating the communist and the green parties in the government lead by Lionel Jospin. The debate on the future of nuclear weapons in France does not include the non-nuclear option, as both the elites and the majority of the French public consider that nuclear weapons retain an important role in European and international security. This view might well prove to be correct, but the government and those who support the principle of deterrence need to come up with strong arguments to sustain the legitimacy of nuclear deterrence in the future.

THE UNITED KINGDOM

Darryl HOWLETT & John SIMPSON

1. Introduction

During the 1990s, the United Kingdom's (UK) nuclear weapon policy has been characterised as much by discontinuity as continuity. A missile submarine force has been retained, with its missiles supplied by the United States and with joint targeting arrangements involving that state, but the remainder of the UK's nuclear capability has either been retired or is about to be stood down. The diverse basing modes, delivery systems and warhead types of the Cold War period are about to be replaced by the Trident delivery system. This will mount an inventory of nuclear warheads that will not exceed 288, will probably be nearer 200, and may even be considerably less[1].

This change in the size and composition of the UK's nuclear force has considerable significance for future UK policies on deterrence, and also for developments concerning disarmament. The Polaris replacement debate occurred during the Cold War, when the only issue was which nuclear system would be the most cost-effective replacement for Polaris, not whether there should be a replacement. By contrast, any Trident replacement debate in 2010-2020, when for technical reasons such a decision will need to be taken, will probably occur in an environment in which the principal question may be not what should the replacement be, but whether there should be one at all.

---

[1] This statement assumes that only three submarines will be operational at any one time, each carrying a maximum of 96 warheads.

One immediate consequence of its change in force structure is that the UK has already embarked on a policy of nuclear reduction or, as one official has put it, nuclear divestment[2]. Whether these unilateral UK decisions could be described as part of an ongoing process of nuclear disarmament, or whether they should be regarded as autonomously motivated actions, stimulated only by a desire to reduce costs and by warheads reaching the end of their technical shelf-life, is a matter for debate. Indeed, given the lack of any official figures for past, present and future stockpile numbers, it remains uncertain whether UK warhead numbers have gone up or down over the period 1993-1997[3].

This chapter indicates that the UK's underlying nuclear weapons policy remains essentially conservative, in that a continuing deterrent role for nuclear weapons is still envisaged. However, by reducing the force to a single warhead design and delivery system, a situation unique among the declared nuclear-weapon states, a door has been opened which could ultimately lead the UK to take a more radical departure from the nuclear policies it pursued during the Cold War.

2. The Security Situation after the End of the Cold War

For policymakers in the UK, the Cold War provided a security environment which created certainty in the assumptions underpinning nuclear defence planning. The Soviet Union and its Warsaw Pact allies constituted a clear and imminent danger, and nuclear forces were

---

[2] Nicholas K.J. WITNEY, *"British Nuclear Policy After the Cold War"*, in: **Survival**, Vol.36, No.4, Winter 1994-95, pp.96-112. The author was an official in the Ministry of Defence who had been seconded to the International Institute of International Studies, London.

[3] The most detailed calculations of numbers of UK weapons were published by Richard GUTHRIE, in: **Trust and Verify**, No.56, April 1995. These were based upon data contained in the *Statement on the Defence Estimates, 1995,* Cm2800, London, HMSO, May 1995, p.39, Fig.6. This indicates that since 1970, there had been significant percentage decreases in numbers of UK operational warheads and the total yield of the operational stockpile of weapons. Guthrie's calculations indicated that the actual numbers of deployed weapons dropped from 244 in 1970 to 196 in 1990 and 142 in 1992, but then rose to 205 in 1995 as Trident came into service and will stabilise at 192 in 1998. Subsequent information, however, suggests that figures of 235 in 1970, 190 in 1990, 135 in 1992, 203 in 1995 and a figure of 180 for 1998 and beyond may be a more accurate interpretation of this data. The initial calculations appear to indicate that 64 warheads will be carried on each of three operational Trident submarines, the later ones that this figure will be 60.

deployed in both a national and NATO context to deter hostile actions by that identifiable enemy. The rapid disintegration of the Warsaw Pact and the Soviet Union, and thus the end of the Cold War, eliminated the principal threat to the security of the UK. Simultaneously, it also removed the sense of certainty and continuity which pervaded nuclear planning for more than four decades.

For those tasked with making policy in this area, this has meant coming to terms with life in a world without a clearly identifiable enemy, and characterized by a greater political fluidity than at any time since the end of the Second World War. Within defence planning circles, the result is seen to be a dramatic change to the context of the UK's security policy, in which the UK no longer confronts "a clear and quantifiable threat from a single dominant adversary [but] uncertainties and risks remain.[4]"

During the Cold War the UK, in conjunction with other NATO allies, planned for a major war in Europe in which an escalating nuclear exchange was regarded as a distinct possibility. As a consequence, the UK's nuclear force structure allowed for both an independent national and a joint NATO role in deterring the Soviet Union and Warsaw Pact. Its nuclear forces possessed a diverse range of capabilities, and were based on land, on aircraft, on surface ships and on submarines. The majority of its warheads were nationally owned, but some of its short-range delivery systems were dependant on the provision of nuclear warheads by the US while, from 1960 onwards, the UK abandoned attempts to develop its own strategic missile delivery systems and chose to rely on their acquisition from the US also.

The land component of the force comprised Lance missiles and 155mm howitzers based in Germany and tasked to deliver US nuclear ordnance under so-called "dual-key" arrangements. The Royal Air Force's Nimrod long-range anti-submarine aircraft also had access to US depth-bombs under this arrangement. The UK had a stockpile of nationally designed, manufactured and owned WE-177 nuclear-gravity bombs which could be delivered to a range of targets by Royal Air Force Jaguar, Tornado and Buccaneer aircraft, and by the Royal Navy's

---

[4] *Statement on the Defence Estimates 1992*, Cm 1981, London, HMSO, July 1992, p.7.

Sea Harriers and anti-submarine helicopters. Finally, from 1968 onwards, when the first Polaris missile submarines entered service, the UK deployed a strategic nuclear force of four boats, each carrying 16 US-supplied Polaris A-3 missiles[5].

The strategic changes induced by the end of the Cold War generated a rapid re-assessment of the UK's defence and security requirements. However, identifying precisely what are now the main challenges to the security of the UK has not proved easy. Official publications after 1991 tended to highlight those "uncertainties and risks" which arose from the collapse of the Soviet Union, such as how to deal with its military capabilities, especially its widespread nuclear infra-structure, and concerns about ethnic and territorial conflicts breaking out in the Former Soviet Union (FSU) and in Central and Eastern Europe. There was also a more general concern about developments outside Europe, particularly the spread of ballistic missiles and weapons of mass destruction (WMD)[6].

In this new context, the principal means of dealing with the "uncertainties and risks" remained the North Atlantic Treaty Organisation (NATO). One outcome of the re-assessment was that the UK's defence forces were restructured around the performance of three vital roles in the post-Cold War world: ensuring the protection and security of the UK and its dependent territories; insuring against any future major external threat to the UK and its allies; and contributing to the promotion of the UK's wider security interests through the maintenance of international peace and stability[7].

Another outcome of the re-assessment was that by the mid-1990s the diversity in nuclear-delivery means, which had characterised the UK's nuclear force during the Cold War, had been much reduced. US and NATO decisions in October 1991 meant that the US ordnance available for use with the UK's Lance missiles, nuclear capable artillery

---

[5] Nicholas K.J. WITNEY, *op.cit.*, p.97. Richard GUTHRIE, in: **Trust and Verify**, *op.cit.*, estimates the numbers of operational UK owned warheads in 1990 as 10 WE177 25 kt. depth bombs, 90 WE177 200 kt. bombs, and 96 Polaris/Chevaline warheads.

[6] See, for example, the annual *Statement on the Defence Estimates,* London, HMSO.

[7] *Statement on the Defence Estimates 1992*, Cm 1981, London, HMSO, July 1992, p.9.

and Nimrod aircraft was transferred from Europe to the US, and the NATO nuclear role of these delivery systems eliminated. Next, in June 1992, the UK announced that all the WE-177 bombs carried on its Royal Naval surface ships were to be removed, together with all ancillary equipment needed for nuclear operations, and the majority of the weapons dismantled[8]. Initially, the UK had plans to replace its WE-177 gravity bombs, first manufactured in the mid-1960s, when they reached the end of their shelf-life in 2003. However, on 18 October 1993 the then Secretary of State for Defence, Malcolm Rifkind, announced that the UK would not proceed with its replacement, known as the Tactical-Air-to-Surface Missile (TASM), as Trident's enhanced capabilities would enable it to perform the sub-strategic role traditionally played by the WE-177[9]. It was then announced in May 1995 that the WE-177 was to be retired in 1998, five years earlier than originally planned, when the third Trident submarine was operational[10].

The Polaris submarine fleet was already scheduled to be phased out over the period from 1994 to 2000 by a new submarine design, the V-class, as a consequence of decisions taken in the early 1980s to acquire Trident D5 missiles from the US[11]. However, by May 1996 the decision had been taken to de-commission the remaining Polaris boats by the end of the year, even though only two out of the planned four Trident submarines would by then be operational[12]. Thus, between 1991 and 1996, a major restructuring of the UK's nuclear forces was undertaken, largely in response to the new security environment[13].

---

[8] **Hansard**, 15 June 1992, col.422.

[9] **Hansard**, 18 October 1993, col.34.

[10] *Statement on the Defence Estimates 1995, op.cit.*, para.303.

[11] The decision to replace Polaris with the Trident system, which was to be purchased from the United States, was first made public in 1980. Two years later, it was also stated the UK had taken the decision to purchase the more advanced Trident II (D5) system rather than the first generation Trident missile. See, *Defence Open Government Document 80/23*, and *Defence Open Government Document 82/1*.

[12] *Statement on the Defence Estimates 1996*, Cm 3223, London, HMSO, May 1996, para.202

[13] The process of defence restructuring had begun in the early 1990s following the publication of *Britain's Defence for the 1990s*, Cm 1559-1, London, HMSO, July 1991.

No official figures have ever been offered on numbers of UK nuclear weapons, though in 1995 some indications were given of how these had declined between the 1970s and 1980s, and how that decline would continue in 1999[14]. However, in a speech in November 1993, outlining the role of nuclear weapons for the UK in the post-Cold War world[15], the then Secretary of State for Defence, Malcolm Rifkind, stated that the deployed number of warheads carried by each Trident submarine would not exceed 96, as against a theoretical maximum of 128, and it could be even lower[16]. Moreover, it was made clear that the case for this ceiling figure for warheads on the UK's Trident missiles was based on the assumption that these figures represented the UK's minimum requirement for deterrence.

At the time of writing, no official statements have been made which would suggest that the Cold War patrol patterns, which guaranteed at least one missile submarine being on patrol at all times, have been altered. The implication of this is that the danger of a surprise disarming attack has been totally discounted. However, through a reciprocal arrangement, the UK has formally agreed not to target its missiles on the Russian federation, at least in peacetime[17].

---

[14] *Statement on the Defence Estimates 1995, op.cit.,* p.39, Fig.6.

[15] *"UK Defence Strategy: A Continuing Role for Nuclear Weapons"*, speech by the Secretary of State for Defence, Malcolm Rifkind, to the Centre for Defence Studies, King's College, London, 16 November 1993, reprinted in edited form in **Arms Control and Disarmament Quarterly Review**, No.32, London, Arms Control and Disarmament Research Unit, Foreign & Commonwealth Office, January 1994, pp.12-29.

[16] Given that the UK's Trident submarines can carry 16 missiles, this statement appeared to imply that each delivery-system can carry up to 8 operational warheads, but that in service they will be deployed with no more than an average of 6 warheads. One implication of this statement is that individual missiles might have different loadings, for example some having only a single warhead. However, as note 3 above indicates, calculations based upon figures in the *Statement on the Defence Estimates, 1995* indicate that actual loadings will probably be much lower, in the range of 60-64 warheads or an average of 4 per missile, on each of three operational submarines.

[17] This decision was a consequence of a joint declaration made by the leaders of the two countries on 15 February 1994 and operative from 30 May 1994. **Trust and Verify**, No.45, March 1994.

3. The Role of Nuclear Weapons in National Security Policy

As noted above, despite the fundamental changes that have occurred in its security context since the end of the East-West confrontation, the UK remains committed to maintaining a nuclear deterrent capability. In so doing, official policy reflects a continuity in thinking which began at the start of the Cold War, has survived changes in government irrespective of the party in power, and is likely to continue with the new government elected after the 1997 General Election[18]. Given the resources already expended on the Trident missile submarine programme, and with the first two V-class missile submarines already in service, the key issues dominating operational policy are to complete the transition from the Polaris to Trident missile force; to eliminate the remaining WE-177 gravity bombs; and to determine the specific targets for the warheads on the new missiles – if any.

In 1997, both before and during the general election campaign, there is very little explicit public debate about nuclear weapons in the UK or whether the country should continue possessing such weapons. In contrast to the "great debates" of the 1950s, 1960s and early 1980s that were driven by advocates of unilateral nuclear disarmament, there has been no public outcry against nuclear weapons in the 1990s or any large-scale Campaign for Nuclear Disarmament (CND) demonstrations of the kind experienced during the Cold War period. This is not to suggest that a movement opposing the UK's deployment of Trident does not exist, for a number of non-government organizations, including CND, are still campaigning against it. But the issue does not have the same political immediacy or significance that it held before 1991, either in the UK media or among the general public[19].

---

[18] The Election Manifesto of the Labour Party, which was in opposition until May 1997, reflects the bi-partisan nature of UK nuclear weapons policy by making a commitment to maintaining the Trident force if elected to office.

[19] The major theme underlying CND's objections to official nuclear policy, that the UK is engaging in both vertical and horizontal proliferation, was articulated in a Memorandum submitted in January 1995 to the House of Commons Foreign Affairs Committee. *"Memorandum submitted by the Campaign for Nuclear Disarmament"*, Wednesday 11 January 1995, Foreign Affairs Committee, Second Report, *UK Policy on Weapons Proliferation and Arms Control in the Post-Cold War Era,* House of Commons, Session 1994-95, London, HMSO, 30 March 1995, pp.194-202.

Despite the lack of a significant public debate over the issue, however, officials are aware that it is more difficult now to offer a cogent and well-articulated defence of the UK's nuclear deterrent force than it was prior to 1991. The annual Statements on the Defence Estimates are the main vehicle for enunciating current nuclear policy to the public, and they contain both material on this and a detailed account of how arms control arrangements support UK security policy. However, this highlights one of the core problems facing those tasked with explaining the UK's nuclear policy: the need to avoid justifications for it which could be used by potential proliferators and which do not conflict with UK support for the nuclear non-proliferation regime.

This dilemma first became apparent in November 1993 in the course of the speech by Malcolm Rifkind, cited above, which was the first extensive national pronouncement on UK nuclear doctrine of the post-Cold War period. This was later reinforced by similar presentations made by senior serving and retired defence officials[20]. Underlying his analysis, known by some as the "Rifkind Doctrine", was an assumption that as nuclear deterrence prevented war between East and West prior to 1991, similar conditions of stable deterrence needed to be recreated to prevent war in the post-1991 period. In Rifkind's speech, stress was placed on the utility of nuclear deterrence as a means of war prevention among the existing nuclear-weapon states, rather than for war fighting or war winning[21]. The speech also highlighted the Alliance's reduced reliance on nuclear weapons following its adoption of a new strategic concept at the Rome summit in November 1991. But the notion of NATO adopting a policy of no-first-use of nuclear weapons was rejected on the grounds that it would imply that conventional

---

[20] For a view by another current official see, David OMAND, *"Nuclear Deterrence in a Changing World: The View from a UK Perspective"*, in: **RUSI Journal**, June 1996, pp.15-22; and for a view by a former official who was instrumental in formulating the UK's nuclear doctrine during the Cold War see, Michael QUINLAN, *"The Future of Nuclear Weapons: Policy for Western Possessors"*, in: **International Affairs**, Vol.69, No.3, 1993, pp.485-496.

[21] "The immense power of nuclear weapons removed long ago any rational basis for a potential adversary believing that a major war could be fought in Europe and won. The potential for miscalculation and escalation in the heat of any crisis or conflict reinforced caution… The value of nuclear weapons in such circumstances lies not in classical concepts of war fighting or war winning, nor just in deterring the use of nuclear weapons by an adversary, but in actually preventing war." Malcolm RIFKIND, *op.cit.*, p.16.

war was a safe option for any aggressor: such a declaration, it was argued, would "take us out of the realm of war prevention and into the realm of war limitation".

The main practical concerns outlined in the speech were how to deal with Russia, "the pre-eminent military power in Europe", and with the consequences of the proliferation of ballistic missiles and weapons of mass destruction around the world. In addressing Russia's residual nuclear capability, emphasis was placed on developing a cooperative relationship with it, in order to construct a stable deterrence system at the lowest possible level of nuclear warheads. The Secretary of State also used Iraq as an example of the potential for conflict situations to arise when a state is seeking a nuclear weapons capability, and for regional nuclear arms races to emerge if one state considers that a neighbour has embarked on a nuclear weapons path.

According to his analysis, an international environment where the proliferation of weapons of mass destruction is a possibility raises several problematic considerations for the UK and nuclear deterrence. Although stressing that the basic ideas of nuclear deterrence do not change, he acknowledged that the rational calculations concerning the use of nuclear weapons which were a feature of the East-West relationship would not necessarily pertain in other regional settings. This implied that nuclear deterrence threats could not be deployed successfully in all cases, and indeed might only work in a limited number of them.

The Rifkind speech then went on to address three related policy issues that had arisen as a result of the Persian Gulf War in 1991: how to respond to an adversary which was not allied to a nuclear weapon state but had a potential nuclear capability; how to respond to a chemical or biological weapons attack from such a state; and whether either situation would justify the use of nuclear weapons? The speech took place at a time when the US was developing its Counter-Proliferation Initiative and the UK, among other states, was concerned that this would lead to it deploying so-called "usable nuclear weapons", capable of performing a war-fighting or surgical strike role to eliminate nuclear, chemical or biological weapon facilities on the territory of regional proliferators. Among the arguments advanced against such a plan was that its adoption would be viewed as an act of hostility towards developing states, and thus undermine attempts to strengthen controls on the spread of WMD.

While the UK opposed moves by the US to introduce new low-yield nuclear devices for use by the NATO allies, the concern about how to respond to chemical and biological weapons remained. This has led to a reluctance by policymakers to offer less-qualified negative security guarantees than those granted during the Cold War and at the time of the 1995 indefinite extension of the Nuclear Non-Proliferation Treaty (NPT).

What is also clear from the November 1993 speech and other pronouncements by officials is that the UK rejects any direct causal linkage between states seeking to acquire WMD, especially nuclear weapons, and its own continued possession of a nuclear capability. Thus, by implication, if the UK were to go down the nuclear disarmament route because it considered that nuclear weapons had no utility in the post-Cold War world, it is believed that this would have little if any impact upon the policies of potential proliferators. Indeed, there is some concern among officials in London that "setting an example of nuclear disarmament" might actually be counter-productive[22]. At least one has argued that an allied state involved in a tense regional confrontation, who was reliant on a nuclear-umbrella offered by a nuclear-weapon state, might consider that the state involved was exhibiting a lack of resolve if it disarmed and either question the future of that relationship or consider whether it should acquire a nuclear capability of its own. Similarly, the enemy of the allied state might interpret such a decision as weakness and pursue a more ambitious strategy. Either way, a dangerous situation could result.

However, it is acknowledged that a political linkage does exist between the need to maintain the nuclear non-proliferation regime and the general policies on nuclear weapons adopted by the nuclear-weapon states[23]. This explains the efforts made to ensure the indefinite extension of the NPT through a pledge to complete a Comprehensive Test Ban Treaty (CTBT) during 1996, and to start negotiations on a fissile

---

[22] Nicholas K.J. WITNEY, *op.cit.*, pp.101-102.
[23] *Ibid.*, p.102.

material cut-off, as well as its commitment to the eventual global elimination of nuclear weapons.

Concerns that nuclear deterrence might not be universally applicable reflect another element in official UK thinking about nuclear weapons in the new international environment. Although there have been several statements of concern about the spread of WMD and ballistic missiles, no attempt has been made to justify the continued existence of the UK's nuclear weapons on the basis of WMD threats from any specific state outside Europe. Instead, the instruments for dealing with any situation in which UK security interests might be concerned are those which seek to deny WMD capabilities to would-be proliferators, including the use of advanced conventional weapons such as submarine launched cruise-missiles, and defensive capabilities. However, it is not denied that the existence of nuclear weapons in the UK's armoury could have the general effect of constraining the behaviour of such states.

The UK has been more reticent than the US to embrace totally the arguments for Ballistic Missile Defences (BMD). Official statements indicate that the UK does have "an active interest" in BMD; has been engaged in a dialogue with the US and France on this issue and is also involved in the NATO group which has been convened to study BMD. However, this interest does not extend to any British interest in the Medium Extended Air Defence System (MEADS), being developed by some of its NATO partners. In addition, between October 1994 and the summer of 1996, British Aerospace was commissioned by the MoD to undertake a preliminary pre-feasibility national study on "possible BMD systems to counter potential threats to the United Kingdom, the Dependent Territories and our forces deployed overseas[24]". Despite industry pressures from both the UK and US to commit itself to such a programme, no firm decision has been taken to proceed with a BMD capability, either nationally or in collaboration with allies. While it is accepted that there is a need for a theatre defence capability to protect UK forces performing peace enforcement missions, grave doubts exist over the cost-effectiveness of any national or regional BMD system. In addition, such systems generate

---

[24] *Statement on the Defence Estimates 1995, op.cit.*, p.62.

the risk of undermining public confidence in the technical credibility of the UK's Trident system.

4. UK-French Collaboration and Nuclear Weapons in Europe

One of the principal areas of discontinuity between the UK's pre- and post-1991 nuclear policies concerns the relationship with France. During the Cold War, and especially after France left NATO's integrated military organisation, there was little formal contact between these two European nuclear-weapon states. Since 1991, however, cooperation between the UK and France over all aspects of military activities, and particularly nuclear policy, has intensified. It has been institutionalised through the Joint Nuclear Commission on Nuclear Policy and Doctrine, established in 1992, as well as a range of other informal contacts and networks.

The significance of these conduits for nuclear dialogue was highlighted in the statements following the meeting between President Chirac and former Prime Minister Major in October 1995, which emphasised the degree of commonality between their respective nuclear policies. This has assisted in persuading France that the way forward in the nuclear context was reintegration into NATO, and therefore opening up the possibility of discussing the European role of French nuclear forces in the NATO Nuclear Planning Group (NSG), rather than in a Western European Union (WEU)/ European Union (EU) context. The UK 1996 Defence White Paper referred to this development as helping "to enhance overall deterrence in Europe...[25]"

It is not surprising that the UK and France have developed closer ties on nuclear issues since 1991, given that the end of the Cold War left both states facing similar questions concerning the roles and doctrines of their national nuclear deterrent forces. However, their continued collaboration has raised additional questions about the future role of these nuclear forces in European security, both in general terms and more specifically in the context of the debate about the enlargement of NATO and the EU. One issue which has sparked considerable controversy in this context is whether the UK and French

---

[25] *Statement on the Defence Estimates 1996, op.cit.,* p.17.

nuclear forces should form the basis for a future European nuclear deterrent force, and what shape it might take[26].

The idea of such a force dates back to the early 1960s, when developments in aircraft and missile technology meant that US strategic forces ceased to need bases on the periphery of the Soviet Union to implement their war-plans. Concerns then arose in Europe that deterrence of a Soviet nuclear attack on the US homeland would become delinked from deterrence of a similar attack upon Western Europe. Several schemes were devised to bridge the gap over extended deterrence that some believed was opening up, including stationing Polaris missiles on land in Western Europe and broadening the involvement of NATO member states, including Germany in particular, in the control of such European-based strategic nuclear forces. None were greeted with great enthusiasm by the UK, though it did not wish to antagonise the US, which was providing its future nuclear delivery vehicles, by openly opposing them.

The institutional ways proposed to achieve these aims included a Multilateral Nuclear Force (MLF) of mixed manned naval vessels carrying Polaris missiles and an Atlantic Nuclear Force (ANF) incorporating the UK strategic nuclear forces. Both the MLF and ANF were not pursued because of practical and political objections from NATO members and implacable hostility from the Soviet Union. Instead other arrangements, in particular the creation of NATO's NPG and the commitment of four US and a similar number of UK Polaris missile submarines to strike at targets requested by the Supreme Allied Commander Europe (SACEUR), NATO's military head, were

---

[26] For discussion of the issues surrounding a European Nuclear Deterrent force see, Marco CARNOVALE, *"Why NATO-Europe Needs a Nuclear Trigger"*, in: **Orbis**, Spring 1991, pp.223-233; Mark HIBBS, *"Tomorrow, a Eurobomb"*, in: **The Bulletin of the Atomic Scientists**, January/February 1996, pp.17-23; Karl-Heinz KAMP, *"Germany and the Future of Nuclear Weapons in Europe"*, in: **Security Dialogue**, Vol.26, No.3, 1995, pp.277-292; Fredric BOZO, *"A West European Deterrence Posture: Prospects and Issues"*, in: Thomas J. MARSHALL & Jerome PAOLINI (eds), **What Future for Nuclear Forces in International Security?**, IFRI, Paris, 1992; Roberto ZADRA, *European Integration and Nuclear Deterrence After the Cold War*, **Chaillot Papers** No.5, Institute for Security Studies, Western European Union, Paris, 1992; Roy REMPEL, *The European Security and Defence Identity and Nuclear Weapons*, **Occasional Paper** No.30, The University of Manitoba, Manitoba, October 1995.

implemented. This arrangement allowed other Western European states to become involved more closely in nuclear planning.

After being buried for a quarter of a century, the idea of a European Nuclear Force (ENF) re-appeared at the end of the 1980s. In its initial formulation, the ENF was to be a deterrent to the Soviet Union, but it has subsequently taken two main forms: a NATO-European Force (NEF); and a European Union Force (EUF). The principal element of the NEF idea is the creation of a distinctive European nuclear force or pillar within the context of NATO, operating alongside a US one. This force would operate within the integrated military structure of NATO and might consist of a small, survivable nuclear force (of around 200 warheads), commanded initially by either a French or British officer, although other European nationals could assume command under agreed conditions.

By contrast, the EUF idea would seek to create a European nuclear force within the context of the EU's Common Foreign and Security Policy (CFSP), thus creating a structure with no direct US involvement in its nuclear decision-making. Such a force would involve radically different political control arrangements to an NEF (although the force composition might look very similar), as well as new nuclear doctrines, command structures and targeting options. It would also mean that the relationship between the non-nuclear-weapon states in the EU and the two nuclear-weapon states would take on new significance: the former would be under the nuclear umbrella of the UK and France, effectively creating a situation of intra-European extended nuclear deterrence[27].

One of the critical elements of any European nuclear deterrent force would be the implications of its basing modes. Over the last decade major changes have occurred to the basing modes of nuclear forces assigned to deterrence roles in Europe. There has been a gradual movement towards sea-based missile systems for nuclear-weapon delivery in both the UK and France, and for nuclear weapons assigned to a tactical role to be marginalised. The trend is for this to continue, to the extent that all land- and air-based nuclear weapons could eventually

---

[27] It was this kind of nuclear force which was at the heart of President Mitterrand's speech at the opening of the National Encounters for Europe, Palais des Congrès, Paris, 10 January 1992.

be removed from European NATO territory, leaving only sea-based strategic systems operational. This movement towards a predominantly sea-based deterrent could create tensions in the future, if it heightens anxieties about the commitment of the US to the defence of Europe, and opens up divisions between the European members of NATO and the US, thus generating a stimulus for Europe to create its own separate nuclear force.

If an ENF were to be developed within the context of the CFSP, it is improbable that it would be able to operate through the Cold War ideas and concepts of extended deterrence. The form in which this functioned through NATO involved the presence of several key elements including: a common nuclear doctrine; a common consultation process for decisions on use; a nuclear planning and targeting organisation; and physical deployments of nuclear weapons on the territories of some of the European non-nuclear weapon states. It seems unlikely that these elements would be present when an ENF was created. As a consequence, it would probably have no option but to settle for a doctrine of existential deterrence. This in turn would mean that EU non-nuclear weapon states would need to believe that the UK-French nuclear forces assigned to the European deterrence role could deter nuclear threats against them, and that those forces would be used if necessary in response to a nuclear attack on their territory. Acceptance of this doctrine would probably require less formal decision-making structures than those needed for the traditional extended deterrence arrangements, though it would not remove the need for them entirely.

The nature of the UK's future nuclear basing modes indicates, however, that in 1998 a significant discontinuity will occur with the past in respect of its nuclear deterrence options. At that point it will become reliant for all its deterrence requirements on the Trident submarine force. Does this eliminate all options for reinforcing the credibility of extended deterrence to allies and potential enemies by the forward basing of nuclear forces, as happened in the Cold War period, given the lack of land-based or air-deliverable nuclear systems to perform such a reassurance role? Or can the sub-strategic role of Trident in some manner substitute for this? More basically, is such reassurance necessary, and can such deterrence be based upon uncertainty, rather than certainty, of response? These questions raise profound political and strategic issues of how a UK nuclear submarine based force, solely or in conjunction with France, might offer extended nuclear deterrence guarantees to other European states, either as part of a European force or on a national basis. This in turn, of course, opens up the question of the future roles, if any, that the UK force might play in such a European deterrent, especially given the bi-partisan opposition in the UK to the EU having a defence role.

5. Attitudes of the Political and Security Elites towards Nuclear Arms Control and Disarmament

Since 1991, the MOD and FCO have taken a very positive view of arms control activities in general, and of certain nuclear arms control initiatives in particular. This is because arms control in general is now considered to be one of the linchpins of UK security policy, and successive Statements on the Defence Estimates since 1993 have reflected this centrality. The 1996 Statement notes the UK's contribution to several initiatives and agreements, including support for the indefinite extension of the NPT, the Chemical Weapons and Biological Weapons Conventions, and the recently agreed CTBT. The UK also supports the negotiation of a Fissile Material Cut-Off Treaty provided that it involves all relevant states, including India, Israel and Pakistan. In addition, in March 1996 the UK signed the protocols to the Treaty of Rarotonga, which created the South Pacific Nuclear-Weapon Free Zone (NWFZ) and has indicate support for other NWFZ "provided that arrangements for these zones are freely arrived at by States of the region concerned[28]".

One central perspective underlying UK policy in multilateral arms control negotiations and discussions has been to give firm support to all negotiations and agreements which have both a disarmament and a non-proliferation function. Its basic position has been that it is prepared to accept limitations on its own capabilities so long as agreements also impose significant limitations on potential proliferators. Hence the support for both the CTBT and fissile-material cut-off

---

[28] *Statement on the Defence Estimates 1996, op.cit.*, p.16.

provided the three threshold states, India, israel and Pakistan, also become party to these agreements, and the hard-line taken with India by its negotiators towards the end of the CTBT negotiations in 1996.

The UK originally took a very firm stance against entering the START negotiations but has subsequently become more flexible. There are currently two considerations which would determine UK entry to these negotiations: first, the US and former Soviet nuclear arsenals would need to be reduced substantially; and, second, that there was no significant improvement in defensive capabilities. The current view is that when US and Russian nuclear weapons can be counted in hundreds rather than thousands, then the UK would consider entering a multilateral discussion on further global reductions.

This position appears to be based on a concern that by entering negotiations, an implicit commitment would be made to participate in reductions, something the UK does not feel able to do given its position that its planned capabilities are the minimum needed for deterrence. Similarly, the minimalist nature of its nuclear forces has consistently driven policies of refusing to reveal exact figures for these forces, and rejecting proposals for all five nuclear weapon states to register details of their warhead and fissile material stockpiles. During the mid-1990s, a different driver for policy may have been operating: numbers of warheads may have increased, rather than decreased, as the increased payloads of the Trident force were commissioned while the WE177 stockpile remained in active service[29]. As a consequence, when the Trident force is fully operational and warhead numbers stabilise, there may be a greater willingness on the part of UK governments to reveal more details of UK nuclear holdings and agree to a nuclear warhead register. What will not change, however, is the UK's reluctance to forgo its nuclear weapon status in advance of the other four declared nuclear weapon states.

Overall therefore, the general tone of the UK's approach to nuclear arms control has been to stress those measures which can contribute to the maximization of national, regional and global security. This relationship between improving security and specific initiatives

---

[29] For detailed arguments supporting this proposition, see Richard GUTHRIE, in: **Trust and Verify**, *op.cit.*

directly impacts on the UK's consideration of any move towards nuclear disarmament. In the 1996 Statement on the Defence Estimates this relationship was made explicit: "The Government believes that it would be irresponsible to dismantle the well-established system of deterrence that exists in Europe before new and reliable systems for preserving stability are in place.[30]"

What is therefore clear is that any discussion involving the prospects of UK nuclear disarmament must be conducted within the context of a broader dialogue on related security measures.

In Rifkind's November 1993 speech, although some reference is made to questions of disarmament, a deep scepticism pervades the discussion of the practical feasibility of such a process in the short to medium term, or the negotiation of a "Nuclear Arms Convention". The possibility is not ruled out entirely, though there remains a concern that even in the longer term nuclear knowledge cannot be disinvented. As David Omand, former Deputy Under Secretary of State (Policy) in the MoD, stated: "I note in passing... what seems to me to be very powerful arguments about the irreversibility of specific knowledge. A world without nuclear weapons is not the same as a world without the knowledge of nuclear weapons. This fact must be an important factor in determining the long term requirement for any form of nuclear deterrence posture.[31]"

Related to this concern about the inability to disinvent nuclear weapons knowledge is that even in a world where nuclear disarmament had occurred there would still be the prospect of a break-out leading to a nuclear rearmament race, with both the prospect and the race itself being regarded as dangerous and de-stabilizing. However, the most significant element in this context is probably the belief held by policymakers that nuclear deterrence represents the most appropriate and cost-effective means for preventing war. Even though the success of operation Desert Storm in 1991 showed how effective advanced conventional technology can be, and raised the question of whether nuclear forces are now a declining asset in the light of advances in conventional weaponry, for the UK, at least, they are not

[30] *Ibid.*, p.17.

[31] David OMAND, *op.cit.*, p.17.

yet perceived to provide an alternative to nuclear forces in a last-resort deterrent role.

The UK's future nuclear force structure also has significant implications for the UK's attitudes towards nuclear disarmament, as well as extended deterrence. One disarmament proposal which has been advanced is for the "neutralization" of nuclear weapons. This is viewed as an interim but realistic step on the road to total elimination. This approach would consist of actions by all states with nuclear weapons to: "irreversibly reduce their arsenals to a minimum number and then to render this remnant unusable for surprise attack by separating warheads from delivery systems and placing both under international monitoring on the territory of the owner state.[32]"

While for the US and Russia, and possibly China, such an initiative might be viewed with some interest because of the diversity of their deployed nuclear forces, policymakers in the UK are unlikely to favour the approach. This is because it would effectively mean the nuclear disarmament of the UK, as once the warhead was removed from the Trident missile and stored ashore there would be no operational nuclear force left and no easy, and above all rapid, possibility of returning the warhead to the submarine delivery vehicle in an emergency. So while total de-mounting has attractions for states with land-based missiles, the different position facing a state with sea-based systems alone may lead to its rejection by UK policymakers.

6. Future UK Policy towards Nuclear Weapons and Disarmament

There remains an underlying pessimism in official circles in the UK about nuclear disarmament both because of the practical problems involved and the lack of credibility of conventional alternatives. Yet, the prospect of nuclear disarmament is not ruled out entirely and a hint of what would be necessary to overcome some of the difficulties envisaged was given in Rifkind's November 1993 speech: "For a

---

[32] See Jonathan DEAN, *"The Final Stage of Nuclear Arms Control"*, in: **The Washington Quarterly**, Vol.17, No.4, Autumn 1994, pp.31-52.

nuclear free world to become a practical objective the community of nations would need to develop robust and dependable solutions to... problems. We may all hope to work towards the day when this is possible but it has not yet arrived.[33]"

Long term considerations of what the world may look like in the year 2010 and beyond, and whether a nuclear deterrent will still be needed at this time, remain issues which do not feature strongly in current thinking either in the MoD or in the FCO. Yet there are those who have begun to give thought to the requirements for UK security when the question of a follow-on to the Trident system will start to become a pressing policy issue. Conducting such an analysis is in-evitably difficult, but providing no major threat emerges of the kind that dominated thinking during the Cold War, the possibility should not be excluded of the UK embracing a more radical nuclear weap-ons outlook at that point in time to the one which currently dictates policy.

Given that there is a scepticism about the practical feasibility, if not the desirability, of the UK moving to a disarmed status, a key question for such an analysis is what would be the precise security requirements which would allow the UK to adopt this more radical nuclear weapons outlook. This question can be broken down into three sub-themes: what would a nuclear disarmament mean in the context of the UK; what would be the means or strategies by which the UK would move to a given disarmed situation; and, what would be the security or other institutional arrangements that would need to accompany such a move. For all three sub-themes a number of dif-ferent issues can be identified.

What would a nuclear disarmed UK look like in practice? Would it mean the absence of assembled weapons; the destruction of key component parts; the prohibition of the production of high-enriched uranium (HEU) and plutonium; the internationally verified storage of all HEU and plutonium; or the abandonment of the entire nuclear industrial complex? Each of these "end states" has implications for the kind of disarmament envisaged for the UK. Is it the case, for

---

[33] Malcolm Rifkind, *op.cit.*, p.14.

example, that a nuclear disarmed UK would be in a position of what has been termed non-weaponized deterrence or virtual nuclear disarmament? Are we talking about a situation whereby the UK is indistinguishable from other industrial states with large nuclear infra-structures like Germany and Japan? Or should it be construed as meaning something more, such as the abandonment of the entire nuclear complex? Are we discussing a series of stages that the UK would progress through, with its ability to rapidly re-assemble its nuclear force becoming less rapid at each successive stage?

Specific questions about the types of political and military arrangements that would be required to enable the UK to move towards any one "disarmed end-state" also need to be addressed as would any limitations on offensive delivery systems and restrictions on civil nuclear trade. Similarly, because of the concerns about nuclear breakout, either during or at the end of the disarmament process, consideration must be given to the kind of enforcement and verification measures necessary to enable the UK to move to a disarmed position.

Beyond these practical questions, there are a range of other issues that need to be addressed: what concepts of security would support such a disarmament process; what additional agreements are required; should the process be incremental or holistic, that is, step-by-step or a move directly towards disarmament within a very short time period; how would the existence of other WMD and delivery systems affect the nuclear disarmament process; and, how would this process impact on the nuclear non-proliferation regime?

Finally, there is a set of issues related to the security debate within Europe: what would constitute nuclear sufficiency for the UK, for France, and for Europe as a whole during a disarmament process; and how will enlargement or remodelling of European defence institutions affect attitudes towards nuclear weapons in Europe?

7. Some Conclusions

The end of the Cold War has stimulated several changes to the UK's nuclear force structure and the country has subsequently undergone a period of hitherto unprecedented nuclear reductions. Although the underlying trend remains one of continuity of nuclear weapons possession and deployment, with the Trident submarine force gradually replacing the Polaris fleet, there are certain elements of discontinuity which indicate that the UK's nuclear weapons future may be considerably different from its nuclear weapons past. In particular, the lack of a specific enemy threat towards which the force can be orientated, other than the residual need to confront Russia's nuclear capability, marks a very significant change in the conduct of planning for the use of the force.

What is also slowly emerging is that a distinction can be drawn between both the roles and utility of nuclear weapons for the UK's territorial security in the specific context of the Cold War, and in the post-1991 period. Before 1991, the threat of nuclear attack upon the UK was perceived to be acute and the argument for the value of the nuclear force as a deterrent was rarely questioned. In policymaking circles, the US and the UK were seen to be in a special relationship of integrated and common defence against the Soviet threat, while the absence of France from the NATO military structure made discussion of a European deterrent force unrealistic.

In the new security context, these foundations for policy have started to dissolve. Indeed, a key issue that may now be starting to surface is how to situate the nuclear force within the structure of national defence planning used by the MoD, which centres upon the identification of specific military tasks and the rational assessment of the forces to fulfil them. This in turn will inevitably raise broader questions concerning the security benefits that the UK derives from the nuclear force in the current context, and whether the defence resources devoted to maintaining it might be more cost-effectively employed elsewhere. Moreover, although the common threat which motivated the UK-US special relationship is receding, this has yet to visibly impact upon the relationship itself, and the UK's nuclear procurement arrangements associated with it. Finally, although France has raised the question of an ENF, there has been no discernable enthusiasm for the UK to pursue this option while current NATO arrangements prevail.

What is clear from this overview of nuclear policy, therefore, is that no immediate technical stimulus exists for the UK to contemplate further nuclear disarmament, though one will emerge in the 2010-2020 period when a decision will have to be taken on whether to replace the Trident force. However, if and when nuclear disarmament becomes an immediate policy issue for the UK, a range of issues would need to be addressed before it could contemplate moving towards a nuclear disarmed status. The questions raised in the final section of this chapter represent an attempt to outline the specific agenda which could allow for this possibility to occur. The accompanying domestic and international dialogue would inevitably have to involve a European element, as it is already apparent that there are fundamental differences of opinion within Europe over the future role of nuclear weapons. At a minimum, this dialogue would seek to achieve a consensus on: the conditions under which Europe might move to having no nuclear weapons deployed on or from its soil; on the steps through which global nuclear disarmament might be achieved and the fora for their negotiation; and finally, what kind of global and regional measures would be necessary to provide credible and acceptable assurances against nuclear breakout before a nuclear-weapon free world came into existence.

Two possibilities for constructing a European dialogue seem appropriate. The first would be to concentrate efforts on the actual process of nuclear disarmament, rather than the end state of total elimination: that is, on how nuclear build-down might proceed. By focusing on the Principles and Objectives approach adopted at the 1995 NPT Extension Conference, the task would consequently be to identify the next incremental steps towards disarmament beyond a CTBT and a Fissile Material Cut-Off. From a UK perspective it would be important for these steps to contain both disarmament and non-proliferation elements. The second, but related, possibility would be to foster a dialogue of a more conceptual nature within Europe on the kind of future security regime that would be desirable within Europe. Achieving consensus on either of these will not be straightforward, but the attempt to do so could provide a solid foundation upon which the UK would contemplate its own nuclear disarmament.

GERMANY

Alexander KELLE

1. The German Security Situation after the End of the East-West Conflict

There can be little doubt that Germany has been the main benefi-
ciary of the ending of the East-West conflict. The two German states
were reunified in 1990, and the country's security situation improved
dramatically; rather than being torn in two along the East-West divide, Germany is surrounded by friendly neighbours.

However, threats to a country's security may emanate from a variety of sources. Depending on the analysis of these threats, one ar-
rives at different assessments as to the function and role of nuclear
weapons in assuring German security now that the Cold War is over.
It took the German government until 1994 to present a comprehensive assessment of the new security situation and of the country's
response to it. The 1994 White Paper acknowledged that the old threat
of a major war in Europe had been replaced by "a variety of risk factors of a different kind", which manifested themselves in regionally
distinct ways. As a consequence, security policy had to address the
roots of the conflicts, if possible before they escalated to the military
level. Risk analyses therefore had to be based on a wide understanding of the term security, encompassing social, economic, and ecological developments. Nor should such analyses be limited to Europe: they
must take into account the interdependence of regional and global

developments and relate these to the security of Germany and its allies[1].

Given this complex understanding of security, it is not surprising
that arms control appears second to last in a list of a dozen security
policy goals, followed only by "supporting the process of democratization in Europe and world-wide[2]". The concept of arms control itself has also changed: its primary aim is now to stabilize political
developments in order to prevent the creation of new military rival-
ries and the perception of a security vacuum in Central and Eastern
Europe. In addition, it is said that future arms control must involve
states outside Europe, so that risks to European security can be properly dealt with and co-operative security relations can be established
in crisis-ridden areas[3].

The main areas in which it is expected that arms control efforts
will be focused in the near future are:

- implementation of existing arms control agreements;
- provision of disarmament aid to those states that have difficulty
  meeting their disarmament obligations by their own efforts;
- reorientation and continuation of arms control efforts in
  Europe within the framework of the CSCE forum on security
  co-operation;
- further development of confidence- and security-building
  measures;
- contributions to regional stability;
- prevention of the spread of weapons of mass destruction[4].

This shift of emphasis away from the negotiating table and towards
the implementation of existing arms control agreements and the provision of disarmament aid to those states finding it hard to live up to
their obligations under these agreements had already been articulated

---

[1] Bundesministerium der Verteidigung, *Weißbuch 1994. Weißbuch zur Sicherheit
der Bundesrepublik Deutschland und zur Lage und Zukunft der Bundeswehr*,
Bonn, April 1994, pp.25 ff.

[2] *Ibid.*, pp.44 ff.

[3] *Ibid.*, p.75.

[4] *Ibid.*, p.75.

in the federal government's 1992 annual report on arms control and disarmament. That report also made it clear that it would be short-sighted to assume that after the end of the East-West conflict there was no need for continuing arms control efforts[5].

Taken together, the two official government statements convey a picture of arms control as a security policy tool which, though now of lower priority, is certainly still useful and not to be dismissed as overtaken by events.

2. The Role of Nuclear Weapons in German Security Policy and the Absence of a Public Debate on Nuclear Disarmament

The official German position on the role of nuclear weapons con-curs with the "Principles and Objectives" agreed at the 1995 NPT Extension Conference and thus acknowledges comprehensive nuclear disarmament as the ultimate goal to work towards. This stance re-flects a long-standing German desire to reduce the discrimination inherent in the nuclear non-proliferation regime. On the other hand, the German government seems content with the present NATO ar-rangement under which European members of NATO continue to enjoy the benefits of the US nuclear umbrella as the ultimate guaran-tor of their security. This ambivalent approach has lead to a rather cautious, status-quo-oriented arms control policy, which has mani-fested itself in a variety of forms.

One example was the conduct of the German during its appear-ance before the International Court of Justice (ICJ). The case which it presented in its oral statement on the legality of the use, or threat of use, of nuclear weapons rested mainly on two pillars[6]. The first was the formal argument that the ICJ ought not to deliver an opinion on the legality of nuclear weapons, since any such statement would

---

[5] Auswärtiges Amt, *Bericht zur Rüstungskontrolle und Abrüstung 1992*, Bonn, September 1993, pp.11 ff.

[6] *Oral Statement of the Federal Republic of Germany at the Public Sitting of the International Court of Justice*, The Hague, 2 Nov. 1995, mimeo.

inevitably influence national security calculations. An opinion of the court in this case would therefore be of a mainly political rather than a legal nature, and this would run counter to the court's long standing "policy" of only voicing its opinion on legal, not political, matters.

The second, material, argument, focused on the fact that nuclear weapons, unlike biological and chemical weapons, have not been banned by the international community. As the federal government sees it, the reasons for this are twofold: first, there is no political consensus in favour of eliminating nuclear weapons; and second, there is a danger that the "politically successful strategy of negotiat-ing international arms control agreements in a step-by-step approach could be undermined by an unrealistic all-or-nothing approach". The incremental approach to arms control, which is evidently favoured by the German government, is then illustrated by reference to the debates on nuclear arms control in the NPT context, culminating in the "Principles and Objectives" adopted during the 1995 NPT Exten-sion Conference. However, the German oral statement does not re-flect the fact that these "Principles and Objectives" contain a renewed pledge to work in earnest to achieve a nuclear-weapon-free world, and that, in this sense, they can be seen as departing from the incre-mental and open-ended approach to arms control, in which the final stage is not clearly defined.

As regards the option of a Eurodeterrent – an idea that was mooted by the French government following the widespread criticism of its resumption of nuclear tests – the German government has kept a low profile here. Following France's offer to "Europeanize" its nuclear deterrent, only the CDU Bundestag faction's spokesman on security, Friedbert Pflüger, showed any interest, travelling to Paris to gather further details of the offer. Although on his return Mr Pflüger identi-fied various points that needed clarification, he strongly rejected the universal outcry against "our French friends"[7].

The low priority accorded to nuclear weapons and nuclear disar-mament by the political elite is reflected in the broader political realm, where only a handful of specialists in the political parties – both in Par-liament and in party headquarters follows the issues closely. Nuclear

---

[7] See **International Herald Tribune**, 25 Aug. and 12 Sept., 1995.

disarmament is certainly not a top priority for German policy makers, which has both as a cause and as a consequence a widespread public disinterest. Consequently, a public debate on the issue of nuclear weapons and their disarmament is practically non-existent in Germany. The only substantive statement that can be made about public opinion in this regard is that, according to a majority of Germans, nuclear weapons should not be tested.

3. The Attitudes of the Political Elite towards Nuclear Arms, Arms Control, and Disarmament

3.1. The Comprehensive Nuclear Test Ban

Until the end of the 1980s Germany advocated the conclusion of a CTBT but at the same time stressed that this could only be a long term goal. This position changed at the 1990 NPT Review Conference, and the new stance was reaffirmed during the PTBT amendment conference held in New York in January of 1991, where the German delegation abandoned the idea of a comprehensive test ban as a long-term goal only. On both occasions, Germany's stance contributed to the isolation of the United States and Britain. On the question of the proper forum for negotiating such a ban, Germany sided with those favouring the Geneva Conference on Disarmament, pointing, in addition, to the interdependence between the negotiations that would eventually lead to such a ban and progress in other arms-control and disarmament forums, and emphasizing that advances in these areas would open up new routes to a nuclear test ban[8].

Although the link between a CTBT and progress in other disarmament forums was not formalized, the federal government incorporated the test ban into a wide-ranging "Ten Point Initiative" unveiled by Foreign Minister Klaus Kinkel in December 1993. This document reiterated the German aim of seeing a comprehensive and verifiable test ban treaty concluded by 1995. In the CTBT negotiations, the German delegation – like its Swedish counterpart – continued for some

---

[8] See the statement by the head of the German delegation, Permanent Mission of the Federal Republic of Germany to the United Nations, 8 Jan. 1991, mimeo.

time to assert that, if the treaty was to be truly comprehensive, preparatory measures for nuclear tests must also be included[9]. In February 1996 this position was abandoned, in order to ensure the timely finalization of the treaty. When announcing this change, the German commissioner for disarmament and arms control, Ambassador Hartmann, said he expected additions on "imminent nuclear explosions"! to be included in the text[10].

Another change in position occured towards the end of the negotiations, when the final treaty was taking shape and the deadline set by the NPT Review and Extension Conference was approaching. A demand for the conclusion of a CTBT to be linked to other disarmament steps – namely, reductions in the strategic nuclear arsenals of declared nuclear-weapon states – was met by German government insistence that no links be created between the CTBT and other (unacceptable) strictly timetabled steps towards the complete elimination of nuclear weapons[11].

Government reaction to the French resumption of nuclear tests was muted, and no criticism was voiced in public. Both Foreign Minister Kinkel and his secretary of state, Helmut Schäfer, acknowledged that they were "not happy" with the resumption but recognized that this was ultimately a national decision and had to be respected. At the same time, they stressed the positive change in the French position at the Geneva test-ban negotiations[12]. The German government's dislike of French testing was only voiced behind closed doors, so that the special Franco-German relationship would not be damaged. That relationship was evidently accorded a higher priority than the continuation of the French moratorium.

---

[9] See Rebecca JOHNSON, *"Geneva Update No.16"*, in: **Nuclear Proliferation News**, No.19, 7 March 1995, p.3.

[10] Rebecca JOHNSON, *"CTB Negotiations: Geneva Update No.26"*, in: **Disarmament Diplomacy**, No.2, Feb. 1996, p.10.

[11] See Presse- und Informationsamt der Bundesregierung, *Jahresabrüstungsbericht 1995*, Bonn, 1996, pp.10 ff.

[12] See the interview with KINKEL, in: **Tagesspiegel**, repr. in: H. MÜLLER & A. SCHAPER (eds), **Fatale Versuche. Zur Wiederaufnahme der französischen Kernwaffentests**, Holos, Bonn, 1995, p.35; the interview with Schäfer on Deutschlandfunk (national German radio) is repr. in: **Stichworte zur Sicherheitspolitik**, No.7, July 1995, pp.51-4.

This stance was also reflected in the parliamentary debate on the resumption of French nuclear tests, during which Chancellor Kohl stressed both the differences in position and the fact that the French decision was a sovereign act: the views of a friend had to be respected even if they differed from one's own. Voicing recommendations in public, or actually calling for French products to be boycotted, was, said Kohl, incomptabible with Franco-German friendship[13]. Members of Kohl's CDU/CSU parliamentary party were the only ones to argue along these lines.

All the other parties in the Bundestag criticized the French decision to varying degrees. This was true even of the junior partner in the governing coalition – the FDP. Its secretary-general, Wolfgang Gerhardt, described the resumption of nuclear tests as "incomprehensible and incapable of being explained to world opinion". Given the continuing nuclear overkill, what the world needed was not further qualitative improvements in nuclear arsenals, but their scrapping. For friends in particular, it should be possible openly to ask for the decision to resume nuclear testing to be reviewed. The FDP, said Gerhardt, appealed to the French to rectify this decision.

The Social Democratic Party whip, Rudolf Scharping, characterized the the French decision as a "militarily pointless undertaking" that entailed serious political risks. It was difficult to ask states to support the idea of nuclear non-proliferation or to accede to a comprehensive test ban treaty when a major country like France decided to expand and test its nuclear capabilities. Similarly, argued the SPD leader, it was difficult to promote the idea of a European Common Foreign and Security Policy when, on a major issue like this, a European state resorted to justifying its decision in terms of national interest.

Joseph Fischer, the whip for Bündnis 90/Die Grünen, was even more pessimistic about the negative repercussions which the French nuclear test would have on European integration. Further integration would be put at risk, he said, if the Europe of the future was based on

---

[13] See the statement by Chancellor Helmut Kohl during the parliamentary debate of 13 July 1995, as quoted in the weekly **Das Parlament**, 45/30, 21 July 1995, pp.2 ff. All other statements *ibid.*

the quest to secure national prestige through nuclear weapons testing. Because of this threat to European integration, because of the risks to the environment, especially around the test site, and because of the danger of a new arms race, Fischer demanded that the Bundestag adopt a clear and unequivoval stance against the tests. It should do this in the interests of European unity, Franco-German friendship, and international disarmament. He conceded the need for the government to observe diplomatic etiquette in its bilateral relations with the French, but he saw no use in seeking refuge in diplomatic formulas in the Bundestag.

The parliamentary debate was followed by the proposal of three motions – two from the Green Party and one from the Social Democrats[14]. In its first motion, the Green Party sought to get a Bundestag vote appealing to the French president to reverse his decision to resume testing and calling on the French National Assembly to try to influence President Chirac in this direction. The second Green motion called for the German federal government to bring the French government before the (European) Court of Justice for violating the EURATOM treaty by resuming nuclear tests. The SPD motion called on the Bundestag to condemn both French and Chinese nuclear testing. Somewhat surprisingly, the parliamentary majority of the governing coalition of CDU/CSU and FDP voted down all three motions. Evidently the criticisms voiced by the FDP during the Bundestag debate in July 1995 were not sufficient to free it from the straightjacket of coalition discipline and enable it to vote for a motion introduced by an opposition party.

3.2. Deeper Cuts versus the Implementation of Existing Disarmament Agreements

Neither the follow-on negotiations to START II nor the inclusion of the smaller nuclear-weapon states in the disarmament process have been widely debated or officially commented on in Germany. However, government experts seem to agree on a number of points,

---

[14] For the Green parliamentary motions, see BT-Drucksache 13/1986 of 13 July 1995 and 13/2270 of 6 Sept. 1995; for the SPD motion, see BT-Drucksache 13/2251 of 5 Sept. 1995.

namely: that the dynamic of the nuclear arms control process must not be lost; that the ABM treaty must remain one of the pillars of relations between the USA and Russia in the strategic nuclear realm; and that the ratification and implementation of START II and the verifiable destruction both of ground-based short-range missiles equipped with nuclear warheads and of nuclear artillery is of prime importance. As regards the latter two categories of nuclear weapons, no legally binding international commitment to disarmament exists: both the USA and the former Soviet Union made unilateral declarations only – in other words, undertakings which could, in principle, be reversed.

German input into the nuclear disarmament process has focused on the implementation of practical disarmament measures. Negotiations which were conducted during 1992 – and which were explicitly endorsed by the German parliament in a resolution of June of the same year – led to the conclusion, in that December, of two bilateral agreements between Germany and Russia on the provision of disarmament aid. The "Framework Agreement on Disarmament Aid" laid the foundations for German contributions to Russian disarmament efforts in the sphere of nuclear and chemical weapons. The second executive agreement provides for practical contributions, mainly to enhance nuclear safety[15]. In addition, a joint study was undertaken to evaluate the possibilities of irreversibly transforming weapons-grade plutonium into nuclear fuel for energy-generating purposes. On the basis of that study, which was completed in February 1995, a follow-up investigation into the technical and economic parameters for the construction of a pilot MOX fuel-fabrication plant was initiated in summer 1995.

A framework agreement similar to the one with Russia was concluded with the Ukraine in June 1993[16]. The project agreement needed to begin implementation of practical measures was concluded in October 1994, and the destruction of the first of the ICBM silos on Ukrainian territory was completed in December 1995[17].

---

[15] See Auswärtiges Amt, *Bericht zur Rüstungskontrolle und Abrüstung 1992*, 54. The German Russian framework agreement is repr. on pp.173-6.

[16] *Ibid.*, 176-9.

[17] Presse- und Informationsamt der Bundesregierung, **Jahresabrüstungsbericht 1995**, pp.25 ff.

Financial contributions to the disarmament process in these two countries amounted to DM 10 million in 1993, DM 9 million in 1994, DM 13 million in 1995, and DM 18 million in 1996, so that by the end of 1996, roughly DM 50 million had been allotted to disarmament in Russia and Ukraine[18] – a figure that was repeatedly criticized by the opposition parties in parliament as being too low. But in the matter of budgets, parliament is master of its own fate, and criticism must be directed more at the majority parties in parliament rather than at the government or its bureaucracies, which have repeatedly requested an increase in funding for disarmament aid to the former Soviet Union republics.

For 1997 another DM 15 million are scheduled to be spent for disarmament aid to Russia and the Ukraine. In the case of Russia, bilateral co-operation will be extended into a trilateral project involving France – which has recently undertaken similar studies on the conversion of weapons-grade plutonium to MOX fuel. France will erect a facility for transforming the plutonium contained in nuclear warheads into plutonium-oxide, while Germany will contribute a MOX fuel fabrication plant, for which it will draw on the experience and equipment of the Hanau MOX plant. The German government is keen that both the plant and the material processed in it should have some kind of safeguards imposed on them. As a means of financing the plants, their (commercial) use for the conversion of non-military plutonium is being considered – to begin once 50 tonnes of excess Russian military plutonium will have been converted.

3.3. The Transfer of Fissile Material from Weapons to Civilian Purposes

The transfer of fissile material from the military to the civilian fuel cycle may be viewed as a complement to existing disarmament agreements. Such transfers may be used to ensure that at least some of the huge amounts of weapons-grade fissile material being released under nuclear arms control agreements between the USA and the successor states of the Soviet Union are no longer available for military reuse.

---

[18] See the 1996 draft budget as proposed by the Federal Government in BT-Drucksache 13/2000-Epl 05, and as quoted in: **Woche im Bundestag**, No.16, 27 Sept. 1995, 31.

In this connection, Foreign Minister Kinkels "Ten-Point Initiative on Non-proliferation" of 16 December 1993 stressed the need for co-operative control over such material, under an international pluto-nium-control system. Multilateral negotiations on this type of inter-national regime have now been started in Vienna, but practical, short-term solutions are needed to deal with the highly enriched ura-nium (HEU) and the plutonium being released as part of the ongoing disarmament process.

HEU from dismantled nuclear warheads can easily be diluted with natural or depleted uranium. The resulting low-enriched uranium can only be used as fuel for light water reactors, but not for weapons. A comparable solution for plutonium would involve either the produc-tion of MOX fuel, which could be used in existing nuclear power reactors, or the mixing of plutonium with radioactive waste, followed by vitrification and disposal in a nuclear waste repository[19]. This lat-ter option would reduce the value of the plutonium, and this runs counter to the Russians' approach of exploiting what they see as the positive aspects of their fissile material. The previously mentioned joint German-Russian study on the feasibility of a MOX production plant in Russia is another example of this policy of offsetting losses in the military value of fissile material by attempting to exploit its perceived economic value.

As regards the possible transfer of the released material from mili-tary to civilian use through the production of MOX fuel elements in the Hanau MOX plant, factors other than disarmament value came into play here[20]. Most prominent amongst these was the problem of securing permission to use the almost complete Hanau facility, which has never gone into operation and has a rather peculiar history[21]. One factor in this history was the resistance shown by the anti-nuclear

---

[19] For a more detailed account of these options, including the "Hanau option", see Annette SCHAPER, *"Using Existing European MOX Fabrication Plants for the Disposal of Plutonium from Dismantled Warheads"*, in: W. G. SUTCLIFFE (ed.), **Selected Papers from Global 95**, LLNL, Livermore, June 1996, pp.197-209.

[20] *Ibid.*, pp. 202-8; the other two factors discussed by Schaper are "proliferation risks" and "costs", which will not be dealt with here.

[21] See Alexander KELLE & Harald MÜLLER, *"Germany"*, in: H. MÜLLER (ed.), **European Non-Proliferation Policy 1993-1995**, European Interuniversity Press, Brussels, 1996, pp.103-28.

regional government of Hesse when the required licences had to be issued for the facility to be completed and brought into operation. The region's willingness to allow the facility to operate temporarily for the purpose of disarming Russian weapons-grade plutonium was equally circumscribed. At any rate, the federal government did not pursue the "Hanau option" seriously, partly because it did not fit in with the governing parties' political agenda (the experience with the Castor transports of nuclear waste had not been encouraging) and partly because the information required from their Russian counterparts was not provided[22]. The reason for this Russian reluctance has, in its turn, to be sought in the preference of the Russian decision-makers to have a facility set up within Russia itself, so that an independent civilian fuel cycle could be created and the valuable material need not be transferred elsewhere.

In the end, the "Hanau option" did not materialize; an equivalent facility in Russia is still at the planning stage; and the plutonium released under the disarmament treaties entered into by Russia is left poorly safeguarded and not properly accounted for[23].

3.4. Cut-off of Fissile Material for Weapons Purposes

It would be difficult to find anyone in Germany opposed to the idea of a cut-off being agreed on the production of weapons-grade fissile material: the positive links between such a cut-off and the goals of nuclear disarmament and non-proliferation are too strong for this. A call for a cut-off was included in Foreign Minister Kinkel's "Ten-Point Initiative on Non-proliferation" and has been repeated by the government on various occasions. Political parties are equally in favour of it. The general assumption seems to have been that negotiations on a cut-off would follow on logically and swiftly once the CTBT had been concluded. However, the detail of such an agreement – its scope, EIF, verification provisions, and so on – have not

---

[22] Information obtained by the author.

[23] See William C. POTTER, *"Before the Deluge? Assessing the Threat of Nuclear Leakage from the Post-Soviet States"*, in: **Arms Control Today**, Oct. 1995, 25, 8, pp.9-16; William SUTCLIFFE & A. RUMYANTSEV, *"The Accounting and Control of Nuclear Material and Radioactive Substances in Russia"*, in: **Yaderni Kontrol, English Digest**, No.1, Spring 1996.

been the subject of public debate. Here too, it is only in expert circles that any of these ideas have been elaborated.

With regard to the scope of a future cut-off treaty: Germany supported resolution 48/75 L of the United Nations General Assembly as a basis for a negotiating mandate, despite the fact that it contained only a narrow interpretation of what negotiations on a cut-off should cover[24]. According to this, only future production of weapons-grade fissile material will be prohibited, and existing stocks will be left untouched. German experts appear to concur that this narrow interpretation should be used as a means of getting negotiations going and that the scope of the future treaty should then be broadened, ultimately producing a document that contains an irreversibility clause precluding the retransfer of excess military material, and material released under disarmament obligations, to military use. This preference for a broader scope is also reflected in the view taken by some experts that a ban on production does not cover all the possible sources of weapons-grade fissile material[25]. In this connection, four other ways in which stocks of weapons-grade fissile material might be increased have been identified:

- future weapons-grade fissile material produced for civilian purposes might be redirected to military use;
- existing civilian weapons-grade fissile material might be redirected to military use;
- weapons-grade fissile material from dismantled nuclear warheads that has been taken out of military control might be reused for military purposes;
- as yet undeclared weapons-grade fissile material in states that are not signatories to the Non-Proliferation Treaty might be used for weapons purposes.

---

[24] In a speech to the CD in Jan. 1997, the German delegate, Ambassador Wolfgang Hoffmann, still cited the resolution as the basis of German policy on the commencement of negotiations on a cut-off: see the *"Statement by the Permanent Representative of the Federal Republic of Germany to the Conference on Disarmament, Ambassador Wolfgang Hoffman"*, Geneva, 23 Jan. 1997.

[25] Interestingly, official German statements also make no mention of a "production cut-off", only of a "cut-off of fissile material": see *ibid.*

As these examples clearly show, there are ways and means in which weapons-grade fissile material can be acquired without any production process being involved. It therefore seems reasonable not to limit the scope of a future cut-off to a ban on production. Instead, the technical parameters of the material to be cut off should be supplemented by a "specific origin criterion" corresponding to the four paths to acquisition listed above.

3.5. Establishment of a Nuclear Weapons Register

In its most innovative part the already mentioned Ten-Point Initiative on Non-proliferation called for the establishment of a nuclear weapons register under the auspices of the UN[26]. This call for greater transparency with respect to the existing nuclear arsenals aimed at establishing a prerequisite for successful and verifiable nuclear arms reduction. The logic behind the request for such a register is that only when the exact amount of nuclear weapons still in place is known can the success of further arms control steps be demonstrated. This original German proposal met with vigorous opposition from Bonn's NWS allies, and it is therefore unlikely to be the subject of specific negotiations in the near future[27]. Nor was it pursued very vigorously at the time of the NPT Extension Conference. None the less, it can be assumed to be waiting in the wings, to be reintroduced at a more propitious moment.

3.6. Application and Scope of IAEA Safeguards

At the 1985 NPT Review Conference, West Germany had led the opposition to making full-scope safeguards on nuclear exports to non-NPT non-nuclear-weapon states a condition of supply. Its statement at the 1990 NPT Review Conference that it would now require such safeguards therefore represented a remarkable shift in position. Even more surprising was the announcement that all existing agreements

---

[26] *Deutsche 10-Punkte Initiative zur Nichtverbreitungspolitik*, Bonn, 15 Dec. 1993, repr. in **Jahresabrüstungsbericht 1993,** Bonn, 1994, pp.201 ff.

[27] See the detailed discussion of this proposal in Harald MÜLLER, *"Transparency in Nuclear Arms: Towards a Nuclear Weapons Register"*, in: **Arms Control Today**, Vol.24 No.8, 1994, pp.3-7.

would have to be renegotiated within five years in order to conform with this new policy.

Following this declaration, German nuclear diplomacy adopted as one of its foremost priorities the harmonization and tightening-up of the requirements on safeguards, both among the NSG countries and among those taking part in the deliberations of the EPC working-group on nuclear non-proliferation. Whilst the German delegation to the NSG urged the adoption of full-scope safeguards as a condition of supplying non-NPT states, the delegation to the EPC working-group focused on the strengthening of safeguards within the NPT framework.

Germany was one of the least voluble participants in the discussions on the "93 + 2" programme on the improvement of safeguards. Though the German position was one of support for the Board of Governors of the IAEA's decision to endorse the "general thrust" of "93 + 2", the German government – more specifically, the ministry of research and technology – and German industry were hesitant even about this. The ambition of the secretariat to create "reliable assurances of the absence of undeclared activities" was seen as unachievable, since assurances of the absence of something cannot be given with total certainty. Germany preferred the less ambitious formula "enhanced capability to detect undeclared activities". All in all, the German government had profound doubts as to whether the measures proposed by the secretariat would actually serve this objective rather than simply leading to discrimination between potential proliferators – who, of course, would not fulfil commitments to report more comprehensively on their activities – and faithful regime members like Germany, who would submit to the enhanced reporting requirements and would probably be rewarded with even more inspections. In other words, the existing disproportionate burden on the advanced industrialized countries would grow, without any tangible improvement in the safeguards aimed at "suspect states". Germany therefore requested guarantees that "enhanced access" would not become part of routine inspections. Enhanced reporting and extended access, in the German view, would lead to grave constitutional problems, as these requirements were not really covered by the NPT itself and could thus be challenged before the Constitutional Court on the grounds that they were threatening the right to property, as defined in Article 14.

Unfortunately, to begin with, Germany (and like-minded countries such as Belgium, Switzerland, Spain, and Japan) failed to come up with a constructive alternative and instead pursued a strategy of procrastination. Although the German objections were clearly not without foundation, this strategy prevented a serious and productive discussion. It was not until the end of 1995 that a more constructive approach emerged. By the end of 1996, the problem areas had been reduced to three:

– universal application of the new safeguards,
– extent to which the requirements in regard to declaration should be expanded,
– extent to which IAEA inspectors would have "universal" and short-notice access under the new safeguards.

As regards universality: the compromise eventually reached stipulated that the nuclear-weapon states would accept those additional safeguards that can meaningfully be applied in their cases and which do not compromise their status as nuclear-weapon states. The principle of universal application will be laid down explicitly in the preamble to the supplementary protocol.

With respect to the declarations required by the new protocol: Germany was of the view that the agency should only be given information whose collection could be justified by government authorities and which could be put to meaningful use by the IAEA. The rights of access of IAEA inspectors had to be limited to agreed facilities, which the inspectors would then have the right to inspect at any time. The way in which these problems were ultimately resolved closely resembled the original German ideas: "Before the IAEA can do monitoring or get extra information under Part 2 [of "93 + 2"] it will have to provide sufficient grounds to justify it." Plans for "strategic sampling" and "wide area monitoring" were also abandoned by the IAEA; instead, a compromise seems to have been reached on "directed sampling[28]".

---

[28] See Mark Hibbs, *"Language Curbing IAEA Access Unlocks Progress on 93-plus-2"*, in: **Nuclear Fuel**, 22/5, 10 Mar. 1997, pp.12 ff.

3.7. Nuclear Weapon Free Zone in Europe / Treaty Banning the Development and Production of New Nuclear Warheads / Convention to Ban Nuclear Weapons

The very limited German debate on nuclear arms control and disarmament takes almost no account of either the creation of a nuclear-weapon-free zone (NWFZ) in Europe or the conclusion of a treaty banning the development and production of new nuclear warheads – let alone a convention to ban nuclear weapons. However, there have been some isolated statements on these matters – and where even these are lacking, it is possible to deduce attitudes towards specific issues from more general positions taken by the federal government or the political parties.

The idea of a NWFZ in Europe was rejected by Chancellor Kohl in an interview in April 1996. Should such a zone none the less be established, German participation in it would, he said, only be considered at some distant point in the future[29]. In contrast, the German government has actively promoted the idea – agreed on within the NATO framework – of not deploying nuclear weapons in those states now joining the alliance. The German government's position on the creation of a NWFZ in Europe, or on the deployment of NATO's remaining nuclear weapons, seems thus to be determined largely by the consensus within the alliance. Any other approach might open up the Pandora's box constituted by the nuclear weapons still deployed on (West) German territory. Given the problems it has to cope with in regard to the transport and disposal of civilian nuclear waste, it is quite understandable that the federal government avoids opening up this flank as well.

Both the Party of Democratic Socialism (PDS) and Bündnis 90/ Die Grünen support the creation of a NWFZ in Europe and the withdrawal of the remaining nuclear weapons on German territory. They

---

[29] The interview, conducted by a correspondent from *Yaderni Kontrol*, is cited in Vladimir A. ORLOV, *"Nuclear Weapon Free Zone in Central and Eastern Europe: Proposals and their Future"*, paper presented at the Kiev nonproliferation workshop sponsored by the Center for Nonproliferation Studies of the Monterey Institute of International Studies, 26-7 Sept. 1996, mimeo.

have made repeated attempts to get a ban on nuclear weapons and their deployment on German territory included in the *Grundgesetz* (Basic Law or constitution). Not surprisingly, these proposals have always been voted down by the Bundestag majority[30]. Most members of the established parties can thus be expected to reject proposals for the creation of a NWFZ in Europe – with the SPD being a reluctant supporter.

Nor can the idea of a convention to ban nuclear weapons be expected to secure majority political support in the foreseeable future. This became clear towards the end of 1996, when both the PDS and Bündnis 90/Die Grünen introduced two motions in support of the notion of a nuclear-weapon-free world (NWFW)[31]. Both motions cited the advisory opinion of the International Court of Justice and the report of the Canberra Commission as the benchmarks which the German government should follow in this area. Practical recommendations to be found in one or other motion, or both (they overlapped a great deal) included:

- supporting the Malaysian resolution for a NWFW in the UNGA;
- urging the nuclear-weapon states to comply with Article VI of the NPT and to commence disarmament negotiations, with the aim of securing a nuclear weapons convention analogous to the conventions on biological and chemical weapons;
- working for the abolition of NATO's strategy of nuclear deterrence and – as a first step – persuading it to abandon its first-use option;
- giving up any European nuclear designs and convincing France and the UK to disarm their nuclear arsenals completely;
- unconditionally renouncing any national nuclear options and, on that basis, a) incorporating the renunciation of nuclear weapons into the German Basic Law, and b) halting the construction of

---

[30] See *Woche im Bundestag, passim.*

[31] See *"Antrag der Abegeordneten Angelika Beer and der Fraktion Bündnis 90/ Die Grünen: Konvention zur Ächtung und Abschaffung aller Atomwaffen"*, Deutscher Bundestag, 13. Wahlperiode, Drucksache 13/6383, 3 Dec. 1996, and *"Antrag der Abgeordneten Andrea Gysi... und der Gruppe der PDS: Eine Welt ohne Atomwaffen"*, BT-Drucksache 13/5987, 6 Nov. 1996.

the FRM-II research reactor and putting an end to the "pluto-nium economy" in Germany.

Both motions were debated in December 1996. During the debate, the CDU/CSU parliamentary party's spokesman on security and de-fence, Friedbert Pflüger, described the idea of a NWFW as utopian. It was, he believed, crucial to keep the momentum of the nuclear disarmament process going, and this included not only ensuring the ratification of START II by the Russian Duma, but securing further drastic reductions in the number of nuclear warheads in all five nu-clear-weapon states. To Pflüger, a convention in which the nuclear-weapon states confirmed the continuation of the nuclear disarmament process for the coming decades was more important than one which aimed at a NWFW. As to the ultimate goal of banning nuclear weap-ons, he called this a "dangerous fantasy", given the existing prolif-eration threats and other security risks[32].

In contrast, Gernot Erler, for the SPD, confirmed his party's will-ingness to support the ultimate goal of a NWFW, though rejecting the method which the two motions proposed for achieving this. It made more sense, thought Erler, to agree the next practical step to a NWFW than to formulate declaratory resolutions with no practical relevance. The measures he recommended were:

- implementing the CTBT and overcoming the objections of India and a number of other countries to it,
- ensuring the long-overdue ratification of START II by the Russian Duma,
- negotiating a cut-off convention,
- negotiating a treaty prohibiting the production, ownership, or use of ballistic missiles with a range of more than 150 km.

The most suitable venue for negotiating, and ensuring the imple-mentation of, these measures was, thought Erler, the "preparatory conferences" (*sic*) of the next NPT Review Conference[33].

---

[32] See Deutscher Bundestag, Plenarprotokoll, 13. Wahlperiode, 145. Sitzung, 5 Dec. 1996, pp.13216 ff.

[33] *Ibid.*, pp.13217 ff.

As these statements show, a ban on the development and production of new nuclear warheads is not a subject on which political comment is forthcoming. In the case of the federal government and the parties in the ruling coalition, the silence may also have something to do with the desire not to embarrass NWS allies. This reticence on the part of the political leadership, and the memory of the allies' response to the German proposal for a nuclear weapons register, are the probable causes of the ruling bureaucracies' unwillingness to push the idea of a treaty on new nuclear warheads. Such a treaty would essentially constitute an attempt to close the gaps left by the CTBT – gaps deliberately left in order to get the nuclear-weapon states behind the idea of a CTBT.

4. Conclusion

There is no consensus or clear trend in the German debate on the future role of nuclear weapons or the most suitable disarmament measures to be taken next. Positions range from continuing adherence to NATO's first-use option to a struggle to achieve greater transparency in the arsenals of the nuclear-weapon states. But a strong and coherent voice in favour of greater efforts towards nuclear disarmament is lacking. This is all the more regrettable given the weight which resolute German support for nuclear disarmament might have in the international discourse.

Germany's ambivalent stance can be traced back to Cold War times, when this clash of interests – between a reduction in nuclear discrimination and the benefits of the US nuclear umbrella – was resolved in favour of the demands of security. Reducing discrimination through disarmament was important, but clearly a lesser priority. Since the end of the East-West conflict, the hierarchy of government priorities has been reversed: the emphasis now is manifestly on increasing transparency and establishing additional controls in the nuclear-weapon states – and not so much in the threshold countries.

The need to implement existing arms control and disarmament agreements and negotiate additional ones is undisputed across the whole political spectrum, provided the discussion remains at a general

level. But talk of making deep cuts that would reduce nuclear arsenals more or less to zero makes many feel uneasy; and posing the
question of how security is to be assured in a nuclear-weapon-free
world causes even more widespread confusion. Hence, the German
debate on how far the nuclear disarmament process should proceed
still has a long way to go before it answers the question of how such
disarmament.

BELGIUM

Quentin MICHEL

1. Introduction

It is difficult to identify a single Belgian nuclear arms control and disarmament policy. The definition and the implementation of this policy fall logically within the competencies of the Ministry of Foreign Affairs and the Ministry of Defence and, on some points, the Ministry of Economic Affairs. The coalition government formed after the general election of June 1994 gave the portfolios of Defence and Foreign Affairs to two different political parties which do not take exactly the same view on the disarmament issue[1]. Moreover, since 1994 these two posts have been held by several different ministers[2].

Nevertheless, Belgium has over the last fifty years fully integrated its defence and security policy within its participation in and commitment to NATO. As the Minister of Defence, Leo Delcroix, wrote in 1994 in the introduction to the Belgian Defence White Paper: "Collective defence was and is our motto. Transatlantic solidarity was and is

---

[1] The Minister of Foreign Affairs, Erik Derijke, is a Dutch-speaking Socialist and the Minister of Defence, Jean Pol Poncelet, is a French-speaking Christian Democrat (1997).

[2] At the Ministry of Foreign Affairs: Willy Claes (resigned in October 1994), Frank Vandenbroucke (resigned March 1995) and presently Erik Derycke. – The Ministry of Defence has been headed by Leo Delcroix (resigned December 1994), Karel Pinxten (resigned June 1995), Melchior Wathelet (September 1995) and presently Jean-Pol Poncelet.

our strength. Recent developments, it is true, are fully in line with a thorough Europeanization of our collective defence apparatus, but the essence of the Alliance remains immutable." Officially, nuclear disarmament is considered as one of the Belgian government's foreign policy priorities.

This affects nuclear weapon states through the dismantling of nuclear arsenals, but also greatly affects non-nuclear weapon states as far as non-proliferation is concerned.

Of these two approaches, prevention and therapy, the first is clearly the more urgent to avoid the risk of horizontal proliferation, but for Belgium the second is obviously essential as a way of reaching the goal of a world without nuclear weapons.

2. The Security Situation after the End of the Cold War

As in many other NATO member states, the end of the Cold War has affected the perception of security in Belgium quite fundamentally.

During the Cold War the major threat perceived was the military potential of the Warsaw Pact. Although there were large demonstrations against the stationing of cruise missiles on Belgian territory in the early 1980s, a consensus to respect NATO policy was widely shared by the population and officialdom.

Officially[3], military security was based on the five following strategic components:

- deterrence and especially nuclear deterrence as the keystone of all strategic thinking. This deterrence was linked with "flexible response", characterised by uncertainty and ambiguity in order to keep open NATO's options;
- arms control to ensure the nuclear balance;
- crisis management focused on the management of crises between the two blocs which might lead to nuclear war;

---

[3] As defined by the *Defence White Paper '94*, p.14.

- limited war to raise the nuclear threshold and therefore render nuclear deterrence more credible;
- and finally collective defence, guaranteed by NATO and Western European Union (WEU) membership, in order to enhance self-defence capability.

Since the end of the Cold War, threat perceptions in Belgium have obviously changed. A direct threat to the nation is no longer assumed and national defence and security policy has been extensively reviewed. This new perception does not differ fundamentally from that of other NATO member states, and has been fully integrated into the European and transatlantic dimensions.

Officially[4], Belgium's security policy pursues two objectives: firstly, maintaining peace and preventing war in Europe, and secondly, protecting human rights and democratic values.

These objectives should be achieved by a security policy based on deterrence, solidarity, stability and continuity.

Deterrence is based on both conventional and nuclear means but also on a range of diplomatic, political, economic and military instruments. Nuclear weapons are considered essential to the preservation of peace by their unique contribution which renders the risks of aggression incalculable and thus unacceptable.

Solidarity is essential to guarantee the security of the non-nuclear weapon states, and should be reinforced by a network of relationships, exchanges and co-operation in all areas which have an influence on security.

Finally, stability and continuity of the different security structures existing or to be created is sought, with the aim of reaching a general balance.

These objectives should be achieved along the following five main lines of policy: developing the European Union, maintaining the transatlantic link, broadening co-operation with other countries, reinforcing the role of the United Nations, and participating in arms control.

---

[4] As specified by the *Defence White Paper '94*, p.25.

As stipulated by the Maastricht Treaty, the European Union (EU) should in the long term develop into a coherent political entity capable of pursuing a common foreign, security, and defence policy. In this context, Belgium intends to support the strengthening of the efficiency of the defence and security structure of the Union. For example, Belgium is unambiguously in favour of a majority system as the basic principle of Union decision-making process, and of integrating into the Union treaty the principles regarding the missions of the WEU defined by the Petersberg Declaration[5].

Belgium also intends to play an active role in favour of the WEU as the armed wing of the EU, and makes its Army, Air Force and Navy available to the WEU. One application of this policy has been Belgian participation in the Eurocorps[6].

Even if the presence of North American troops in Europe is seen as essential for security in Europe, a strengthening of the European pillar is regarded as necessary to demonstrate the willingness of the European countries to fulfill their responsibilities.

At the regional level, Belgium is endeavouring to participate in building up a pan-European architecture based on several institutions of which the Organization for Security and Cooperation in Europe is the largest. The OSCE is seen as an important forum for negotiation as part of the effort to prevent the development of regional conflicts.

Belgium also favours strengthening the United Nations' role in preventing and settling conflicts and maintaining peace in the world[7].

Finally, Belgium supports within the various forums, such as the United Nations and the OSCE, efforts to pursue arms control and reduction. For example, Belgium has supported, like the other members of the European Union, the indefinite and unconditional extension of the Nuclear Non-proliferation Treaty and the adoption of a Comprehensive Test Ban Treaty. It is a co-signatory of the convention

---

[5] The Petersberg declaration was issued by the WEU Council of Ministers for Foreign Affairs and Defence (19 June 1992).

[6] The Belgian mechanised division has been integrated into the Eurocorps.

[7] Belgian has participated in peacekeeping operations in the former Yugoslavia, in Somalia, and in Rwanda.

on chemical weapons and advocates a common European policy on arms exports.

There is no doubt that the end of the Cold War caused some questions on the usefulness of the armed forces to be raised in Belgium, and initiated a complete redefinition of the defence tasks assigned to them. A consequence of this redefinition was the necessity of a complete reorganisation of the different forces, to provide them with the flexibility and specialised training required for international peacekeeping and peace enforcement tasks. However, the problem raised by public finance questions and the necessity to reduce the large government deficit has been seen by successive governments as a primary consideration in the reorganisation of the armed forces' structures. Major savings efforts have been imposed on the Defence Ministry and its budget was reduced during the 1985-1994 period by 20.7 percent in real terms.

Early in 1993[8], the government approved the project of Minister Delcroix entitled "Bear 97", which started a major restructuring process within the armed forces. The plan practically ended conscription and set in train a progressive shift to a professional army, with a maximum strength of 40,000 servicemen in active service and a maximum of 5,000 civilians[9]. Consequently, a reduction of the number of units and the elimination or reduction of weapon systems and equipment have followed[10]. Hardware like battle tanks and fighter aircraft,

---

[8] 29 January 1993.

[9] From around 80,000 in 1992.

[10] The new Armed Forces will be structured as follows :

The interservice territorial command, which will centralise tasks formerly allotted to different services. This command will be divided into a staff and four groups (General Support Group, Infrastructure Group, Telecommunication Group and Medical Group).

The Army: Intervention Force (divided into 5 combat units), Combat Support Division (includes all the organisations and centres responsible for instructions and specialised training), Logistical Support Division (provides direct and general support in the areas of supplies, maintenance and transport).

The Air Force: Operations Headquarters (coordination and execution of all operations, including training), four Tactical Units (Two Tactical Wings of 36 F16, an Air Transport Wing and a Heli Search and Rescue Squadron), Operational Support Units (Meteorological Wing, Air Traffic Control Centre, Radar Control Centre), Schools (Flying and technical schools), Logistical Units.

The Navy: Naval Operation Command, Logistics Command, Training Command, Belgian-Netherlands School of Mine Warfare.

and also real estate property, uniforms, wheeled vehicles, and ammunition have been put on sale. If most of the smaller items of equipment could be sold without restrictions and will yield a reasonable return[11], it will be harder to find buyers for larger items such as a frigate or the 24 HAWK launchers which meet the conditions imposed by arms export legislation.

The restructuring plan has also frozen the national defence budget at a ceiling of 98 billion francs in nominal terms until the end of 1997. This continuous reduction in real terms imposed on the defence budget has begun to affect the effective fulfilment of the new defence tasks. Moreover, the budget restrictions imposed by the plan "Bear 97" are considered by the new Minister of Defence, Jean-Pol Poncelet, to be so drastic that he has not authorised the complete implementation of the plan[12]. At present, an increase in the defence budget is not conceivable. The government clearly has other priorities, and any such proposal would be unlikely to find the necessary political support from all the parties making up the government coalition. Finally, the government has agreed, at the request of the Minister of Defence, to postpone the completion of the restructuring plan to the end of 1998, which will make it possible to reconsider its budgetary impact[13].

3. The Role of Nuclear Weapons in National Security

Belgium has traditionally been a strong supporter of NATO, and despite the dissolution of the USSR NATO is still considered officially as an essential component of West European security. The Belgian authorities fully support the new tasks of NATO nuclear forces as defined by the Alliance's new strategic concept, adopted at the Rome summit in November 1991[14].

---

[11] By January 1996, 2 billions Belgian francs worth of hardware had been sold.

[12] *"Le ministre Poncelet tente de corriger les excès des prédécesseurs : l'armée saignée par le plan Delcroix"*, in: **Le Soir**, 17 November 1995, p.5. The retirement conditions offered to Army personnel were not sufficiently attractive, and only a very small number accepted them. It would have been politically and economically difficult to force more personnel to resign.

[13] See National Defence Budget 1997, introduced by the Minister, 6 November 1997.

[14] The Alliance's Strategic concept agreed by the Heads of State and Government participating in the meeting of the North Atlantic Council in Rome on 7th-8th November, 1991.

This document sets out the tasks of NATO nuclear forces as follows:

> "The fundamental purpose of the nuclear forces of the Allies is political : to preserve peace and prevent coercion and any kind of war. [...]
>
> A credible Alliance nuclear posture and the demonstration of Alliance solidarity and common commitment to war prevention continue to require widespread participation by European Allies involved in collective defence planning in nuclear roles, in peacetime basing of nuclear forces on their territory and in command, control and consultation arrangements. Nuclear forces based in Europe and committed to NATO provide an essential political link between the European and the North American members of the Alliance. The Alliance will therefore maintain adequate nuclear forces in Europe. [...]
>
> The circumstances in which any use of nuclear weapons might have to be contemplated by them are therefore even more remote. They can therefore significantly reduce their sub-strategic nuclear forces. They will maintain adequate sub-strategic forces based in Europe which will provide an essential link with strategic nuclear forces, reinforcing the trans-Atlantic link. These will consist solely of dual capable aircraft which could, if necessary, be supplemented by offshore systems[15]".

The maintenance for the foreseeable future of an appropriate (reduced) mix of nuclear and conventional forces based in Europe is seen as essential to guarantee the Belgian security. These forces should have the necessary capabilities and the appropriate flexibility and survivability to be perceived as credible and effective. In conformity with NATO nuclear policy, Belgium has organised and put at the disposal of the Alliance air forces and storage facilities which could play a role in this field.

The political role of nuclear weapons is widely accepted by Belgian politicians, but some doubts have been expressed about their capacity to deter the potential use of weapons of mass destruction against an ally. If this was true during the Cold War because the

---

[15] Paragraphs 55, 56 and 57 of the Alliance's Strategic concept.

adversaries shared the same kind of rationality and the relationship was essentially based on a kind of trust, it is not self-evident that this is still the case. Present conditions differ greatly from the Cold War situation, and some aspects will need to be carefully analysed. For example, are we convinced:

- that the adversary is deterred by a potential use of nuclear weapons?;
- that his rationality is the same as ours?;
- that we can communicate effectively with the proliferant and that we appear credible (i.e. our declaratory policy is convincing)?;
- that we know exactly what is to be deterred?

4. Public Debate on Nuclear Weapons and Nuclear Disarmament

Public interest in nuclear issues in Belgium is usually rather low, except when the population feels directly threatened for some reason. Most public debates on nuclear issues are related to nuclear power generation. For example, there has been an intensive debate on the question of the most suitable site for the permanent storage facility for low-level and short mid-life radioactive waste which is to be built on Belgian territory. Nuclear weapons and nuclear disarmament in particular do not provoke any special reactions. Most of the population is in favour of nuclear disarmament and the policy followed by the government does not seem to be contested by the mass media or by Parliament[16].

The resumption of French nuclear testing in the summer 1995 gave rise to a renewal of public interest in nuclear disarmament, but it did not mobilise the population to anything like the same extent as the planned stationing of cruise missiles on Belgian territory in the early 1980s[17]. A small demonstration was organised in front of the French

---

[16] Only three parliamentary questions were put to the government during the 1991-1995 period. All those three came from H. Van Dienderen, a member of AGALEV, the Green Dutch-speaking political party, and requested clarification of government policy concerning nuclear disarmament.

[17] Large demonstrations against the stationing of cruise missiles on Belgian territory took place in Brussels in 1981, 1983 and 1985.

Embassy on July 14, 1995[18] and at the end of September a larger one brought more than eleven thousand demonstrators to Brussels. The participants in this last demonstration were mostly Dutch-speaking citizens and representatives of different nongovernmental organisations (Greenpeace, Pax Christi, Oxfam), of youth associations, trade unions and some political parties (Dutch-speaking Christian Democrats, French and Dutch-speaking Socialists, French and Dutch-speaking Greens, Dutch-speaking Liberals and some extreme right and left-wingers such as the Vlaams Blok and the Belgian Workers Party).

The reaction of the Federal authorities was surprisingly strong and widely supported by most of the political parties. Less than 24 hours after the French President's announcement of the nuclear tests, the Belgian Federal Government, after consultation with its Benelux partners, issued a communiqué which "deplored" the French decision[19].

Furthermore, a resolution was adopted in September 1995 by the Senate[20] and by the House of Representatives[21] which required the Federal Government to protest formally against the French tests and to undertake, in the context of bilateral relations within the European Union or at the Conference on Disarmament in Geneva, action to persuade nuclear weapon states to give up nuclear testing. Some members of parliament[22] even embarked in the "Kaunitoni", which should have participated in the "peace fleet" but for technical reasons[23] never reached Mururoa.

In July 1995, Eric Derijcke, the Minister of Foreign Affairs, met Hervé de Charette, the French Minister of Foreign Affairs, in Paris. During the meeting, a resumption of the nuclear tests was discussed and Derijcke advocated a reversal of the French decision.

---

[18] Most of the demonstrators were supporters of Greenpeace or members of Ecolo (Green party).

[19] After each test the government issued a similar communiqué which "regretted" the French decision.

[20] Senate Resolution of October 12 1995 (Document 32/1).

[21] House of Representatives Resolution of November 11, 1995 (Document 49/1).

[22] Olivier Deleuze and Vera Dua (Greens), Philippe Coene and Philippe Mahoux (Socialists), Marc Van Peel (Christian Democrat).

[23] The main reason was that the engine broke down completely halfway to Mururoa.

In October 1995 the Minister of Foreign Affairs declared that "Belgium will follow the position of the Commission[24]" following the declaration of EU Commission President Jacques Santer, who stated that the EU Commission had the right to ensure that peaceful and military activities which generate radiation respected radioactive protection norms.

Finally, in December 1995, Belgium, along with ten other EU member states, voted for a resolution in the General Assembly of the United Nations which condemned French and Chinese nuclear tests. The Belgian vote and that of the two other Benelux members[25], was explained in terms of the need to make clear "Benelux disappointment regarding any initiative which goes against the nuclear disarmament objective, even if they could not fully agree with the text of the resolution". In retaliation, the French President Jacques Chirac decided to postpone sine die a meeting planned with the Belgian Prime Minister Jean Luc Dehaenne.

5. *Attitudes of the Political and Security Elites towards Nuclear Arms, Nuclear Arms Control and Disarmament*

It is rather difficult to define precisely the Belgian political and security elites' views on nuclear arms control and disarmament. All political parties support nuclear disarmament in general terms, and also the final goal of complete nuclear disarmament, but the question has never, except occasionally with regard to specific issues[26], been the subject of a major debate in Parliament. Government policy seems to be widely supported and has never been openly contested.

---

[24] Declaration made at the External Relations Commission of the House of Representatives (CRB 1995-1996. Commission of External Relations, Minutes of the plenary session, Wednesday 11 October 1995).

The main argument is based on Article 34 of the Treaty establishing the European Atomic Energy Community, which requires Member States to consult the Commission before conducting experimental explosions.

[25] The Netherlands and Luxembourg. See Declaration made by the Belgian delegation in the name of the Benelux countries.

[26] Mainly in summer 1995 in connection with the resumption of French nuclear testing.

To increase the chances of success of the final objective of complete disarmament, the prevention of nuclear weapons proliferation should, to guarantee its universality, be dealt with in a multilateral framework. In this context, Belgium regards the NPT as the cornerstone of the non-proliferation regime and regrets that some states which continuously claim to support nuclear disarmament do not follow that policy and refuse to ratify the treaty.

To reinforce prevention, the Belgian government has consistently supported and contributed to work on the Comprehensive Test Band Treaty (CTBT) initiated during the Conference on Disarmament (CD)[27]. When in June 1996 no consensus could be reached in the Ad Hoc Committee of the CD, the Belgian delegation supported the Australian initiative to submit the draft CTBT, identical to that negotiated in the CD, for adoption by the General Assembly even though the draft was considered to be far from perfect. The Belgian delegation underlined in particular three deficiencies of the draft treaty :

> "To begin with, we would have preferred in the Preamble a firmer text on the question of nuclear disarmament. As the representative of Belgium said before the Conference on Disarmament on 15 February 1996, 'the Conference on Disarmament has a role to play in nuclear disarmament, as it is proving with the current CTBT negotiations'. That being so, it would have been normal if, in the preamble, the CTBT had been placed in the context of the process of nuclear disarmament.
>
> In addition, Belgium is disappointed with respect to the verification machinery, particularly on-site inspections, for it considers that this system should have been fundamentally deterrent in nature – an aspect that seems totally to have vanished, so cumbersome and complicated is the procedure provided for.
>
> Lastly Belgium also has reservations regarding entry into force: the wording decided on is not bad in itself, but it lacks flexibility, which could have adverse effects for the universality of the treaty. Belgium, for its part, advocated entry into force immediately upon the signing of the treaty.[28]"

---

[27] Nevertheless, the adoption of a Comprehensive Test Ban Treaty was not, before or after the United Nations resolution, an issue of public interest.

[28] *Report of the Conference on Disarmament to the General Assembly of the United Nations*, 12 September 1996, CD/1436, p.47.

A cut-off of the production of fissile materials for weapons purposes is supported by Belgium. Negotiation on that issue should take place within the framework of the CD as long as this conference is the only multilateral forum which is dedicated to negotiating universal treaties. The Belgian delegation was rather disappointed that the CD did not re-establish an Ad-Hoc Committee on this issue during its 1996 session.

Negotiations on the reduction of nuclear arsenals should be conducted exclusively, in the interests of efficiency and political realism, by the nuclear weapon states. To set these debates in the context of multilateral fora would even be counterproductive. Nevertheless, non-nuclear weapon states should urge the USA and Russia to pursue their disarmament negotiations to a point where they could be joined by the three other nuclear weapon states. In general Belgium supports, at least through its diplomacy, any initiative taken to reach the final goal of complete nuclear disarmament. So, for example, the conclusion of a START III treaty would be welcomed.

Belgium advocates the application of IAEA Safeguards to all peaceful activities of nuclear weapon states and also to all nuclear material resulting from the dismantling of nuclear warheads. For Belgium, the application of IAEA safeguards has over the years imposed an ever-increasing burden, especially in financial terms, on Belgian nuclear facilities. In this context, the application of the safeguards to the whole fuel cycle for civil use in the NWS appears to be necessary to balance the unfair economic advantage gained by NWS. It should be noted that the Belgian nuclear industry is an important power source; more than fifty percent of Belgian power generation is derived from nuclear energy[29].

It should also be noted that the Belgian nuclear industry has developed important MOX fuel manufacturing activities. For these reasons, as long the MOX option is a possible choice for the disposal of plutonium leftover from the dismantling of nuclear warheads, it will be of interest for the Belgium industry.

---

[29] 55, 2% in 1995 (OECD Nuclear Energy Data 1996).

6. *Conclusion*

Nuclear disarmament is not a major concern of the Belgian political and security elites, nor that of the population. There are no fundamental conflicts of opinion and most of the elites consciously or unconsciously support government policy. On questions of national security, Belgium lies within the Alliance consensus and supports, for economic and political reasons, any initiative which could reinforce the role of the European Union in this field.

Officially, Belgium pursues the final goal of complete nuclear disarmament but the authorities are well aware that this will not materialise soon. For that reason Belgium, as a non-nuclear weapon state with a large nuclear industry, contributes to and co-operates with all fora related to nuclear non-proliferation. Non-proliferation and promotion of peaceful uses of nuclear energy can be identified as the two central concerns of its policy in this field.

THE NETHERLANDS

Marianne VAN LEEUWEN

1. The Security Situation after the End of the Cold War

In the Netherlands, changes in perceptions of security risks after the end of the Cold War do not differ fundamentally from those in many other West European countries.

During the period of the Cold War, the feeling that the Soviet Union presented the major threat to Dutch security was widely shared, although there was no consensus. As a consequence, the Netherlands' membership of NATO was widely accepted as necessary and proper, although here again there was no full agreement. At the end of the 1970s and in the early 1980s the NATO decision to station cruise missiles on Dutch territory triggered a major political and public debate in the country as well as mass protest. The Dutch government, without explicitly refusing to implement the NATO decision, successfully adopted a policy of stalling by making implementation conditional upon the results of arms control negotiations. Eventually, the controversial NATO decision was in effect reversed in the INF Treaty as a result of the arms control policies of the Soviet Union under Michael Gorbachev.

With the end of communist rule in the Soviet Union and the subsequent dissolution of the USSR, threat perceptions in the Netherlands obviously changed – as did views on the usefulness of the military apparatus. The main consequence was that military expenditure was cut, while the functioning of the Dutch armed forces was reconsidered and adapted to make it more flexible and better suited to international peace-keeping and peace-enforcement tasks[1]. Conscription was ended in 1996. Dutch soldiers, for the first time in more than twenty years, have to wear their hair cut short[2]. In all, the trend is for the armed forces to become leaner, meaner and strictly professional.

A direct military threat to the nation is hard to imagine at the moment. People worry – if they concern themselves with "external dangers" at all – about developments like alleged increases in cross-border organised crime or in ordinary immigration, and their consequences for Dutch society.

2. The Role of Nuclear Weapons in National Security Policy

Nuclear weapons have, strictly speaking, no function in national security policy. The Netherlands, however, values its membership of NATO very highly. The Dutch decision-making elites continue to accept that nuclear weapons are part of NATO strategy. The cabinet as a whole has discussed NATO expansion extensively. These – closed – debates may well have touched on aspects concerning NATO's nuclear deterrent, but not as the principal issue. In segments of the political and military elites, the position of the Baltic states in the context of NATO expansion is considered in the light of Article V. Some feel that one of the reasons why these countries should be excluded from NATO membership is that their accession would mean extending Article V protection to them. This would imply a nuclear guarantee – which might provoke adverse Russian reactions[3].

---

[1] See, for example: Tweede Kamer der Staten-Generaal, vergaderjaar 1990-1991, *Defensienota 1991: Herstructurering en verkleining*, 21 991, Nos 2-3; Tweede Kamer der Staten-Generaal, vergaderjaar 1991-1992, *Nota Buitenlanduitgaven*, 22 610, Nos 1-2; Tweede Kamer der Staten-Generaal, vergaderjaar 1992-1993, *Prioriteitennota 1993: Een andere wereld, een andere defensie*, 22 975, No.1. Further analyses can be found in: J.G. SICCAMA, *"Defensie en Buitenlandse Zaken"*, in: H. DE GROOT & C.A. DE KAM (eds), **Jaarboek Overheidsuitgaven 1994**, Academic Service, Schoonhoven, 1993, pp.163-180; and, Gert DE NOOY & Jan GEERT SICCAMA, *"De kosten van de krijgsmacht: en sleutel tot de herijking?"*, in: **Atlantisch Perspectief**, No.4/5, 1995.

[2] It appears that this measure is no guarantee of better morale. Drug consumption is reported to be heavier among the ranks of new-style young Dutch soldiers (professionals on a short contract).

[3] Information derived largely from interviews with experts from the ministries of Defense and Foreign Affairs.

Dutch participation in NATO nuclear planning or NATO discussions on the role of a nuclear deterrent in the context of counterproliferation and the taming of rogue states falls under the responsibility of the Minister of Defence in the first instance, and the Minister of Foreign Affairs in the second instance. Experts from these two ministries participate on a regular basis in the NATO Senior Political Group and in the Senior Military Group debates on what to do about threats from rogue states and other proliferation-connected issues. Potential security threats caused by rogue state behaviour are taken very seriously, as is the potential role of NATO's nuclear capabilities to deter such threats. Counterproliferation issues are not topics for detailed debate in full cabinet meetings, however, and the political parties have remained silent on the subject for years. In sum, counterproliferation is left to the experts.

In the context of Dutch NATO membership, nuclear weapons are still stored in the Netherlands at Volkel airbase[4].

3. Public Debate about Nuclear Weapons and Nuclear Disarmament

There is virtually no public debate on nuclear weapons and nuclear disarmament, perhaps the only exception worth mentioning being occasional interventions by an "old style" Pacifist-Socialist member of the First Chamber of Parliament, Tom Pitstra[5]. He persists in advocating full nuclear disarmament and Dutch withdrawal from NATO, a view popular at the end of the 1970s which has since lost its relevance for most politicians.

Few among the general public are aware that nuclear weapons are still stored at Volkel, and those who are aware probably do not care. Nor is there currently any public concern about interpretations of Article V of the NATO Agreement, because a threat to NATO in general and the Netherlands in particular that would be serious enough as to warrant a nuclear response seems to be utterly unlikely. There is

---

[4] This is generally assumed to be the case, although the authorities do not confirm or deny this information.

[5] For example his statement in the First Chamber on Tuesday, March 11, 1997.

no public or political drive to "denuclearise" NATO. The only recent public stir about nuclear issues was related to the French and Chinese testing of explosive devices, and that concern was focused on the environmental effects more than anything else. The main lobbying group on this issue was Greenpeace, not the Interkerkelijk Vredesberaad or Pax Christi, the traditional anti-nuclear-weapon groups[6].

There are no fundamental conflicts of opinion between the government and the public on nuclear arms: in principle, both support (eventual) nuclear disarmament – although many politicians accept that the golden future of full nuclear disarmament by the "official" nuclear weapon states will not materialise any time soon. By and large, Dutch politicians and Dutch governments are principled within reason about the issue. Thus, when the General Assembly of the United Nations, in the early summer of 1995, asked the International Court of Justice in The Hague for its opinion on the question whether the threat or use of nuclear weapons is permitted under international law in any circumstance, the Netherlands government's reaction (which contained a host of juridical and political considerations) argued that the Court should steer clear of making a pronouncement that might undermine the effectiveness of the Nuclear Non-Proliferation Treaty: "The Netherlands Government believes that the risks involved in the threat or use of nuclear weapons will be more effectively countered by further negotiations in the field of disarmament and non-proliferation of nuclear weapons, in line with the provisions of the NPT. Any judgement of the Court in reply to the request submitted by the General Assembly would create a real danger of undermining the ongoing process of nuclear non-proliferation and disarmament.[7]" In The Hague, the NPT is considered the fundament of the international nuclear non-proliferation regime. The Treaty, of course, recognises the existence of five "official" nuclear weapon states while emphasis-

---

[6] See my comments in Harald MÜLLER (Ed.), **European Non-Proliferation Policy 1993-1995**, PRIF, European Interuniversity Press (EIP), Brussels, 1996, pp.170-171.

[7] Letter from H.F. Dijkstal, Minister of Foreign Affairs ad interim, to the Registrar of the International Court of Justice in The Hague dated June 16, 1995. In this letter, the Minister also pointed out that a pronouncement by the Court that the threat or use of nuclear weapons is legitimate under certain circumstances might undermine the NPT by stimulating ambivalent non-nuclear weapon states to read **a justification of proliferation** into such a pronouncement.

ing the obligation of all adherents to engage in sincere negotiations to abolish nuclear arsenals. And in October 1996, the Netherlands enthusiastically supported a resolution introduced by the Japanese in the First Committee of the General Assembly, aimed basically at supporting the Nuclear Non-Proliferation Treaty and combining a call for future nuclear disarmament with the actual acceptance – for the time being – of the existence of nuclear weapon states[8].

The Netherlands have contributed to the process of arms reduction by providing a tenacious and resourceful chairman to the CTBT negotiations in Geneva. But even this fact has not attracted much attention in the media. A focus on international respect for and implementation of human rights will gain diplomats or mediators more national renown – a fact which illustrates public priorities at the moment.

At present, decision-making elites seem actually to prefer to keep certain issues connected with nuclear disarmament off the public agenda. This has been the case with the financial controversy with the Americans with regard to Volkel. Similarly, the practical effectiveness of a Comprehensive Test Ban Treaty as a means of arms control, as contrasted with its symbolic value, has not been subjected to public scrutiny. Such an approach might have hampered the Dutch negotiating role in Geneva. And the government and political elite have also avoided public debate of the French suggestion that a European nuclear guarantee could protect Western Europe, as such a debate would not have been opportune and might only have thwarted progress in negotiations on Combined Joint Task Forces. An independent European nuclear component might endanger the American commitment to European security, and the government would consider this highly undesirable. A very small number of experts have discussed the issue of a Eurodeterrent on the op-ed pages of the elite press, but without noticeable reverberations outside their own circle.

---

[8] Information based mainly on interviews with experts from the Ministries of Defense and Foreign Affairs.

4. Political and Security Elites' Attitudes on Nuclear Arms, Nuclear Arms Control and Disarmament[9]

Despite the low-profile of the issue, the Dutch Foreign Ministry conducts an active and committed policy on nuclear disarmament.

A comprehensive ban on nuclear testing has been consistently supported by the political and security elites. It should be noted, however, that in their view the degree of comprehensiveness is defined by the possibilities of effective verification and monitoring. Computer simulations, for instance, would not fall under a CTBT. Dutch diplomats have played a prominent part in recent CTBT negotiations, as noted above. Dutch policy-makers argue for greater efforts to enhance the Treaty's prospects of entering into force.

A cut-off of the production of fissile materials for weapons purposes is supported by the elites. The Dutch advocated this measure during the negotiations on the extension of the Nuclear Non-Proliferation Treaty in 1995, as a desirable quid pro quo which could be offered by the nuclear weapon states to the non-nuclear states. There is some recognition that the issue of existing stocks should be addressed but the most that is hoped for is some gesture of transparency by the existing nuclear weapon states.

A change in NATO strategy from first use to no-first-use, on the other hand, is not something Dutch political or security elites will advocate on their own. In general, where issues directly connected with the functioning of the North Atlantic Treaty Organization are concerned, Dutch politicians and military leaders will almost always follow the prevailing NATO trends – often, admittedly, with special consideration for US preferences.

A START III Treaty. The Dutch policy-making elite favours nuclear disarmament in principle. In practice, it believes in first things first, and feels that the implementation of START II would be a respectable priority. As the Dutch envisage further disarmament following a step-by-step approach, START III would be a logical consequence.

---

[9] Information based mainly on interviews with experts from the Ministries of Defense and Foreign Affairs.

The inclusion of the French, British and Chinese nuclear arsenals in international nuclear arms limitation and reduction treaties is favoured by the Netherlands, as a logical consequence of their support for the final goal of global nuclear disarmament. The Netherlands do not, however, present their position in the form of demands or detailed wish lists. Such an approach might not improve generally constructive and friendly relations with the French and the British, and the Netherlands is in no position to try and influence Chinese behaviour in this respect by unilateral diplomatic initiatives.

A nuclear weapons register is considered too impracticable an idea in the Ministries of Defence and Foreign Affairs. In view of the known opposition of the nuclear weapon states, it is felt that it makes little sense to waste diplomatic resources on what looks like a lost case.

The transfer of fissile material from weapons to civilian purposes, with the concomitant application of safeguards has been advocated by the Netherlands delegations involved in the preparation of the Review and Extension Conference of the NPT and at the conference itself, and is still supported wholeheartedly. The first priority should be to place all fissile materials derived from the dismantling of nuclear weapons under IAEA safeguards. The material should be recycled for civilian purposes as far as possible.

The extension of IAEA standards to the whole civilian fuel cycle in nuclear weapon states was also very actively advocated by the Netherlands during the run-up to the extension of the NPT, and is still favoured in The Hague. Apart from the practical effects, the symbolic meaning of this measure is valued highly. It would remove at least part of the inequality between nuclear weapon and non-nuclear states that has bedevilled international negotiations on nuclear arms control. Cost considerations are not unimportant, but secondary compared to the advantages.

A treaty banning the development and production of new nuclear warheads. It is felt in The Hague that a Comprehensive Test Ban Treaty in effect implies a commitment not to produce new weapons on the part of all states that ratify. As a consequence, a separate treaty has not been actively promoted and is seen as a rather unnecessary duplication.

A nuclear-weapon-free zone in Central Europe is opposed by the Netherlands. For the time being, at least, it should be enough if NATO unilaterally decides not to station nuclear weapons in the newly-to-be-admitted Central European member states, while stipulating that it retains the prerogative to do so in future. On the other hand, The Hague is sympathetic to the security needs of Ukraine – the main proponent of such a nuclear-weapon-free zone – and the Baltic states. Yet it feels that other reassurance measures should be taken in this context. Decision-makers in The Hague feel that NATO has a special responsibility to foster relations with those countries that cannot or will not join NATO in the near or at least foreseeable future. Ukraine is arguably the most important country in that category, although the Baltic states are generally considered with more sympathy because of their small size and because of close contacts between various "twin" cities.

A convention to ban nuclear weapons would conflict with the Netherlands' view that nuclear weapons have for the time being a role to play in the deterrence of attacks with weapons of mass destruction (whether nuclear or other). It also contradicts the conviction that realistic nuclear disarmament is possible only as a step-by-step process.

Is nuclear deterrence needed against the proliferation of chemical and biological weapons? The Netherlands follow NATO policy in these matters. As has been discussed above, the potential security threats emanating from rogue states, which may use chemical or biological weapons, is an important issue in various NATO fora. Nuclear deterrence is one acceptable way of countering such threats. Again, as discussed above, these issues are by and large dealt with by the expert ministries, Defence and Foreign Affairs. Other members of the cabinet as a rule do not concern themselves intensively with these issues. The same goes for most members of parliament.

Is ballistic missile defence an area of high priority as a counter-measure to the proliferation of weapons of mass destruction? The Netherlands participates actively in NATO's political and military consultations on this subject, because it considers the issues at stake to be important. Its involvement also reflects its loyal support of NATO projects. The Dutch military, which has been suffering from substantial budget cutting after the end of the Cold War, also has some vested interests in promoting ballistic missile defence.

As to the weight of the issue of nuclear arms control and disarmament: it is considered important, although opportunities for the Dutch to influence the nuclear weapon states in this area are clearly limited. Horizontal nuclear non-proliferation is probably deemed even more important in practice, as that is an area where the Dutch elites feel they can contribute, at least diplomatically.

5. Conclusions

Issues of nuclear disarmament have not created any public excitement in the Netherlands for more than ten years now. In this respect, the end of the Cold War has served to prolong an already existing situation.

Dutch elites continue to adopt positions concerning nuclear disarmament that may be defined as principled within reason. Complete global nuclear disarmament is embraced by almost all as an ideal. In practice, disarmament measures are seen as something that should not work against security imperatives (which in the view of most Dutch decision-makers include firm US commitments to NATO and European security in general), and they should be verifiable.

The Netherlands will not as a rule diverge from the positions concerning nuclear arms reductions prevailing within NATO. This is another important, perhaps the most important, parameter to Dutch thinking on nuclear disarmament.

Interviews

The author wishes to thank Mr. Joost A. Klarenbeek of the department of nuclear disarmament and non-proliferation of the Ministry of Foreign Affairs and Commander Gert C. de Nooy, a colleague at the Netherlands Institute of International Relations Clingendael and previously a member of the Arms Control Desk in the Military Strategic Affairs Division of the Netherlands Defence Staff, for their information and comments, provided during several interviews in the fall of 1996 and the early spring of 1997. Any factual or interpretational mistakes, however, are her own.

SPAIN

Vicente GARRIDO REBOLLEDO

1. General Remarks:
The Spanish Position on Nuclear Issues

There is no doubt that Spain considered developing a nuclear bomb under the Franco regime. This has been admitted by the political and security elites and by the nuclear scientists who worked on the Spanish nuclear programme at that time. Nevertheless, all of them recognised that there were many obstacles, especially economic ones, to this project[1].

Officially, Spain gave up its nuclear aspirations on October 29, 1981, at the time of the parliamentary debates on the country's membership of NATO. At that time, a proposal from the Basque Nationalist Party (PNV), by which the non-nuclear status of the Iberian peninsula was defined, was approved with the support of all political parties. It was stated that Spain would be a non-nuclear state and that any subsequent decision on this matter would require express authorisation by Parliament[2]. This decision confirmed and completed the Spanish non-nuclear policy which had already been defined in the

---

[1] On this issue see Vicente GARRIDO REBOLLEDO, *El Régimen de No-Proliferación Nuclear: participación e implicaciones para España* (doctoral dissertation), Universidad Complutense, Madrid, 1995.

[2] Diario de Sesiones del Congreso de los Diputados, Sesión Plenaria Number 193, October 29, 1981.

bilateral Defense Cooperation Agreement between the USA and Spain of January 24, 1976, and by which the USA was obliged not to store either nuclear arms or their components on Spanish territory. This decision led to the withdrawal of US nuclear submarines from the Rota base, an operation not completely concluded until 1979. Finally, the ratification by the socialist government of the Nuclear Non-Proliferation Treaty (NPT) on November 5, 1987, definitely confirmed Spain's status as a non-nuclear weapon state.

Nonetheless, we should not forget that when the Spanish Parliament authorised Madrid's adhesion to NATO, governmental decisions on the transit of nuclear arms through Spanish territory (including territorial waters and airspace) were expressly excluded from parliamentary control. In this sense, the possibility of a temporary nuclearisation of Spanish territory was at the discretion of the government. With the signing of the Agreements on Defense Cooperation between the United States and Spain dated 2nd July 1982 (by which the regime applied to calls by US warships at Spanish ports was established), this policy was confirmed. US warships were granted the right of innocent passage through Spanish territorial waters (without any obligation to specify their cargo)[3]. These agreements, renewed on 1st December 1988 with the signing of a new defence agreement for a period of eight years[4], and again in 1996 for another year[5], are still in force. Nor has there been any change in Spanish nuclear policy towards NATO, as we shall see.

All this has caused problems for successive Spanish governments with domestic public opinion. In June 1988, in order to justify the claim that the policy of free transit of nuclear armament through Spanish territory was compatible with the Iberian peninsula's status as a nuclear weapon free zone, the then Foreign Affairs Minister, Fernández Ordoñez, was obliged to resort in the Spanish Parliament to a distinction between the term "introduction of nuclear armaments

---

[3] Appendix A, Annex 4 of the 2nd Complementary Agreement of the 2nd July 1982 Defense Cooperation Agrement.

[4] On the contents of the 1989 agreements see Vicente GARRIDO REBOLLEDO, *"Spain"*, in: Harald MÜLLER (ed.), **European Non-Proliferation Policy, 1988-1992**, European Interuniversity Press (EIP), Brussels, 1993, pp.162-163.

[5] *"España prorroga por un año el convenio con EEUU"*, in: **El País**, November 3, 1996.

with the purpose of installation or storage" and "simple introduction" without that purpose, which, he argued, was not prohibited[6].

This policy stance has had a very important influence on the Spanish position on nuclear arms and disarmament issues. Since Spain joined NATO in 1982 (and especially up to 1986, when permanent membership of the Alliance was established in a referendum), the country has not played a very important role with any innovative or adventurous proposals on nuclear disarmament. On the contrary, it has tried to be a "good partner" within NATO by backing the Alliance's nuclear deterrent policy and by attempting to reconcile its non-nuclear status with a special relationship with the United States. The traditional policy maintained by successive Spanish governments, both internally and externally, has been: "Spain, as a non-nuclear weapon state, is not the appropriate country to tell the nuclear-armed powers how to control and manage their nuclear arsenals.[7]" This policy did, as we shall see, not change substantially until the 1995 NPT Review and Extension Conference and the Spanish Presidency of the European Union during the second half of 1995. This change of position, however, was also motivated by changes in NATO and US policies on arms control and disarmament questions.

No major changes in this area were introduced by the conservative party, Partido Popular (PP), which won the 3rd March 1996 general elections. The fact that the PP did not obtain an absolute majority in Parliament, and enjoyed only a small margin of advantage over the socialist party (PSOE) (1.4 points and only 360,000 votes more), forced it to negotiate with the small regional parties (the Catalan CiU, the Basque PNV and the Canarian Coalicin Canaria). On May 3, 1996, Prime Minister José María Aznar formed his first Cabinet, with three independent ministers including the Defence Minister Eduardo Serra. This decision was severely criticised both by members of the PP and by the security elites. Some PP members considered that there were other candidates from the PP who would have been better able

---

[6] See Carlos MIRANDA, *"La position de l'Espagne sur les questions nucléaires"*, in: **Relations Internationales et Stratégiques**, No.21, IRIS, Université Paris-Nord, Spring 1996, p.123.

[7] Vicente GARRIDO REBOLLEDO, *"Spain"*, in: Harald MÜLLER (ed.), **European Non-Proliferation Policy, 1988-1992**, European Interuniversity Press (EIP), Brussels, 1993, p.162.

to implement the party's defence programme, and considered Serra a "stranger within the PP". As a result, he did not get full support from all PP representatives, or even from all the PP members of parliament. The security elites considered that it was not possible to solve structural problems of defence policy with a minister who had been a member of successive socialist governments from 1981 until 1987 as State Defence Secretary. On the other hand, it was also obvious that both military officials and many members of the PP regarded Serra's appointment as little more than an interim measure.

At the time of writing (March 1997), it can be said that there is no real debate on nuclear non-proliferation and disarmament issues in Spain. The main reason for this is that these issues are neither an objective nor a priority of Spanish defence and foreign policy. It has been stated by officials from both the ministries concerned that three centrepieces on which Spanish defence policy is based are professionalisation of the Spanish army (elimination of compulsory military service), modernisation of the defence budget and the full integration of Spain into NATO. The last point means joining the NATO Military Command and participation in the new structures of the Alliance (by demanding a subregional NATO Command controlling all Iberian peninsula territory and access to the Mediterranean through the Straits of Gibraltar)[8]. Nevertheless, Spanish integration into the NATO military structure has been precisely the topic which has indirectly reopened the debate on Spanish non-nuclear status.

As the Foreign Minister stated in May 1996, Spanish foreign policy will be characterised by continuity with the policy pursued by the Socialist Party[9].

2. The Security Situation after the End of the Cold War

The main difference with respect to the Spanish security situation before and immediately after the end of the Cold War was defined by the President of the Partido Popular Defence Commission in Parliament in the following terms: "Spain has converted itself from a rearguard to a

---

[8] Interviews with officials from the Defense and Foreign Affairs ministries.

[9] **El País**, May 31st, 1996.

vanguard state in the security field.[10]" Nevertheless, an analysis of Spanish defence policy by two specialists very closely linked to the PP party in 1994, and currently occupying responsible posts in the government, stressed that "Spain has not paid much attention to defence issues… Democracy did not bring a new reflection on the state and the role of the Spanish armed forces. The first democratic governments only paid attention to the military problem in the sense of the political control of the military…[11]" In the opinion of these two defence analysts, the end of the Cold War caused a deterioration of the Spanish army due to "the lack of interest of successive Spanish governments in the army since 1990, a fact that represents a paradox, since this period coincides with increasing demands on Spanish soldiers, such as observation missions in Central America, the monitoring of disarmament agreements in Africa and of UN embargoes against Iraq and the former Yugoslavia, and the participation of the Spanish army in peace enforcement and peacekeeping operations as well as humanitarian missions abroad, among others.[12]" In short, these analysts see the reduction of resources and the increase of missions, combined with a practically unchanging military force structure, as leading to a virtual "technical collapse" of Spanish defence by 1994 (this view is also held by the security elites). All of this represents a "danger not only for the effective fulfilment of the new defence tasks assigned to Spain abroad and for its contribution to NATO, the WEU and the Eurocorps…, but also for the survival of the Spanish army. The result will be an increase in Spanish vulnerability in relation to its minimal military reaction capacity, due to a Spanish defence policy which adopts international commitments in excess of the army's capacity.[13]"

With respect to risks and threats to Spanish security, three documents show the evolution of the Spanish position during and after the Cold War. First, the so-called "Peace and Security Decalogue" set up by the President, Felipe González, in the Spanish Parliament

---

[10] Personal interview, September 1996.

[11] Rafael BARDAJÍ & Ignacio COSIDÓ, **España y su defensa. 1994: El aumento de la vulnerabilidad**, Instituto de Cuestiones Internacionales y Política Exterior (INCIPE), Madrid, 1994, p.7.

[12] *Ibid.*

[13] *Ibid.*, p.63.

on October 23, 1984. At this time, Spain was a signatory of the Washington Treaty but was not integrated into the NATO military structure – González saw this as unnecessary[14]. As a result of the Decalogue, and once the referendum of March 1986 had accepted Spain's permanent membership of NATO, the National Defence Directive (DDN 1/86) was promulgated on October 29, 1986; at that time, the threat was identified as coming from the Warsaw Pact countries.

Second, the DDN 1/92 of March 27, 1992, in which, in a post-Cold War context, Spain considered that there was no threat from the Eastern countries. In this new directive, special mention was made of Spain's support for and participation in international operations related to security in Europe and the implementation of confidence-building and security measures in the framework of the CSCE[15]. With respect to relations with the Mediterranean countries, there were two different theses at this time. At an official level, as stated in the 1992 Directive, "Spain considers that it should continue to support initiatives which help to promote stability and security in the Mediterranean region and to consolidate bilateral relations with the Southern rim countries.[16]" Therefore, at an official level, the necessity of co-operation with the Southern countries, which do not represent any threat to Spain, is stressed. On the other hand, there was another view taken by the military elites and some conservative party representatives, who accused the government of over-confidence in the Southern countries and of not being prepared to "see the reality of the situation". Therefore, they promoted a discourse based on the "**necessity of protecting** Spanish territory against a **hypothetical Southern threat** (military threat, but also human threat, i.e. migration, and especially the risk of the spread of political fundamentalism).[17]"

---

[14] Point 2 of the Decalogue.

[15] DDN 1/92, Part IV, point 7° in: *Política de Defensa y Seguridad*, Dirección General de Política de Defensa, Ministerio de Defensa/Secretaría General Técnica, Madrid, 1993, pp.115-119.

[16] *Ibid.*, Part IV, point 10°.

[17] Interviews conducted during October 1994 – April 1995. On this issue see: Vicente GARRIDO REBOLLEDO, *España y el Magreb, percepciones de Seguridad. El Caso de la No-proliferación Nuclear*, **CIP Working Document** No.11, Peace Research Center (CIP), Madrid – Ploughshares Fund (USA), 1995.

In this context, the Spanish socialist governments made a very important effort to eliminate in public opinion the perception of the Maghrebian and Middle Eastern countries as "enemies", threats to Spanish stability and security (for example, by revising the history of the Islamic world taught in the school books), especially in the mass media. Nevertheless, it should not be forgotten that although representatives of the PP stressed in September 1996 that "there was no threat whatsoever to Spain from the Mediterranean countries", the current Spanish Vice-President, Rodrigo Rato, stressed in October 1995 in a North Atlantic Assembly Report: "The political fundamentalists may be the catalysts of multiple risks, which are currently arising on the Southern flank of the Mediterranean. Population boom, political instability, poverty and the proliferation of weapons of mass destruction... The weakness of the West in confronting the new risks is not only psychological, but is also the result of a decrease in real military capacity... This means in the first place, that the Southern Mediterranean countries' net superiority in conventional terms is being substantially reduced, and in the second place, that the technological superiority is disappearing due to the refusal to develop new defence systems, such as antimissile systems.[18]"

Nonetheless, such ideas have not been backed by the current conservative government. In the opinion of Defence Ministry officials who have close links with the conservative party, **threat** means not only **will**, but also **capability**, which does not exist in the case of the North African countries, and therefore there is no reason to see a hypothetical military threat or risk originating from that region, in view of Spain's superiority and the fact that the country is a member of NATO[19]. This is the policy which has been shaped in the new National Defence Directive 1/96, dated December 12, 1996. In point 3.1.d it says: "Bilateral and multilateral relations with the North African countries will be improved, in order to contribute to stability in the Mediterranean region...[20]"

---

[18] Rodrigo RATO, *"Co-operation and Security in the Mediterranean"*, in: North Atlantic Assembly – Political Committee, 1995 Reports, AM 295 PC/SR (95)2, October 1995, pp.7-8.

[19] Interviews with officials from the Defense Ministry and representatives of the PP, March 1997.

[20] *Text of the DDN 1/96*, in: **Revista Española de Defensa**, No.108, Spanish Defence Ministry, February 1997, pp.33-37.

3. The Role of NATO Nuclear Weapons in Spanish Security Policy

Spain, both a non-nuclear weapon state and a "loyal member" of NATO, has traditionally been a staunch supporter of the Alliance's nuclear deterrence policy. In this sense, the communiqués, declarations and ministerial documents from the North Atlantic Council and from the Defence Planning Committee related to the nuclear deterrent, as well as the declarations and documents especially adopted by the Nuclear Planning Group, have received support from Spain, which considers NATO and Spanish nuclear policies to be compatible. Spain has also backed the nuclear deterrence doctrine in the framework of the WEU[21]. None of this means that there have not been conflicts in relations between NATO and Spain. Madrid does not receive NATO documents relating to nuclear armaments issues, because of Spain's dual membership status within NATO as a member of the Nuclear Planning Group who is not fully integrated into the NATO Military Command. For this reason, Spain should have ratified a secret agreement on protection of the NATO NPG documents, but since Spanish law does not permit the ratification of international treaties or agreements of a secret character, the government has not presented this agreement to Parliament (all international treaties have to be published in the Spanish Official State Bulletin, BOE). This abnormal situation should be resolved with the full integration of Spain into NATO[22].

Nevertheless, Spanish ideas of how the nuclear deterrence doctrine should be understood have also changed with the end of the Cold War. For instance, in 1992 officials from the Foreign Ministry stressed that it was "necessary to maintain only a minimum deterrent... pressing for drastic cuts in nuclear weapons to the lowest possible level, but not for their total elimination.[23]" In 1995 the same officials backed

---

[21] Carlos MIRANDA, *"La position de l'Espagne sur les questions nucléaires"*, in: **Relations Internationales et Stratégiques**, No.21, IRIS, Université Paris-Nord, Spring 1996, p.123.

[22] On this issue, see *"La OTAN excluye a España de la entrega de sus documentos secretos sobre armas nucleares"*, in: **El País**, March 9, 1997.

[23] See my chapter on Spain in: Harald MÜLLER (ed.), **European Non-Proliferation Policy, 1988-1992**, European Interuniversity Press (EIP), Brussels, 1993, pp.152-153.

the idea that a gradual elimination of nuclear weapons up to and including complete disarmament was necessary, considering that this
should also include reductions in the nuclear arsenals of France, the
UK and China, countries also subject, like the USA and Russia, to
Article VI of the NPT[24]. Therefore, it can be said that for the first
time, and especially during the Spanish Presidency of the European
Union, Spain passed from a "passive" to a "combative" attitude on
nuclear arms control and disarmament issues.

But on the other hand, both the new conservative government and
the security elites support NATO's efforts to develop military means
to counter the threat of weapons of mass destruction. This includes
consideration of ballistic missile defences, particularly as a counter
to chemical warheads. Nuclear deterrence by NATO against the threat
or use of chemical, biological or nuclear weapons against Spain or
another NATO member is also supported. It appears that there is a
certain exaggeration in the Spanish military of military counter-
proliferation against all kinds of proliferation, and a misunderstand-
ing as to the priority given by NATO to traditional, diplomatic instruments of non-proliferation. Representatives of the PP stress that:
"Spain supports the NPT philosophy and nuclear disarmament, but
at the moment the total elimination of nuclear weapons is not possible; therefore, there is no reason for NATO – or the USA – to re-
nounce totally its nuclear component, since a minimum nuclear deterrent is still needed." If this policy is confirmed by the present
conservative government, it would mean a substantial change with
respect to the policy pursued by the last socialist government. We
should remember that general and complete disarmament, as mentioned in Article VI of the NPT, was supported by the Spanish Foreign Minister and today's NATO General Secretary, Javier Solana, in
his speech to the General Assembly during the 1995 NPT Review
and Extension Conference[25]. The promotion of this goal was also one

---

[24] Interviews with officials from the General Directorate for Security and Disarmament
Matters, September 1995. See also my chapter on Spain in: Harald MÜLLER (ed.),
European Non-Proliferation Policy, 1993-1995, European Interuniversity Press
(EIP), Brussels, 1996, pp.202-204.

[25] Intervención del Ministro de Asuntos Exteriores de España, Excmo. Sr. D. Javier
Solana, en la Conferencia de Examen y Prórroga del Tratado de No-Proliferación
Nuclear (TNP), New York, April 18, 1995.

of the priorities of the Spanish EU Presidency[26]. After the end of the Cold War, Madrid has also intensified its cooperation with NATO with the signing of two coordination agreements with the Alliance: the first relates to the use of Spanish territory for logistic support of NATO operations, and the second to the control of the Straits of Gibraltar. Under the terms of the first agreement, Spain will be a "rearguard base providing logistic support[27]", a fact that, on the other hand, had already been confirmed by the joint use of Spanish military bases during the Gulf War. Nevertheless it should be mentioned that under the terms of the 1986 referendum on permanent Spanish membership of NATO, in case of a military crisis involving NATO, "nuclear weapons would be permitted to transit through Spanish territory, but would not be deployed there." This means that although Madrid supports the NATO policy of deployment of nuclear weapons in Europe, Spain should remain free of nuclear weapons, a condition which was also attached to the resolution approved on November 14, 1996, by which the Spanish Parliament conceded to the government the authorisation to join the NATO military command. The resolution was passed with 293 votes in favour, and opposed by the left coalition Izquierda Unida (IU); the Canarian regional Party Coalición Canaria (CC) abstained[28].

The main argument used by Solana in favour of Spain's full integration into NATO was that there was no reason to maintain two parallel military structures (taking into consideration Spain's participation in all NATO military planning bodies, including the Nuclear Planning Group), and therefore Madrid should be present in "all military and political NATO operations in the future[29]". But this argument, which coincides with the position of the present Spanish government,

---

[26] See Román OYARZUN, *"The EU and Nuclear Non-Proliferation"*, in: Vicente GARRIDO, Antonio MARQUINA & Harald MÜLLER (eds), **The Implications of the NPT Review and Extension Conference. A Spanish Point of View**, UNISCI Papers, No.7, Madrid, 1996.

[27] The agreements were signed on June 24, 1992.

[28] See *"Madrid Endorses Joining NATO Military Command"*, in: **International Herald Tribune**, November 15, 1996; *"Le Parlament espagnol doit se prononcer en faveur de l'integration à la structure militaire de l'OTAN"*, in: **Le Monde**, November 15, 1996.

[29] *"España debe de ser capaz de jugar todas sus bazas en la Alianza Atlántica"*, in: **El País**, September 8, 1996.

has also caused the reopening of the debate on the consequences and significance of integration at both the public opinion and the military levels. Firstly, because the Spanish mass media suggested that the nomination of Solana as NATO Secretary General (backed by the USA) was due to his favourable position towards full Spanish integration into the Atlantic Alliance (although he had been strongly against it when the socialist party was in opposition)[30]. Secondly, due to the allegations of the only political party opposed to full integration, the left coalition Izquierda Unida, which argued that this step was explicitly not foreseen in the 1986 referendum, and therefore a new referendum was needed[31]. Thirdly, because full integration reopened the debate on the status of the Straits of Gibraltar and the NATO command there (GIMBED), which Spain does not recognise. Finally, due to the dual nature of the Canary Islands' status within the Alliance; under the future Spanish NATO command (at the third level) in peacetime, but in case of any conflict in the zone under the USA SACLANT Command (Supreme Allied Commander Atlantic)[32]. This was the reason why the Canarian Party Coalicin Canaria (CC) abstained during the parliamentary vote on the resolution concerning full Spanish integration into NATO.

This conflict could also have other consequences related to the fulfilment of the mandate provided by Parliament in order to negotiate for the Spanish military full integration "in accordance with the Spanish military contribution and its political weight, especially in those zones of Spanish strategic interest in the Atlantic and the Mediterranean". Firstly, Spain considers itself discriminated against in being allotted a third level rather than a second level command, when Portugal has obtained one of the latter. Secondly, because putting the Canary Islands under a US command is seen as problematic by both the conservative government and the security elites with respect to the ratification by Spain of Protocol III of the Pelindaba Treaty. Madrid has not yet ratified this treaty, arguing that there are political problems

---

[30] *"Solana reveló a EE.UU. que él es partidario de que España entre en la estructura militar de la OTAN"*, in: **El País**, December 3, 1995.

[31] *"IU exige al Gobierno de Aznar celebrar un nuevo referéndum de la OTAN"*, in: **El Mundo**, May 17, 1996.

[32] *"La OTAN premia a España con un mando de último nivel"*, in: **El Mundo**, December 5, 1996; *"La OTAN quiere que el grueso de la Armada y la Aviación españolas dependan de mandos en Italia"*, in: **El País**, December 15, 1996.

(this means the recognition of the "Africanness" of the Canary Islands[33]. Article 1 of the Pelindaba Treaty states that the term "stationing" should be understood to mean "implementation, emplacement, **transport on land or inland waters**, stockpiling, storage, installation and deployment". Therefore, some officials from the Foreign Ministry and army officers take the view (though they do not state this openly) that since the transit of nuclear armaments through Canarian territorial waters and the airspace above is also prohibited under the terms of the Pelindaba Treaty, it is impossible for Spain to deny permission for such transit as a NATO member state and State Party in Pelindaba, especially if Canarian territory also falls under the SACLANT Command in the event of conflict. But there are also other problems delaying the final decision on the ratification of the Pelindaba Treaty: Madrid cannot understand why the Canaries have been included within the zone of application of Pelindaba while the Portuguese territory of Madeira has been expressly excluded[34]. Although the decision on the Spanish ratification of the Pelindaba Treaty has been delayed since May 1996, the military elites consider the treaty as contrary to Spain's strategic interests and incompatible with Spain's obligations as a member of NATO.

3.1. Public Debate on Nuclear Weapons and Nuclear Disarmament

In general terms, it can be said that Spanish public opinion is against anything connected with the term nuclear, and does not distinguish between civilian or military uses of nuclear energy[35]. This feeling has its origin in the Palomares nuclear accident back in January 1966, when the Franco regime kept secret the real consequences of the nuclear accident for the inhabitants of the affected zone. In this accident, two USA aircraft transporting four hydrogen nuclear bombs collided in mid-air; three of the four bombs were immediately recovered

---

[33] Vicente Garrido Rebolledo, *"Africa: tierra no nuclear"*, in: **El Mundo**, April 13, 1996.

[34] Interviews with officials from the Foreign Ministry and with military officers, February 1997.

[35] See also Carlos Miranda, *"La position de l'Espagne sur les questions nucléaires"*, in: **Relations Internationales et Stratégiques**, No.21, IRIS, Université Paris-Nord, Spring 1996, p.125.

but the fourth which fell to the sea bed, was only discovered by the US navy 57 days after the accident, with several fissures and a leak of radioactivity which was never officially admitted[36].

The question of the necessity of possession and deployment of nuclear weapons was a matter of major concern for Spanish public opinion and the political parties during the period of the French nuclear tests in 1995 and 1996. Concerning the opinion of Spaniards on nuclear weapons, 83 percent were against them in 1995 and 82 percent were also against the "Eurodeterrent", the idea of having European nuclear arms[37]. The Spanish opposition to the French nuclear tests in Mururoa was also very strong, with frequent public demonstrations. Spanish parliamentarians also showed their disagreement, with the exception of the conservative party Partido Popular, which said that it was exclusively "a question of French national interest[38]".

Nevertheless, there was also criticism abroad of the Spanish attitude towards the French tests. On October 10, 1995, Spain's President Felipe González said during a meeting with President Chirac in Madrid, speaking at a joint press conference: "I'm not going to allow myself to be dragged along by public emotions on the French tests… We must respect the solidarity between European Union countries.[39]" For the Spanish Foreign Ministry, this position was justified as a way of maintaining the EU solidarity principle and avoiding differences between EU members that might endanger advances on other disarmament issues. Therefore, the Spanish position during the UN First Committee was to search for the maximum consensus among Europeans. Although it was not possible to avoid condemning French nuclear testing in the resolution (A/C.1/50/L.3)[40] (with abstentions

---

[36] On this issue, see Vicente GARRIDO REBOLLEDO, *"El secreto mejor guardado"*, in: **Cuadernos de Ecología**, Dossier Especial No.1, February 1996 and *"Contacto 261"*, in: **El País**, May 26, 1996.

[37] MORI opinion poll commissioned by Greenpeace, conducted in September 1995. Sample size in Spain: 1,000 respondents. Figures in: **Nuclear Proliferation News**, Issue Number 35, October 26, 1995, p.6.

[38] *"Los españoles callaron por Mururoa"*, in: **El País**, September 15, 1995.

[39] **El País**, October 11, 1995; **Nuclear Proliferation News**, Issue Number 35, October 26, 1995, p.10.

[40] First Committee, November 16: 95 for, 12 against and 45 abstentions. General Assembly Resolution (December 12, 1995) A/RES/50/70 A: 85 for, 18 against and 43 abstentions.

from Spain, Germany and Greece and votes against from France and the UK), Madrid considers that thanks to its "good offices action" the consequences of this resolution were not as serious as they might have been. It was still possible to adopt other resolutions in areas such as the conclusion of a CTBT, nuclear weapon free zones, verification, NPT universality, and the question of negative security assurances (this resolution was adopted with all EU states abstaining)[41]. The same could be said with respect to Spain's abstention during the 1995 UNGA vote censuring France for its tests (A/50/590, Resolution A)[42]. In the view of the Spanish Ambassador to NATO, Carlos Miranda, the Spanish attitude towards the French tests has always been prudent, since Madrid considered at that time that small-scale testing in order to maintain the credibility of the nuclear deterrent was necessary. But this diplomat also recognises that the French decision to resume nuclear testing put the Spanish government in a "difficult situation", which finally resulted in a position that reflected "the friendship between the two countries and their common participation in NATO and the WEU". The Spanish Ambassador to NATO considers that France was very grateful for Spain's attitude in this respect[43].

4. Spanish Views on Nuclear Arms, Nuclear Arms Control and Disarmament Issues

Spanish policy on nuclear arms control and disarmament[44] was carefully formulated during the period of the Spanish Presidency of the EU in the second half of 1995. The essentials of this policy were

---

[41] Vicente GARRIDO REBOLLEDO, *"Spain"*, in: Harald MÜLLER (ed.), **European Non-Proliferation Policy, 1992-1995**, European Interuniversity Press (EIP), Brussels, 1996, pp.210-211.

[42] Vote: 85 for, 18 against and 43 abstentions including Spain.

[43] Carlos MIRANDA, *"La position de l'Espagne sur les questions nucléaires"*, in: **Relations Internationales et Stratégiques**, No.21, IRIS, Université Paris-Nord, Spring 1996, pp.124-125.

[44] In order to ascertain the opinions of the political and security elites towards nuclear arms, nuclear arms control and disarmament issues, about 15 interviews were conducted with new officials from the General Directorate for Disarmament and Security International Matters (from the Foreign Ministry), the Defence Policy General Directorate (DIGENPOL, Defence Ministry), the presidents of the PP Defence and Foreign Affairs Commissions in the Spanish

set out in the speech of the then Foreign Minister, Javier Solana, to the inaugural session of the NPT Review and Extension Conference[45]:

- *Test Ban:* After the indefinite extension of the NPT, the main objective of the Spanish EU Presidency in nuclear arms control and disarmament matters was to promote negotiations to conclude a universal, effective and verifiable CTBT with a real "zero option", meaning that all kinds of nuclear tests must be forbidden. Some interviewed army officers were very sceptical with respect to the implementation of the treaty because of China's attitude especially because there would always be countries outside the treaty, such as India. Therefore, they do not have much confidence in the CTBT. This position was not shared by officials from the Foreign Ministry, who consider the Treaty as the first and most important step towards general and complete disarmament.

- *Cut-off of the production of fissile materials for weapons purposes:* During the Spanish EU Presidency this was considered a secondary objective of the presidency, which could not be realised until after the conclusion of a CTBT. It was also present in the inaugural speech of the Spanish Presidency to the UN first Disarmament Commission. Spain supports the conclusion of such a treaty, but all those interviewed see the negotiations as very problematic. For the officials from the Foreign Ministry, the ideal solution would be its conclusion within the CD.

- *A change in NATO strategy to no-first use:* Those interviewed refused to make declarations on this question (they only said that Spain, as a NATO member state, enjoys the positive assurances given by the Washington Treaty). Representatives

---

Parliament, some military officers and civil advisers from the Defence Ministry, and officials of the Safeguards Department from the Industry and Energy Ministry. One of the most important findings was the lack of coordination between these bodies, and especially between the representatives of the PP in charge of the definition of Spanish defence policy and the officials in charge of its implementation. These interviews were conducted between September 1996 and March 1997 (where necessary, two interviews with the same person were conducted during that period). In general, those interviewed did not wish to be quoted in this study.

[45] Intervención del Ministro de Asuntos Exteriores de España, Excmo. Sr. D. Javier Solana, en la Conferencia de Examen y Prórroga del Tratado de No-Proliferación Nuclear (TNP), New York, April 18, 1995.

from the Partido Popular recognise that NATO should change in order to deal better with its new military objectives, but state that "Spain will respect the decisions adopted by the Atlantic Alliance". Representatives from the Foreign Ministry stressed that this is not a matter of concern for Spain.

– *START III Treaty and the inclusion of French, British and Chinese nuclear arsenals in international nuclear arms limitations and reduction treaties:* Although full implementation of the START II Treaty was also an objective of the Spanish EU Presidency, the chances of implementation of the START III Treaty are viewed with pessimism – even if START II is ratified by the Russian Duma. Some army officers see the treaty as contrary to Russian interests, since it allows the possibility of deploying nuclear arms on the territory of the new NATO members. On the other hand, representatives from both the Partido Popular and the Defence Ministry refused to make any declaration on the management of the arsenals of the five nuclear weapon states, arguing that it is a question of national interest and sovereignty – a position that once again differs from the one adopted by the socialist governments in favour of a global treaty to achieve general and complete disarmament. In the opinion of some officials from the Foreign Ministry, the only way to avoid a Russian boycott of the START II Treaty could be to go directly to START III by offering the ratification of an additional "protocol II and a half". In this respect, these officials are more optimistic than the military officers, and consider that START III could be ready to be signed by the year 2000. In the opinion of the same officials, the inclusion of the French, British and Chinese nuclear arsenals in international negotiations is also necessary in order to achieve general and complete disarmament.

– *The extension of IAEA safeguards to the whole civilian fuel cycle in nuclear weapon states:* During the Spanish EU Presidency, Madrid supported the IAEA safeguards regime and its inspection system as the best verification instrument able to guarantee NPT members' compliance with their obligations. At the political level, it also supported the necessity of reinforcing the application of the system with the "93+2" programme, especially inspection without previous notification and free access to strategic zones in routine inspections. In this sense, the adoption of a common EU position on the implementation of the "93+2" programme was a priority of the Spanish Presidency. Both in the UN and in the IAEA, resolutions were adopted giving greater powers to the Agency. Spain also initiated negotiations in order to put into practice the "expanded declaration" of IAEA member states, and backed the role of the Agency in matters of nuclear export controls to prevent nuclear smuggling[46]. Nevertheless, it is well known that Spain is highly critical of some points of the "93+2" programme. Officials from the Industry Ministry stressed that the biggest problem is the extension of the IAEA verification system to activities which, although related to the nuclear fuel cycle, do not imply the use of nuclear materials, a fact that implies the establishment of controls and administrative intervention in countries with a freely-operating market economy protected by the constitution[47]. As for the "Expanded Declaration", Spanish criticisms are based on the idea that providing more information than initially foreseen in the Safeguards Agreements is very difficult in other fields such as research and development, simply because states only have knowledge of the R & D activities carried out in public centres or included in state plans, and do not know what private bodies are doing. Another criticism of the 93+2 programme is the lack of a clear definition of its objectives, which could cause many mistakes in implementation. This problem could be resolved, in the opinion of these officials, by a clearer distinction between the reinforcement of the declared nuclear facilities included in the safeguard system and an improved capability to detect indications, which could reveal the existence of non-declared nuclear activities[48]. Nevertheless, no concrete ideas were presented on the application of safeguards to the

---

[46] Vicente GARRIDO REBOLLEDO, *"Spain"*, in: Harald MÜLLER (ed.), **European Non-Proliferation Policy, 1992-1995**, European Interuniversity Press (EIP), Brussels, 1996, p.210.

[47] José SANCHEZ, *"Comments to the intervention of Mr. Fischer on what European could do to reinforce the IAEA safeguards system"*, in: Vicente GARRIDO, Antonio MARQUINA & Harald MÜLLER (eds), **The implications of the NPT Review and Extension Conference. A Spanish point of view**, UNISCI Papers, No.7, Madrid, 1996, pp.35-37.

[48] *Ibid.*

whole civilian fuel cycle in the nuclear weapon states. Officials from the Foreign Ministry consider that although this is a very difficult issue, if the idea were accepted by the NWS it would not be impossible to implement it.

– *A convention to ban nuclear weapons:* Those interviewed (both the political and the security elites) do not see any necessity to negotiate such a convention, since they believe that in the nuclear field there is already the NPT, backed by the IAEA and the UN Security Council. Therefore, these efforts should be focused on other questions, especially on the negotiation of a cut-off treaty. Officials from the Foreign Ministry consider that the idea of such a convention is at present rather utopian.

– *A nuclear weapons register:* This is not a matter of concern for the Spanish political and security elites. Some of them consider that the main problem of implementing such a register is the lack of will on the part of the nuclear weapon states.

– *A treaty banning the development and production of new nuclear warheads:* Like the previous points this does not constitute a matter of concern for Spain. Some officials from the Foreign Ministry consider that with the START II Treaty in force, there is no necessity to negotiate new treaties with analogous purposes.

– *Transfer of fissile material from weapons to the civilian fuel cycle in the NWS:* There is no debate on this topic. Those interviewed declared that it is only relevant for Russia.

– *A nuclear-weapon-free zone in Central Europe:* Both the political and the security elites recognise that there is no debate on this question in Spain. Some officials from the Defence and Foreign Ministry are totally against this proposal, since they consider it as incompatible with NATO enlargement to include the former Eastern Bloc countries and with the possibility of deploying nuclear weapons there. In the opinion of those interviewed, there are other zones in which the creation of a nuclear-weapon-free zone is more important, above all the Middle East.

- *Complete withdrawal of nuclear weapons from the territories of the non-NWS:* This proposal does not receive much support, since Spain backs all initiatives adopted by NATO on the deployment of nuclear weapons in the non-nuclear weapon states. Although the deployment and storage of nuclear weapons in the Iberian peninsula is strictly prohibited by law, those interviewed are clearly against this proposal.

5. Conclusion

In general terms, it can be said that there is no real debate on nuclear disarmament and arms control in Spain. The reason is very simple: such a debate is neither a foreign affairs nor a defence policy priority for Spain, which at this moment is more concerned about questions such as the professionalisation of the army and the definition of the future Spanish role within NATO.

Traditionally, Spain has backed all initiatives on nuclear issues adopted by the NATO and the WEU, without forgetting Madrid's special relationship with the USA. This policy is unlikely to change. A change with respect to the non-asking clause is also unlikely in the short to medium term. Nevertheless, ratification of the Pelindaba Treaty by the conservative government is still uncertain, since the treaty is perceived both by the foreign affairs officials and the security elites as contrary to Spanish security interests.

To sum up, there are three ideas on which it seems the conservative government will base its arms control and disarmament (non-)policy:

- Spain, as a non-nuclear weapon state, cannot tell the NWS how to control and manage their nuclear arsenals;
- Spain/the conservative government considers decisions on the possession or development of nuclear weapons as a question of national interest, which falls within the sovereignty of each nuclear state;
- Spain should support all initiatives adopted in this field by NATO, the WEU and the EU.

GREECE

Thanos DOKOS & Panayotis TSAKONAS

1. Introduction

Greece is situated on the periphery of an "arc of nuclear crisis", extending from Russia in the north to Japan in the east, India in the south and the Maghreb in the south-west. This region contains a potentially explosive mix of overt and covert nuclear-weapon states (NWS), inheritors of the Soviet nuclear arsenal, nuclear aspirants, and states which would feel threatened by the nuclearization of their neighbours and have the technological capability to develop their own nuclear weapons. There is also widespread proliferation of other types of weapons of mass destruction (chemical, biological) and of delivery systems (ballistic missiles and, in the future, cruise missiles).

Despite this situation, Greece has not been very active in the field of nuclear non-proliferation and disarmament[1], the main reasons being Greek perceptions about a "conventional" threat to national security,

---

[1] Despite the lack of an active non-proliferation policy, however, Greece has participated in international efforts to stem the spread of nuclear weapons. It ratified the NPT in 1970, and when it became a member of the EC in 1981, it acceded to the agreement between the NWS of EURATOM and the IAEA. Although it exports virtually no nuclear or nuclear-usable items, Athens complies fully with the Zangger Committee's "trigger" lists and applies safeguards in the rare case of trans-shipments of nuclear technology through its territory. In 1991, Greece declared its intention to observe the Nuclear Exports Guidelines and became a member of the London Club. Greece has also signed the Biological Weapons Convention and the Chemical Weapons Convention and is a member of the Australia Group for the Control of Chemical Exports, the Missile Technology Control Regime (MTCR), and the Wassenaar Agreement.

the absence of a nuclear-armed competitor or opponent in the immediate region, and a certain short-sightedness on the part of Greek diplomacy.

As part of a PRIF research project on nuclear disarmament, representatives of the Greek "nuclear/security élite" (diplomats, politicians, academics, military officers, and journalists) were asked for their views on the subject. The following is a summary of the results of these interviews.

2. The Security Situation after the End of the Cold War

There was general agreement as to the lack of stability and predictability in the international system after the end of the Cold War. The exact structure and characteristics of the new world order were a matter of considerable uncertainty, but it was clear from the interviews that security experts and decision-makers in Greece are slowly becoming aware of the need for new thinking and for a broader definition of security. It was felt that such a definition should include non-military dimensions, given that many emerging security challenges and problems in the neighbourhood (the Mediterranean) are of a non-military nature and therefore cannot be dealt with effectively using military means.

There was less agreement as to the nature and extent of the major threats facing Greece and Europe in the post-Cold War era. Significantly, a majority considered the proliferation of weapons of mass destruction (WMD) and the emergence of new nuclear or potential nuclear powers on the periphery as a threat to Greek and international security[2].

There was concern about general instability in the eastern Mediterranean and the Middle East, including problems such as terrorism, mass migration, scarcity of water resources, and religious fundamentalism. Some voiced worries about instability in the former USSR and about the future orientation of Russia, but the majority rejected these

---

[2] The threat posed by the proliferation of WMD was explicitly mentioned in the 1995 and 1996 Greek defence White Papers.

fears, arguing that the economic and political crisis which Russia was experiencing precluded any aggressive behaviour. Not surprisingly, Turkey's revisionist policy was seen as a serious and immediate threat to Greek security. Other actual or potential threats to international, regional, or national security cited by the interviewees were:

- the possible renationalization of Western foreign policy (shift towards unilateralism), perhaps leading to estrangement between the USA, the EU, and Japan, and to the transfer of economic competition to the political field;
- the future role of China as a potential superpower;
- oil-energy security;
- the North-South divide, especially as manifested in the Mediterranean region;
- environmental problems;
- transnational crime.

3. The Role of Nuclear Weapons in National Security Policy

During the 1980s, perhaps for the wrong reasons, Greece was opposed to NATO's nuclear policies. Today, its attitude has shifted from opposition to indifference. There is a feeling that after the collapse of the Soviet Union, NATO's nuclear weapons are somewhat irrelevant as a means of dealing with the new threats to European security, although they still have some value as a deterrent. In any case, Greece is a member of NATO and the WEU, which implies acceptance of a certain deterrent role for nuclear weapons. Greece would not be prepared to oppose NATO on the issue of a nuclear-weapon-free zone (NWFZ) in the Balkans. As for the existence of nuclear weapons in Greece (a small number of gravity bombs), few are aware of this, and even fewer consider it a problem.

There is a widespread feeling that, in order to avoid alienating Russia, the option to deploy nuclear weapons in Central/Eastern Europe, though permissible in principle, should not be taken up. However, a small minority of those interviewed strongly disagreed with this view. It was not considered necessary for such a prohibition to be formalized through the creation of a NWFZ in Central Europe.

There is strong Greek interest in NATO's command structure and new role (especially out-of-area missions), although nuclear weapons are not perceived as having a substantial role to play in this context. It should be noted that Greece is generally adopting a more multilateralist approach towards NATO and international organizations (with active participation in peacekeeping operations, humanitarian missions, and other activities).

4. The Public Debate about Nuclear Weapons and Nuclear Disarmament

In the period under examination, there was no domestic debate on nuclear disarmament. The security agenda – for the public, for policymakers, and for the experts – was dominated by the conflict in the former Yugoslavia and by problems with neighbouring Turkey. During the early months of 1997, Albania's internal problems became a major concern.

One issue that did arouse public concern was the use of nuclear energy and the associated risks, with some concern being shown about Kozlodui, Chernobyl, and Akkuyu in Turkey[3]. Most members of the Greek "nuclear élite" are opposed to the development of nuclear energy. They also feel that because of the widespread and powerful antinuclear feeling among the Greek public, no ruling party would dare introduce nuclear energy in the near future.

There was also public opposition to French nuclear testing. This mainly took the form of protest rallies and demonstrations, organized, in most cases, by Greenpeace. The offical response was rather muted, and in the UN vote on a resolution condemning French nuclear testing, Greece was one of only three EU countries to abstain (the others were Germany and Spain; Britain oposed the resolution). Responding to domestic criticism, the Greek government explained its rather unusual stance in terms of "solidarity" with an EU partner. In a subsequent UN vote on the same issue, the position of the Greek government remained the same.

---

[3] Strong feeling about the building of a power station at this site has been displayed within Turkey itself, on account of the environmental and safety factors involved.

The re-election of the Socialist Party in the September 1996 elections has not affected disarmament policy, although the new government's foreign policy will probably be slightly more "activist". One encouraging aspect in this context is the appointment of an under-secretary for strategic planning at the Ministry of Foreign Affairs. Whether this new "activism" will extend to disarmament remains to be seen[4].

There were relatively few reports in the press about the CTBT, or about other developments in the arms control and disarmament fields.

5. The Attitude of the Political and Security Elites towards Nuclear Arms, Nuclear Arms Control, and Disarmament

Three categories of proposed agreement are discernible in this area: (a) those of high visibility (CTBT, START III, etc.); (b) those of lower visibility but of equal usefulness and value; and (c) those of a rather symbolic nature, which would make a limited contribution to arms-control efforts (some analysts would place the CTBT in this category).

Test Ban

There is strong unconditional support for the implementation of the CTBT. Although one interviewee considered a CTBT important only from an environmental viewpoint, and all agreed that it would not have quite the same impact as during the Cold War, the great majority argued that a complete cessation of testing would help block potential proliferants' efforts to develop nuclear weapons. (It must be said, however, that of those interviewed, very few were aware that testing is not necessary for the development of Hiroshima-type weapons.)

START III Treaty

There is strong support for the treaty, although the strategic arsenals of the superpowers are no longer perceived as a major cause for

---

[4] Greek governments have undertaken some arms control initiatives in the past, such as the active promotion of a NWFZ in the Balkans and the Five Continent Peace Initiative (also known as the Initiative of the Six – the Six being Argentina, India, Tanzania, Mexico, Sweden, and Greece). Despite the widespread publicity about the Initiative, it met with little success. Greece still officially supports the scheme, but it is unlikely that it will be pursued with any great zeal.

concern. But START III is regarded as a distant prospect, given that (at the time of the interviews) the Russian Duma had not yet ratified START II. There was also a feeling that the poor state of the Russian economy would considerably delay implementation (i.e. the destruction/de-activation of warheads).

Inclusion of French, British, and Chinese Nuclear Arsenals in International Nuclear Arms Limitation and Reduction Treaties

There was general agreement as to the importance of this proposal, but no great optimism about its short-term prospects. For France and Britain, two great powers "in relative decline", nuclear weapons have an important, if rather symbolic, role. For China, an emerging great power – indeed, superpower – nuclear weapons are the "great equalizer" vis-à-vis US military might.

A NWFZ in Central Europe

A majority perceived this to be an important and feasible scheme. It would probably be the price NATO would have to pay for its expansion into Central and Eastern Europe, since it would go some way to assuaging Russian concerns. A small minority of those interviewed were strongly opposed to the scheme, because they considered nuclear weapons important as a deterrent against any future change in Russian plans and intentions.

Convention to Ban Nuclear Weapons
(Analogous to the Chemical Weapons Convention)

A majority considered this an important option, but not feasible in the near future, because nuclear weapons were still valuable to their owners for purposes of prestige, influence, or deterrence.

Cut-Off on the Production of Fissile Materials for Weapons Purposes

Most considered this an important and feasible arms-control scheme, albeit of symbolic rather than practical value. There was little awareness of the progress of UN efforts in this area.

Transfer of Fissile Material from Weapons to Civilian Purposes, with Concomitant Safeguards

This was seen as an interesting and quite important idea, but most believed the effective application of safeguards would present a major problem. Some interviewees argued that there was already a surplus of fissile material from the dismantling of nuclear weapons and wondered if all the material could be absorbed by civilian nuclear plants.

Extension of IAEA Safeguards to the Whole Civilian Fuel Cycle in Nuclear-Weapon States

This proposal was generally considered very important, as it would go some way to alleviating the discriminatory nature of the international non-proliferation regime. However, few were aware of the additional costs involved in this (or the following) proposals.

Extension of IAEA Safeguards to the Whole Military Fuel Cycle in Nuclear-Weapon States

Although it was generally accepted that such an extension would probably contribute to nuclear disarmament efforts, some doubted whether it should be a high priority. It was generally felt that the focus of non-proliferation efforts should be more on threshold states, and less on NWS.

Treaty Banning the Development and Production of New Nuclear Warheads

This proposal was perceived as important, but also as requiring strict verification. Furthermore, it would not affect existing warheads, and since NWS are not expected to produce great numbers of nuclear warheads, the impact of the proposed treaty would be rather limited.

Change in NATO Strategy to No-First-Use

A majority perceived this as important, but as no longer of the first priority, now that East-West confrontation in Europe had come to an end. The issue was linked to the acquisition of nuclear and other weapons of mass destruction by developing states on Europe's periphery, to the threat this poses to Europe, and to the necessary response. Although very few argued that nuclear weapons should be used against an opponent, some valued them for their deterrent capability.

International Treaty on No-First-Use of Nuclear Weapons

Despite the rather low priority accorded to a NATO "no-first-use" policy (see response to previous proposal), a sizeable majority argued that such a treaty should be a priority, as it would constitute a significant Confidence and Security Building Measure (CSBM) and would decrease tension in regions such as South Asia (India and Pakistan).

Nuclear Weapons Register

This was seen as quite important, provided the following two conditions were met: (a) it would have to be comprehensive; and (b) there must be adequate verification. However, some expressed doubts about the usefulness of a register, arguing that expending effort simultaneously on a large number of arms-control proposals of different priority and importance would negatively affect progress towards agreement and implementation.

Nuclear Deterrence against other Weapons

One crucial question was whether interviewees believed that nuclear deterrence was needed to combat the proliferation of chemical and biological weapons (CBWs), and whether ballistic missile defence should be given high priority as a countermeasure to the proliferation of all weapons of mass destruction.

The majority believed that nuclear deterrence was not essential to combat the spread of CBWs, as the threat of use would not be credible. Although there was a large majority in favour of ballistic missile defence as a countermeasure to the proliferation of weapons of mass destruction, some felt that the deployment of theatre missile defences (TMDs) would probably lead to the development of more sophisticated offensive systems[5]. There was strong opposition to pre-emptive or preventive strikes, because of the political and military problems involved.

It was argued that a military counterproliferation strategy should remain an option of last resort, and that ATBM deployment should not be regarded as a panacea, but should be viewed only as an effective first step towards regional deterrence. Care should be taken to ensure that Arab states were not antagonized. It was felt that NATO should be prepared to deal with the threat of WMD proliferation, without, however, exaggerating the dangers involved.

Non-proliferation efforts should receive increased support from all states concerned, and a serious effort should be made to resolve regional conflict. Greece would follow US/NATO policy on TMDs – but not, it seems, with much enthusiasm, if substantial financial costs were involved. (The Greek economy is in a poor state, and levels of defence spending are high.)

As mentioned above, there is uncertainty about the future role of NATO. While almost everyone agreed that it was instrumental in guaranteeing European security, there was some uneasiness about out-of-area missions.

Priorities

The issue of nuclear arms control and disarmament is clearly of low priority amongst the Greek political and security élites. This follows a period of high-profile but low-content efforts by the late Andreas Papandreou, within the framework of the Five Continent Initiative and the Balkan NWFZ. The lack of urgency is due mainly to the existence of a conventional external threat and the absence of a "clear and present danger" in the NBC field.

---

[5] Some argued that the possibility of acts of terrorism involving the use or threat of use, of nuclear, biological, or chemical weapons should not be ignored. In fact, such acts constitute a more serious threat to Western states (including the USA) than the launch of ballistic missiles. Greece, like most European states, lacks an effective mechanism for dealing with NBC terrorism. There is also a lack of specialized equipment.

In addition, there is a severe, semi-permanent problem of under-staffing at the Directorate for International Organizations and Disarmament, whose handful of diplomats are making valiant efforts to cover numerous international arms-control forums[6].

Notes on Interviewees

Because of the highly technical nature of some of the proposed nuclear agreements, the interviewees were generally obliged to ask for explanations and then gave stereotypical (usually positive) answers, without really understanding the issue.

On the methodology: interviewees were asked to indicate whether they thought a particular nuclear agreement was "very important", "important", or "neither". In a (very) limited number of cases, agreements were described as harmful to general disarmament efforts.

One would be hard put to it to find substantive differences between the interviewees. The Greek "nuclear élite", a subgroup of the foreign

---

[6] The foreign ministry is the overall co-ordinator and driving force in this area. In addition to the directorate mentioned above, the Directorate for International Economic Relations, dealing with former COCOM issues, also plays a role – albeit a secondary one. Where no vital issues are involved, NATO delegations play an important part in shaping national policy. The Ministry of National Economy (and more specifically the Directorate for External Trade Procedures) has prime responsibility in the area of export controls. The Ministry of Finance, and more specifically the Customs Directorate, acts as its executive arm. Since 1996, the agency dealing with nuclear issues within the Ministry of National Defence has been the General Directorate for Armaments. The defence ministry has no policy-making functions or direct involvement in non-proliferation matters, playing only an advisory role. Finally, despite Greek reservations about the perceived risks and benefits of counterproliferation, the Ministry of National Defence (in the form both of the joint chiefs of staff and the ministerial staff) is involved in the NATO discussions on counterproliferation, together with the NATO Directorate of the Ministry of Foreign Affairs.

As far as the Greek Atomic Energy Committee is concerned, there has been no major change in its role, activities, or staffing recently, apart from one concerning the president and board of directors. The GAEC is the most professional of all the agencies involved in the Greek nuclear export-control system.

The National Intelligence Agency has an advisory role in matters relating to export controls. It has power to veto the granting of a licence where national security may be threatened. Because of developments in the CIS states and the growth in nuclear smuggling, there has been a slight increase of interest in, and monitoring of, nuclear issues, but nuclear non-proliferation is certainly no the agency's highest priority.

and security policy élite, has only a few members. They tend to think along the same lines, and their opinions on nuclear disarmament and WMD proliferation are neither determined nor influenced by the official position.

There has been scant overt public interest in, and hence little public debate about, nuclear disarmament. Newspapers have published very few articles about the issue, and very few scholarly books or articles on the subject have been produced in Greek. Despite this, the Greek public does display a considerable sensitivity to the issues of nuclear disarmament and WMD proliferation.

6. General Conclusion

Greece has no national economic or security interests in the field of non-proliferation and disarmament. However, for the sake of regional and international stability, and in view of the prospect of the future nuclearization of other countries in its area, it supports relevant efforts.

The general picture is a rather passive one, in which initiatives are lacking and Greece simply follows the lead of its European partners. The Ministry of Foreign Affairs has in fact clearly stated that "we follow our European partners", whilst other bodies involved claim, in their turn, that they follow the ministry.

There is nothing wrong with this policy. Small countries that do not engage in any nuclear activities[7] sometimes cannot afford the luxury of national policies and initiatives on issues they consider of rather low priority, especially when faced with other external threats they regard as very real. Following the lead of one's partners and allies is perfectly acceptable, provided that all decisions and control systems are properly implemented.

What can one expect from Greece in the future? There will be support for disarmament initiatives; the country will sign whatever

---

[7] Greece has no nuclear industry. The only nuclear installations in the country are a 5 MW pool-type research reactor which uses 20% enriched uranium, situated at the Democritos National Research Centre, and a subcritical installation at the Polytechnic School of Athens. The Democritos reactor is mainly used to train scientists and for the production of radioisotopes for medical use.

international agreements are reached, and make serious efforts to implement them. But sometimes good intentions and good will are not enough. Greece is a small country that does not engage in nuclear activities and has no related interests of its own, other than a rather nebulous (at least in the mind of many policy-makers) general interest in the prevention of the spread of weapons of mass destruction, and thus also in maintaining international stability. No proliferators are to be found in the immediate neighbourhood (especially if one takes the rather short-sighted view that North Africa and the Middle East are distant places). Furthermore, there are many other foreign-policy priorities (such as the turbulent situation in the Balkans and eastern Mediterranean), and the foreign ministry's budget is very limited. As a result, it is easy to fall into the trap of being a free-rider on issues considered as low priorities. Economic and vocational assistance from the European Commission can play a significant role in strengthening the Greek nuclear export-control system[8].

Greece's long-standing objective is to play a stabilizing role in the Balkans, the Black Sea, and the eastern Mediterranean, and it firmly believes that arms-control efforts in the Middle East and the eastern Mediterranean would be much more likely to succeed if the European Union were involved: the EU – or at least some of its member states – have better credentials than the United States among many Arab countries. If there is a West European initiative on the limitation of weapons of mass destruction in the Middle East and the eastern Mediterranean, the good relations which Greece has traditionally enjoyed with the Arab world may prove a significant factor in facilitating such a process.

---

[8] For this purpose, and to facilitate interception of contraband nuclear material, there is a pressing need for an overhaul of intelligence agencies. Information-exchange systems and closer co-operation between EU states (and others) are crucial elements here.

List of Interviewees

1. Professor Dimitri Konstas, Director, Institute for International Relations (IDIS), Panteion University, Athens
2. Professor Yannis Valinakis, Director-General, Hellenic Foundation for European and Foreign Policy (ELIAMEP), Athens
3. Professor Theodore Couloumbis, Secretary-General, ELIAMEP, Athens
4. Associate Professor Athanasios Platias, Panteion University, Athens
5. Assistant Professor Dimitris Bourantonis, Athens University of Economics and Business
6. Ioannis Varvitsiotis, MP, New Democracy (Conservative Party), former Minister of National Defence
7. Eleftherios Verivakis, MP (Socialist Party), Chairman of the Parliamentary Committee on Foreign Affairs and Defence
8. Kostas Karamanlis, MP, New Democracy
9. Michalis Papakonstantinou, MP (independent), former Minister of Foreign Affairs
10. Michalis Papayiannakis, MEP ("Left and Progress" Coalition)
11. Lt. General (ret.) Richard Kapellos, Director-General, Ministry of National Defence
12. George Koutrouboussis, Defence Advisor, Greek delegation to NATO (Brussels)
13. Colonel Dionysios Kypriotis, Arms Control Division, Hellenic Army General Staff
14. Major Alexandros Kolovos, Director, National Space Research Center
15. Anny Potamianou, NATO and Arms Control Office, Ministry of National Defence
16. Amb. Ioannis Souliotis, Disarmament Division, Ministry of Foreign Affairs
17. Dr. Nikos Liousis, Adviser to the Minister of Foreign Affairs
18. Dr. Kostas Schinas, Special Adviser, Ministry of Foreign Affairs
19. Ambassador (ret). George Sekeris, Diplomatic analyst
20. Theodosis Georgiou, President, Greek North-Atlantic Association (NGO)
21. Dr. Antonis Verganelakis, Democritos Center for Research, Chairman, Greek Pugwash Committee
22. Michalis Myrianthis, Executive-Director, Public Energy Company
23. Philippos Pierros, former MEP, DG1A, European Commission, Brussels
24. Costas Iordanidis, Diplomatic Editor, Kathimerini newspaper
25. Stefanos Kassimatis, Assistant-Diplomatic Editor, Eleftherotypia newspaper
26. George Christoyiannakis, Editor, Stratigiki (monthly journal)

TURKEY

Mustafa KIBAROGLU

1. Introduction

A study on **Turkey and nuclear disarmament** should primarily revolve around the status of Turkey within the North Atlantic Treaty Organization (NATO) and Turkey's bilateral relations with the United States in the military sphere. An equal emphasis should also be placed on Turkey's highly strategic geopolitical position, which has sometimes offered opportunities and sometimes generated disincentives for the Turkish political and security elites[1] to adopt policies congruent with global and/or regional nuclear disarmament efforts. The deployment of nuclear weapons in Turkey was a consequence of the country's admittance to the NATO alliance and the geostrategic imperatives of its immediate neighbourhood. Policies adopted by the Turkish political and security elites which have also fitted in with global nuclear disarmament efforts have essentially been an outgrowth of the fundamental principles and objectives of Turkish foreign and security policy, insofar as they were not constrained by regional security considerations. More often than not, however, the Turkish political and security elites have faced dilemmas arising from conflicts between their regional and global security concerns.

---

[1] Although the phrase **political and security elites** might be considered self-explanatory, it is still worth noting that throughout this chapter **security elites** will denote civilian or military officials from the Ministry of Foreign Affairs, Ministry of Defense, and the military, as well as others, not necessarily officials, who are known to take a scholarly interest in the field of security.

In their formal statements, the Turkish political and security elites consider nuclear disarmament to be "an absolutely necessary but at the same time a long process during which steps must be taken very carefully by the international community.[2]" As this rather oblique statement may suggest, Turkey has not pursued a very consistent policy with regard to nuclear disarmament. For that reason, Turkey should be categorised neither as a strictly anti – nor as an absolutely pro-nuclear weapons country. Turkey's attitude has shifted from one side to the other depending on the circumstances and on the threat assessments of the security elites in specific periods. Variations in the Turkish attitude to nuclear matters can best be observed in the different strategies adopted vis-à-vis the proposals aimed at establishing nuclear-weapon-free zones (NWFZ) in the region to which Turkey belongs[3]. Proposals for the immediate and complete withdrawal of nuclear weapons from the territories of all non-nuclear-weapons states (NNWS) are not well-received by Turkey unless there is some provision to replace these weapons systems with other powerful instruments that would provide comparable security assurances. In view of the fact that uncertainty still reigns in world politics, and military builds in weapons of mass destruction by so-called "rogue states", especially in the Middle East, are in progress, Turkey considers nuclear deterrence worth keeping, at least for the time being[4].

2. The Security Situation After the End of the Cold War

The end of the Cold War had a powerful impact on the security of Turkey in many respects. Since 1952 and throughout the Cold War

---

[2] E-mail correspondence with experts in the Turkish Ministry of Foreign Affairs, December 1996.

[3] As will be discussed later at length, Turkey opposed the idea of a NWFZ in the Balkans while endorsing a similar arrangement for the Middle East. More recently, the Turkish security elites have implied that a NWFZ in Central and Eastern Europe is not desirable for Turkey, while such a zone in Central Asia would be welcome.

[4] In 1991, NATO decided to reduce its land based nuclear stockpile in Europe by 80 percent, and this reduction was completed by 1993. See *"Focus on NATO: Facts on NATO's Nuclear Posture"*, in: **NATO Review**, No.4, July 1996, p.19. Nuclear weapons are still deployed, as of February 1997, in four non-nuclear-weapons state members of NATO, namely Belgium, the Netherlands, Italy and Turkey. Conversations with Tariq Rauf from the Center for Nonproliferation Studies of the Monterey Institute of International Studies, January 1997.

years, Turkey had enjoyed the rather privileged status of being one of NATO's sixteen nations. With its geostrategic location as a flank country and the second largest standing army in the Alliance after the United States, Turkey became an indispensable ingredient of the security of the Western world. Hence, not much room was left for the Turkish political elites to worry about national security. These serious matters were left to the military, which was primarily concerned with the preservation of the unity and sovereignty of the Turkish Republic. The Turkish security elites believed they could count to a considerable extent on the United States in the first place, and on NATO in general, as far as the Soviet threat was concerned.

However, the other side of the coin should also be mentioned. When Turkey joined NATO, the parties tacitly agreed that Turkey would help contain the Soviet Union. Should deterrence fail, Turkey would have made its facilities available to NATO and would have distracted as many Soviet forces as possible from a campaign in Central Europe[5]. In other words, Turkey risked its own devastation and invasion as a NATO ally by virtue of its location in the immediate neighbourhood of the Soviet Union, simply because the military thinking of the Alliance focused on the central front as the main area of Soviet/Warsaw Pact threat, putting an overwhelming emphasis on the contingency of a massive attack through Germany into Western Europe. NATO's strategic calculations developed around this priority, and Turkey's contribution was considered a function of such a contingency[6]. Nevertheless, thinking in terms of the paradoxical logic of strategy, the more threatening the Soviet Union appeared, the more the West was expected to contribute – in the view of the Turkish political and security elites. Their overwhelming belief was that in return for the risks Turkey exposed itself to as a front-line state, the country would fall under NATO's deterrent and defence umbrella, and the Alliance would provide economic and military assistance to modernise the Turkish armed forces. In a nutshell, during the Cold War, international politics were generally seen as "business as usual" from

---

[5] Bruce R. KUNIHOLM, *"Turkey and the West"*, in: **Foreign Affairs**, Vol.70, No.2, 1991, p.41.

[6] A detailed account of this issue can be found in Ali L. KARAOSMANOGLU, *"Europe's Geopolitical Parameters"*, paper presented at an international conference at Bilkent University, Ankara, March 1996, p.12.

Turkey's standpoint in respect of the country's military capabilities and political constraints.

The end of the Cold War, however, which literally meant the disappearance of the threat perceived from the Soviet Union, caused drastic changes in Turkey's security environment. Not all of these changes were unfavourable. New independent states emerged from the territory of the Soviet Union, and the most striking outcome of this development is that, for the first time in the four-century-old history of Turco-Russian relations, the two nations have been geographically separated[7]. This dissolution of common borders with the Russian-led "Soviet empire" contributed greatly to the security of Turkey. The minimum time required for Turkey's colossal ex-neighbour to launch a surprise attack has increased to one year from a figure that used to be expressed in weeks, if not days[8]. Conventional force reduction levels that were achieved with the CFE Treaty had improved the disproportionate situation between the two actors in that area, but not so dramatically. It must be mentioned, however, that the change in Russian military doctrine decided in October 1993, intended to be commensurate with the requirements of the so called "near abroad" doctrine, and Russia's related demand for a revision of the terms of the CFE Treaty for the Caucasus region, gave rise to serious concerns among the security elites in Turkey[9].

The emergence of new independent states in the former Soviet Union as well as the former Yugoslavia brought with it both new hopes and opportunities and worries and dilemmas related to coexistence in regions where nations had lived together for decades. The most practical end result of this evolution was that the number of Turkey's geographical neighbours doubled overnight; among these were nations with which Turkey had deep historical and cultural ties. Turkey was widely regarded by the Western community as the

---

[7] If one excludes the rather distant neighbourhood across the Black Sea and the common borders with the Commonwealth of Independent States (CIS).

[8] Interviews with Turkish military experts.

[9] For an excellent discussion of the importance of the CFE Treaty in European security as well as an assessment of the threat to Western interests arising from the Russian demand for revision of the CFE rules applying to the flank zone, see Richard A. FALKENRATH, *"The CFE Flank Dispute: Waiting in the Wings"*, in: **International Security,** Vol.19, No.4, 1995, pp.118-144.

role-model for the newly emerged republics of Central Asia and the Caucasus[10] and its historical and cultural ties compelled Turkey to offer solutions to the problems of the "turkic world". Clashes between turkic and non-turkic identities in that region increased as the Soviet system disintegrated. Specifically, the conflict between Armenia and Azerbaijan arising from the dispute over the status of the Nagorno-Karabakh region has become a test case for Turkey with regard to its capabilities and ability to properly "lead" the newly independent states of turkic identity. The most Turkey could achieve in this regard, however, was to participate in the Minsk Group established under the auspices of the then Conference on Security and Co-operation in Europe (CSCE)[11]. This dispute remains largely unresolved in spite of Turkey's efforts. As war erupted on the territory of the former Yugoslavia, and especially with the Serbian atrocities committed against Bosnians, Turkey found itself in a still more difficult situation. The Muslim identity of Turkish citizens and the pressure arising from the fact that approximately two million of them are of Bosnian descent compelled Turks to help their Muslim brothers living in the troubled lands of the *Rumelia*[12]. These communities, of different ethnic

---

[10] The so-called Newly Independent States (NIS) in the Caucasus and Central Asia, with few exceptions, share many aspects of their history, culture, religion and linguistics with both Turkey and Iran, albeit to varying degrees. Hence, the possibility that Iran would establish comprehensive relations with these states caused alarm in Western capitals. The fundamentalist Iranian regime and its generally hostile attitude towards the West were the main sources of this concern. One major objective of the Western countries was to contain Iran's expansionist ambitions by not allowing it to export its fundamentalist regime to the NIS. Turkey, with its secular democracy and market economy, was considered in Western capitals to be a feasible alternative to Iran. Turkey was also thought to be well equipped to act as a role model for the NIS and to help the new states survive the painful and dangerous period of transition after the collapse of the Soviet system.

[11] Armenia, Azerbaijan, Belarus, the Czech and Slovak Republics, France, Germany, Italy, Russia, Sweden, Turkey, and the United States participated in the CSCE (now OSCE) negotiations that took place within the framework of the Minsk Group. The function of the Group was to define the emergency measures required to ensure a cessation of hostilities. Later, the Minsk Group served to monitor the cease-fire imposed by UN Security Council Resolution 882, of which Turkey was a co-sponsor together with Russia and the United States. For a fuller discussion of this question, see Mustafa KIBAROGLU, *"Impact of the Northern Tier on the Middle East: A Rejoinder"*, in: **Security Dialogue**, Vol.27, No.3, September 1996, pp.319-324.

[12] The term Rumelia denotes former Ottoman territory in western Thrace and the portion of the Balkans inhabited by Turks and other Muslim communities such as the Bosnians, Albanians, and Kosovans.

origins, had lived together in peace and harmony for centuries under Ottoman rule. However, Turkey's efforts and contributions, whether economic or military, were insufficient to find a solution or save the lives of hundreds of thousands of Bosnians.

The extreme discontent of the public with the performance of the Turkish government and military caused deep distrust of the administration and eventually even weakened central authority as demonstrations were frequently staged in big cities like Istanbul and Ankara. The alleged failure of Turkish foreign policy on all fronts had serious repercussions on domestic politics, which acquired further momentum with the increasing insurgencies of the PKK terrorist organisation that had launched a campaign against the central political authority. The 14-year-old low-intensity war that has been taking place mostly in the south-eastern part of Turkey bordering the Middle East has so far claimed the lives of thousands of people, both military personnel and civilians. The invasion of Kuwait by Iraq and its repercussions in the early 1990s eliminated the authority of the Iraqi government in its northern territory. This further complicated Turkey's security situation. The region became a sanctuary for PKK terrorists, which enabled them to flourish and wage more frequent attacks on targets inside Turkey.

Turkey lies at the pivotal point of a geographical location encircled by the Caucasus, the Middle East and the Balkans, and is therefore exposed to the side-effects of intra- and inter-state conflicts in all of these regions. In this period, the country's unity and state sovereignty started to be questioned and even threatened internally. Such an internal threat unavoidably attracted most of the attention of the Turkish political and security elites, and largely undermined their interest in many global issues. Interest in international problems such as the proliferation of weapons of mass destruction or NATO expansion was thus confined to a handful of security specialists from the government and academia[13].

---

[13] For some broad considerations of these matters, see for instance Nezihi CAKAR, *"Turkey's Security Challenges"*, in: **Perceptions**, June-August 1996, Center for Strategic Studies (SAM), Ankara, Vol.1, No.2, pp.12-21; and, Olgan BEKAR, *"NATO's Enlargement: Russia and Turkey"*, in: **Eurasian Studies**, Vol.3, No.1, Yeni Forum Corporation, Ankara, Spring 1996, pp.65-80. The author of the first article is a retired Turkish army general, while the author of the second works for the Turkish Ministry of Foreign Affairs. For an elaborate and alternative perspective from academia, see Duygu B. SEZER, *"Turkey's New Security Environment, Nuclear Weapons and Proliferation"*, in: **Comparative Strategy**, Vol.14, No.2, 1995, pp.149-173.

3. Public Opinion on Nuclear Weapons and Nuclear Disarmament

There has not been a serious discussion, let alone a public debate, in Turkey about nuclear weapons or nuclear disarmament[14]. One of the main reasons for this has been the ultimate authority of the military in matters relating to national security. The military has done its best to prohibit the slightest leakage of relevant information to the public. Hence, partly because of the silence of the political and security elites and partly because of the lack of public interest in nuclear weapons and nuclear disarmament, governments in Turkey have not experienced any difficulty in adopting policies regarding nuclear weapons deployment on Turkish territory. By comparison with some other NATO countries such as Norway, which preferred to remain nuclear-weapon-free, or Germany, where serious debates took place over the deployment of nuclear weapons, it would be fair to say that there was no discussion in Turkey. Even the disclosure of the clandestine Iraqi nuclear weapons programme was not enough to prompt a substantial public debate.

However, this ought not to be the case for a country like Turkey, which sits in the immediate proximity of the Middle East – the most volatile region in the world and a region acknowledged to be fertile soil for state aspirations to develop all sorts of weapons of mass destruction. Turkey's most strategic power stations, dams, communication and transportation lines, and above all, an important proportion of its population are already exposed to the threat of ballistic missiles that exist in the arsenals of potentially hostile states in the Middle East. Hence, there is every reason for Turks to wonder and to

---

[14] During the period of short-lived and limited public interest in the deployment of the US Jupiter missiles, the Cuban missile crisis of October 1962, and the developments that followed, nuclear issues were only sporadically and superficially debated in the public domain. Even then, the discussion focussed on the domestic political repercussions of these issues without touching their substance. It is interesting to note that the word "nuclear" was not spelled out in this debate; words like "rockets" and "bases" were enough to denote the whole subject matter. This unique period is worthy of detailed investigation, and luckily just such a study will appear shortly. For an excellent account of the period covering the introduction of nuclear forces to Turkey, the Cuban missile crisis, and its aftermath, see Nur Bilge CRISS, *"Strategic Nuclear Missiles in Turkey: The Jupiter Affair (1959-1963)"*, in: **Journal of Strategic Studies**, 1997 (forthcoming).

discuss publicly whether their neighbours are attempting to develop mass destruction weapons, their delivery means already having been acquired[15]. The Turkish political and security elites should also seriously consider the possibility of the acquisition of fissile or radioactive materials by the numerous terrorist groups active in the Middle East. As control over the stockpile of tons of fissile and radioactive materials on the territory of the former Soviet Union is weakened to an unprecedented extent, the possibility that terrorist groups could seize such material or even a nuclear explosive device directly affects Turkish interests. Nevertheless, these issues are barely raised or discussed even in the various publications of the Turkish Ministry of Foreign Affairs[16], or in the article written by the former Foreign Minister (also the Deputy Prime Minister of the coalition government) published by the Center for Strategic Studies newly established in Ankara under the auspices of the Ministry of Foreign Affairs[17]. Turkey may soon have to suffer the consequences of neglecting these issues. The limited scholarly interest paid to these issues in Turkey means that no substantial debate commensurate with the dimension of the threat associated with them can take place[18].

---

[15] Ironically, during the war in the Gulf in the early 1990s, the only discussion of this hot topic was related to whether Scud missiles in the Iraqi arsenal were sophisticated enough to hit their intended targets. In other words, Turks preferred to hope for a lack of precision in the ballistic weapons systems at the disposal of their potential enemies rather than to discuss the issue publicly and/or suggest counter-measures.

[16] The web site of the Ministry of Foreign Affairs (MFA) on the internet is http://www.mfa.gov.tr.

[17] Tansu CILLER, *"Turkish Foreign Policy in Its Dynamic Tradition"*, in: **Perceptions**, Vol.1, No.3, Center for Strategic Studies (SAM), Ankara, September-November 1996, pp.5-16. These concerns were mentioned in passing during the premiership of Tansu Ciller in a NATO publication which is, however, only rarely accessible in the public domain. See Tansu CILLER, *"Turkey and NATO: Stability in the Vortex of Change"*, in: **NATO Review**, No.2, April 1994, pp.3-6. During the final revision of this chapter the government has changed in Turkey in early July 1997. The attitude of the government towards such issues is yet to be clarified.

[18] For a detailed discussion of ballistic missiles in the Middle East and an assessment of the threat posed to Turkey, see Sitki EGELI, *Balistik Fuzeler ve Turkiye* ("Ballistic Missiles and Turkey"), Ankara, Under-Secretariat of Defense Industries, Turkish Ministry of Defense, (Sales no: SSM-10 Strateji-1), 1993; for an account of Iran's nuclear policy and the implications of the recent Bushehr nuclear reactor deal between Iran and Russia, see Mustafa KIBARAOGLU, *"Is Iran Going Nuclear?"*, in: **Foreign Policy**, Vol.XX, Nos 3-4, Foreign Policy Institute, Ankara, Winter 1996, pp.35-55.

4. The Role of Nuclear Weapons in National Security Policy and Attitudes towards NWFZ

During the Cold War years, Turkey relied heavily on the presence of nuclear weapons on its territory for national security. The Turkish political and security elites considered these weapons systems to be a credible (albeit limited) deterrent against the Warsaw Treaty Organization (WTO) in general and the huge military might of the USSR in particular. Nuclear weapons were deployed according to the mutual commitments of Turkey and NATO. However, the deployment of nuclear weapons in Turkey under the terms of its NATO membership owed more to the geostrategic significance of the country for the United States in its confrontation with the Soviet Union[19]. The North Atlantic Treaty did not involve any concrete undertaking on the part of the member states with reference to the deployment of nuclear weapons or any other specific weapons systems. There were, however, good reasons for Turkey to rely on a nuclear deterrent. Soviet claims on the Turkish Straits[20] and on some of the eastern provinces of Turkey under Stalin gave rise to grave security concerns in the Turkish political and security elites. Turkey's vulnerable situation in the aftermath of World War II and the USA's timely pledge to extend its security umbrella to Turkey marked the beginning of substantial US-Turkish bilateral military cooperation[21]. During the

---

[19] At the NATO meeting in Washington, D.C., in December 1957, it was decided to deploy long-range ballistic missiles in Europe. Around 1960, US Thor and Jupiter missiles became operational in the UK, Italy and Turkey. They had a range of approximately 3,000 km and a warhead yield of 1.5 megatons. Jupiters in Italy (30) and in Turkey (15) were phased out by 1965. See **World Armaments and Disarmament, SIPRI Yearbook 1982,** for Stockholm Peace Research Institute, Taylor & Francis Ltd, London, 1982, p.7.

[20] The straits of Istanbul (Bosphorus) and Canakkale (the Dardanneles) in northwestern Turkey are highly strategic sea routes for the countries littoral to the Black Sea. The status of the straits was agreed in the Treaty of Montreux of 1936.

[21] It may also be worth noting that Turkish-American military relations suffered from two periods of distrust. Both were related to Turkey's strategy towards and hence interventions in Cyprus. First, US President Johnson sent a bitter letter to the Turkish Prime Minister Ismet Inonu in June 1964 when Turkey dispatched military aircraft to Cyprus to pressurize the Greek-dominated Cypriot administration, with a view to inducing the Greek Cypriots to treat the Turkish Cypriots fairly and equally. With the so-called "Johnson letter" the US administration warned its Turkish counterpart that Turkey could not be permitted

1960s and 1970s, the Soviet threat was felt more explicitly both in Turkey and in the United States as the Soviet Union closed the gap with the US in the nuclear field. The Soviets increased their military presence and capabilities both in conventional and unconventional weaponry along Turkey's eastern frontier as well as their naval presence in the Mediterranean. That period also witnessed intensifying relations between the Soviets and Syria in all respects, including the military field. The Soviet Union's growing military presence both in quantitative and qualitative terms across the southern flank of NATO prompted the Alliance in general and Turkey in particular to rely extensively (though gradually) on nuclear forces.

During the Cold War, fully aware of the overwhelming superiority of the Warsaw Pact countries in conventional weapons systems, Turkey opposed the proposal to establish a NWFZ in the Balkans[22]. It was believed that the non-deployment or removal of nuclear weapons from the territory of Turkey would expose the country to a very difficult military situation. For Turkey, the existence of nuclear weapons on its soil meant the active presence and full backing of NATO in general and the United States in particular in contingency plans involving the WTO countries. Hence, the Turkish security elites did not opt for a nuclear-weapon-free Balkans even though this proposal

---

to use any military equipment of US origin in its intervention in Cyprus. The US also threatened that NATO might not defend Turkey should the Soviets launch an attack as a result of Turkish military intervention in Cyprus. The second period of poor relations came when the US Senate imposed a military embargo on Turkey in July 1975 in the aftermath of the Turkish military intervention in Cyprus in July 1974, which followed a Greek-sponsored military coup that aimed to annex the island to Greece. The military embargo lasted until September 1978 but had some lasting effects on the mindset of the Turkish political and security elites. A clear indication of this were Turkey's attempts to diversify its military cooperation and procurement strategies by including other countries such as Germany and France among its suppliers, and ist attempts to develop an indigenous military industry in order to become as self-reliant as possible.

[22] A proposal for a nuclear-weapons free Balkans was first put forward by the Soviet Union on June 25, 1959. As the deployment of US medium range nuclear missiles to Turkey was seen on the horizon, the Soviets initiated counter-measures at the international level, and "recommended" to the Turks not to accept these weapons, which could hit targets in the Soviet Union and would therefore be targetted by Soviet nuclear missiles. However, Turkey did not give way to this Soviet threat. The proposal was reiterated by the Balkan members of the WTO in the early 1980s.

had political advantages for some countries and politicians in the region in terms of the opportunities it presented to conduct "high politics" with the help of disarmament rhetoric[23]. Notwithstanding its opposition to a Balkan NWFZ, Turkey fully supported the proposal that aimed at establishing a nuclear-weapon-free zone in the Middle East (NWFZ/ME), originally co-sponsored by Egypt and Iran as early as 1974. Turkey also expressed its concern that such a zone should encompass all kinds of weapons of mass destruction as well as their delivery means. One principal reason for supporting the idea of a NWFZ/ME was the threat perceived from the spread of nuclear, chemical and biological (NCB) weapons of mass destruction into the Middle East. Such a threat, however, was not the primary concern of NATO in its relations with Turkey[24]. The Middle East was generally considered by most of the NATO countries to be "out of area". Therefore, it was not clear to the Turkish political and security elites whether or not the NATO "nuclear umbrella" would be effective in defending Turkey in the event of a conventional or non-conventional attack launched by any (or a combination) of its Middle Eastern neighbours. Since Turkey was confident that its conventional arsenal could cope with its Middle Eastern neighbours, any proposal that would eliminate the non-conventional capabilities of these states would be to the advantage of Turkey's security. Thus, Turkey supported the idea of a Middle East free of weapons of mass destruction.

The concept of "out of area" and the Turkish attitude to this question may serve as an indicator of the chronic dilemma inherent in Turkey's foreign and security policy. Whereas the United States suggested the inclusion of an "out of area" intervention in contingency plans encompassing the Persian Gulf region, the West European members of NATO generally opposed the idea as the threat perceived from Eastern Europe was of primary importance for them[25]. So did Turkey,

---

[23] For instance, Greece, despite the fact that it was a NATO ally, not only welcomed the idea of a Balkan NWFZ but also became a co-sponsor of subsequent proposals.

[24] See Article 6 of the North Atlantic Treaty.

[25] The debate between the European members of NATO and the United States is not new and can be traced back to the original drafting of the North Atlantic Treaty. For a comprehensive discussion of this question see Douglas T. STUART & William Tow, **The Limits of Alliance: NATO Out-of-Area Problems Since 1949**, Johns Hopkins University Press, Baltimore, 1990.

because the Turkish political and security elites did not want to get into a bilateral commitment with the United States alone in contingencies including the Middle East, where the West Europeans would probably not be present. The possibility of such an undertaking was not desirable politically or militarily for Turkey for a number of reasons. The Turkish security elites believed that the United States did not have a clearly defined strategy with regard to contingencies in the Middle East, especially those falling short of Soviet involvement. Hence they feared that the Turkish military would have to be involved in US operations specifically designed to back Israel against the Arab states. Even though Turkey kept its diplomatic relations with Israel at very low levels both *de facto* and *de jure*[26], and at the same time tried to keep clear of inter-Arab disputes, the Turkish political elites did not want to be seen as taking sides in the Arab-Israeli dispute. Furthermore, memories of unsuccessful attempts to institutionalise cooperation among the states in the northern tier of the Middle East (e.g., the Baghdad Pact and RCD) reminded the Turks of the significance of their institutional ties with Europe and the need to strengthen them[27]. Hence, based on lessons learned, the Turkish political and security elites wanted to keep out of the highly intricate intra-regional

---

[26] Turkey was one of the first countries to recognize the State of Israel in March 1949. Nonetheless, Turkish politicians have expressed their regrets as regards Israel's invasion and occupation of Arab lands. Turkey also repeatedly urged Israel to return to its pre-1967 frontiers and to comply with UN Security Council Resolutions 242 and 338. Turkey decided to recall all of its high level diplomatic staff from the Turkish Embassy in Tel Aviv in December 1980 (immediately after the military coup staged in Turkey) and asked Israel to match this move. Eventually, as a reflection of the growing pace of recent Arab-Israeli rapprochement, Turkish-Israeli relations gained a new momentum. As an expression of this, a senior Turkish diplomat again assumed his office in the Embassy in Tel Aviv after the Peace Accord between Israel and the PLO signed in Washington, D.C., in September 1995. The framework of multifaceted relations between Turkey and Israel will be mentioned later in this chapter.

[27] Following its accession to NATO, Turkey tried to pursue an active policy in the Middle East as a regional actor which promoted Western (namely US and British) policies. The Pact of Mutual Cooperation or Baghdad Pact, signed at Baghdad on 24 February, 1955, was an outcome of this policy. See CRISS, *"Strategic Nuclear Missiles in Turkey: The Jupiter Affair (1959-1963)"*, in: **Journal of Strategic Studies**, 1997 (forthcoming). The RCD, the agreement of Regional Cooperation for Development, was another link in the chain of US efforts to contain the Soviets by strengthening cooperation among countries such as Turkey, Iran and Pakistan. The RCD remained in existence from 1964 to 1979.

politics of the Middle East. In sum, due to their national and regional security concerns and foreign policy principles and objectives, the Turkish political and security elites preferred to keep their political and military freedom to be able to decide independently on whether or not to get involved in contingencies in the Middle East, taking into consideration the attitude of the West European members of NATO as well.

As for the recent proposal to establish a NWFZ in Central and Eastern Europe, the Turkish attitude is again negative. Although the proposal has been informally discussed in Western political and scholarly circles, the Turkish security elites apparently prefer to remain aloof. The reasons for and likely implications of this attitude will be discussed later. However, it should suffice to say that the assessment by the Turkish elites of the political and military repercussions of a NWFZ in Central and Eastern Europe vis-à-vis Turkey's national security interests is not a promising one.

4.1. The Threat Posed to Turkey by Weapons of Mass Destruction in the Middle East

Turkey is within range of all sorts of Weapons of Mass Destruction (WMD) that are strongly believed to exist in the Middle East. Only five states in the world are formally recognised to have a nuclear weapons arsenal, namely the United States, Russia, UK, France and P. R. China, and only three states have formally admitted having a chemical weapons arsenal, namely the United States, Russia and Iraq. Moreover, Iraq has also admitted to have weaponised biological agents for military purposes. Iraq's formal acknowledgement of its possession of chemical and biological weapons is due to the efforts of the United Nations Special Committee (UNSCOM) which disclosed, destroyed, removed, or rendered harmless Iraq's WMD programme as mandated by UN Security Council Resolution 687 following the defeat of that country in the Persian Gulf in 1991. Regardless of what UNSCOM has unearthed so far, however, Iraq is strongly suspected of having hidden militarily significant number of operational chemical (and possibly biological) weapons, and of pursuing clandestine efforts to rebuild its devastated infrastructure for manufacturing mass destruction weapons[28]. Whether or not formally admitted, there is strong evidence that a combination of nuclear, chemical and biological weapons and their delivery vehicles do exist in a number of countries in the Middle East, which poses a serious threat to Turkey. Six particular Middle Eastern states are believed to possess WMD arsenals, although the risk of further proliferation is not confined solely to these states. The six states that potentially constitute a threat to Turkey are: Iran, Iraq, Syria, Libya, Egypt and Israel.

Whereas the first four can be seen as posing a more serious threat, the latter two should be treated as less serious threats by virtue of their apparently unproblematic and even friendly relations with Turkey. For instance, Egypt, being a NNWS party to the NPT, may pose a much less serious threat for two main reasons. First, the final status of the Egyptian chemical weapons arsenal is unclear[29]. Secondly, in view of Egypt's improving relations with Turkey, one would hardly argue that Egypt is likely to have the intention, let alone the necessary technical capabilities, to wage a chemical weapons offensive against Turkey across the Mediterranean.

Israel is also thought to be a less serious threat even though it is believed to have a considerable nuclear weapons stockpile. Relations between the two countries are improving considerably, especially since the restoration of diplomatic relations that followed Israel's peace initiatives with the PLO and Jordan in late 1995. Furthermore, Turkish-Israeli relations entered a new phase with the recent military cooperation agreement which apparently includes clauses aimed at improving bilateral military cooperation such as can be found in many agreements of this type. For instance, Israeli military aircraft will be allowed to overfly Turkish territory during training. And, Israel will

---

[28] There is convincing evidence that Iraq has reestablished its procurement network, and despite the UN embargo, succeeded in selling significant amounts of oil since the end of the Gulf War by land and sea through three main routes. Conversations with a UNSCOM inspector who participated in more than a dozen inspection missions in Iraq, February 1997.

[29] Moreover, Egypt is also the originator of the proposal to turn the previous NWFZ/ ME proposal into a zone free of all weapons of mass destruction. The proposal is also known as the "Mubarak Zone". For a comprehensive study of the feasibility of such a zone and policy recommendations, see Jan PRAWITZ & James F. LEONARD (eds), **A Zone Free of Weapons of Mass Destruction in the Middle East**, UNIDIR Research Report, New York/Geneva, May 1996.

upgrade 54 Turkish F-4 class military aircraft and will provide the Turkish airforce with electronic warfare equipment. However, the significance of this military cooperation goes beyond these transactions. Putting aside the meaning of the agreement for Israel, the perception of the rapprochement between Turkey and Israel in the Middle East is of utmost importance for the Turkish political and security elites. For instance, Turkey has serious problems with some of its neighbours, especially with Syria[30]. The recent military cooperation agreement between Greece and Syria exacerbated tension in the region and Turkish threat perceptions. The agreement allows, among other things, Greek military aircraft to be stationed at Syrian bases as both parties "deem" necessary. Greece has also entered into similar agreements with Armenia and has attempted to do the same with Georgia, these states being newly independent former Soviet republics adjoining Turkey's eastern and north-eastern frontier. Such moves by Greece, including its initiatives to develop and diversify its relations with Iran in a number of spheres including the military, have caused a sense of encirclement in the minds of the Turkish political and security elites[31]. Furthermore, the threat posed by the fundamentalist aspirations of Iran and its alleged efforts to destabilise the democratic regime in Turkey by proxy have raised the perceived value of relations with Israel. The state of affairs in the region and the state of

---

[30] The principal sources of conflict between Syria and Turkey are the following: Syria has claims on the waters of the Euphrates and Tigris rivers originating from Turkey; there is good evidence that Syria gives support to the terrorist organization PKK, which is engaged in insurgencies inside Turkey against both military and civilians which cause heavy casualties; Syria never recognized the status of the city of Hatay (Alexandretta) which was annexed by Turkey in 1939 as the result of a local referendum. On Syrian official maps, Hatay is still depicted as "belonging" to that country.

[31] The Turkish stance in this regard was made clear in a press release of the Ministry of Foreign Affairs on April 5, 1996 stating that "... Greece [was] adopting a more antagonistic attitude not only toward resolving the dispute in the Aegean but toward Turkish-Greek relations overall. In a speech to university students in Thessaloniki, Greek Defense Minister Arsenis called for the formation of alliances with Turkey's neighbours, Russia, Armenia, Bulgaria, Iraq, Iran, and Syria in order to pressure Turkey. In conjunction with the Minister's new plan of pressuring Turkey through its neighbours, the Minister also ominously announced that Greece has entered into a military agreement which would permit Greek fighter plans to land in Syria and fly over Syrian airspace. Clearly the purpose of such an agreement would be for Greece and Syria to join forces against Turkey." For details see the web site of Turkish Ministry of Foreign Affairs (http://www.turkey.org).

mind of the Turkish political and security elites were highly conducive to an improvement of relations with Israel that could result in a Turkish-Israeli axis crosscutting the one set up by the enemies and rivals of both countries[32].

In addition to Iraq, Syria and Libya are also believed to have elaborate WMD development programmes, especially in the chemical and biological fields. There are indications that these two countries have already established large procurement networks for this purpose. These networks pursue not only the procurement of technological items and chemical or biological agents, but also the recruitment of scientists and experts in these fields from "supplier" states like Russia and South Africa[33]. Iran is strongly suspected of having nuclear aspirations. Although Iran adamantly rejects allegations that it has a clandestine nuclear weapons programme, its most recent nuclear reactor deals with Russia and China, and its overall nuclear infra- and super-structure, tend to strengthen these suspicions[34]. Iran is also suspected

---

[32] A fuller discussion of this topic would be necessary to highlight many obscure points that could not be dealt with here. However, such a discussion would far exceed the scope of this study.

[33] In the case of Libya, Western intelligence received reliable information in the late summer of 1994 that the Libyan government was attempting to recruit scientists from the South African Biological Weapons (BW) project to come to Tripoli to establish a similar program for Libya. US and British intelligence services (CIA and SIS, respectively) mounted a large intelligence operation which was designed to thwart this effort. As part of that operation the British and US governments put private political pressure on President Mandela, which was not initially successful. However, this leaked to the press and revelations appeared in the London *Sunday Times* on February 26, 1995. The political storm then created in South Africa halted the Libyan effort. For details, see James ADAMS, *"The Dangerous New World of Chemical and Biological Weapons"*, in: Brad ROBERTS (ed.), **Terrorism with Chemical and Biological Weapons**, Chemical and Biological Arms Control Institute, Alexandria, VA, 1997, pp.23-42.

[34] With the January 1995 protocol signed between the Russian Ministry of Atomic Energy (Minatom) and the Atomic Energy Agency of Iran (AEOI), Russia agreed to construct two 1,000 MW(e) and two 440 MW(e) VVER light-water reactors (LWR) at the Bushehr nuclear site in the south of Iran on the Persian Gulf. The construction of two Siemens 1,300 MW(e) LWR at the same site was initially undertaken by the German firm Kraftwerk Union (KWU), but then halted because of the Islamic revolution in Iran. China has also agreed to install at least two 330 MW(e) LWR in Iran. Since Iran is one of the richest countries in proven oil and natural gas reserves, its argument that it needs so much installed nuclear power capacity to generate electricity is unwarranted.

of having a chemical weapons arsenal and of making recent efforts to enlarge its capability in that field[35].

4.2. The Threat Posed to Turkey by Ballistic Missiles in the Middle East

The existence of ballistic missiles in the Middle East with a range sufficient to reach Turkish territory is a more categorical threat than that posed by the ambiguity surrounding the status of mass destruction weapons in the region. The open source literature provides detailed graphic information as to which country has which category of ballistic missiles in its arsenal[36]. These sources paint an alarming picture of that situation in the Middle East. To date, the profile of the missile arsenals of Iran, Iraq, Syria and Egypt reveals above all the deployment of Soviet-origin Scud missiles of varying degrees of sophistication and hence varying ranges and payloads. Nonetheless, ongoing research and developments efforts to manufacture indigenously the derivatives of Scuds or non-Scud based missiles with longer ranges and higher payloads constitute a significant threat not only to the Middle Eastern countries and Turkey, but also to states in the southern parts of the European continent[37]. The profile of the missiles deployed in the Middle East can be summarised as follows:

4.2.1. Iraq: All missile development programmes of Iraq over 150 km range were halted by the United Nations. However, Iraq's alleged renewed procurement attempts in the field of WMD also apply to the missile area[38].

---

[35] In May 1996, India concluded a $15 million deal with Iran to construct a plant to produce phosphorus pentasulfide, a chemical that can be used to make pesticide but has been identified by the Australia Group as a component of some chemical weapons. See James ADAMS, *ibid.*

[36] See for example Yiftah SHAPIR, *"Proliferation of Nonconventional Weapons in the Middle East"*, in: Shlomo GAZIT (ed.), **The Middle East Military Balance 1993-1994**, Jaffee Center for Strategic Studies, Tel Aviv University, Westview Press, 1994, pp.216-238. For a more recent account, see Ian O. LESSER & Ashley J. TELLIS, **Strategic Exposure: Proliferation Around the Mediterranean**, RAND, Santa Monica, CA, 1996.

[37] A comprehensive assessment of the the threat posed by ballistic missile programs in the Middle East and North Africa to southern European states can be found in Ian O. LESSER & Ashley J. TELLIS, **Strategic Exposure,** *ibid.*

[38] UNSCOM sources substantiate these allegations with their findings pertaining to the detailed intitiatives and contracts of Iraq's worldwide procurement network operating through front companies. Conversations with a UNSCOM inspector, February 1997.

4.2.2. Iran: Iran's first Scud missiles were gifts from Libya, which enabled the former to launch missile attacks on Baghdad beginning in 1985. During the 1988 "War of the Cities" Iran received Scud missiles from North Korea. After 1992, North Korea delivered modified Scud-C missiles whose range exceeds 500 km. Iran's attempt to acquire 1,000 km range Nodong-1 (Scud-D) missiles has not borne fruit to date. Iran is reportedly working on a medium range (800 km) missile called Thondar-68.

4.2.3 Syria: Syria has possessed operational Scud missiles since 1975. These missiles were acquired from the Soviet Union. The first Scud-C missiles were delivered to Syria from North Korea in late 1991 and early 1992. North Korea also provided Syria with Scud-C launchers in 1993. China agreed to sell Syria M-9 missiles with a range of 600 km, but partly due to pressure put on China by the United States, it appears that no missiles have been delivered.

4.2.4. Libya: Libya received Scuds from the Soviet Union in the late 1970s. Libya was reportedly involved in the 1980s in a project called al-Fatah, a liquid-fuelled missile with a range of at least 1,000 km. Progress on the project, developed by German engineers, was slow. To date, the fate of the missile project is unknown.

4.2.5. Egypt: The first country in the Middle East to operate ballistic missiles on the battlefield was Egypt, which fired three Scuds at Israeli forces in Sinai in October 1973. In the early 1980s, Egypt transferred a few Soviet-made Scud missiles to North Korea. The North Koreans studied the missile through reverse engineering, and then produced and exported them. Egypt is believed to have Scud-B and Scud-C missiles, while the status of efforts to manufacture Scud-C missiles indigenously is not known for sure.

4.2.6. Israel: The first ballistic missiles acquired by Israel in the 1960s were based on the French missile Dassault MD-660. That missile system, then known as Jericho-1, had a range of 480 km. The modified Jericho-2 developed in the mid-1980s had a longer range. In 1989 and in 1990 Israel succeeded in launching its experimental satellites, Ofeq-1 and then Ofeq-2, delivered by the Shavit missile launcher. The Shavit missile was reportedly capable of carrying a payload of 1,000 kg over 4,500 km[39].

5. The Attitude of the Political and Security Elites towards Nuclear Issues[40]

The fundamental thrust of Turkish foreign and security policy is to become a state party to international agreements in the security field so as to contribute to their effective implementation and also to reiterate the guiding principle of Turkish foreign policy: "peace at home and peace in the world". This guiding principle was laid down by the founding father and the first President of the Turkish Republic, Mustafa Kemal Ataturk. Issues pertaining to nuclear arms, nuclear arms control and disarmament are principally seen by the Turkish security elites from this perspective. Accordingly, Turkey has become a state party to the Nuclear Non-Proliferation Treaty (NPT) by signing it on 28 January 1969, and subsequently ratifying it on 17 April 1980[41]. Turkey has also become a state party to the Biological

---

[39] For details see Yiftah SHAPIR, *ibid.*

[40] The information summarized in this section is partly derived from the author's personal correspondence with members of the political and security elites belonging to different institutions in Turkey. Some of this correspondence, however, took place during the author's doctoral research (1993-96). Nonetheless, in view of the fact that no drastic changes have occurred in the fundamental thrust of Turkish foreign policy since then, these views are thought to be still relevant to the subject matter of this study and are therefore brought into the discussion at this point.

[41] Turkey's rather late ratification of the NPT may give rise to the question of whether Turkish politicians wanted to keep the nuclear option open. The conventional wisdom does not suggest that this is likely. However, the traditional weight and hence the undisputed influence of the military on the decision-making process on matters relating to national security was probably a factor that delayed ratification for some time. During the 1970s, when interest in nuclear as well as other weapons of mass destruction and their delivery means was growing in neighbouring countries like Iran, Iraq, and Syria, the Turkish military elites might not have wanted to give an impression by means of a hasty ratification that Turkey would definitely forgo the nuclear option. Although they had no real intention in that respect, the Turkish elites might have wished to leave the issue ambiguous as a deterrent to regional rivals and enemies. The other side of the coin should also be mentioned. In the second half of 1970s, Turkey went through a period of chaos which prompted the military intervention in 1980, which, according to many political analysts, rescued the country from the brink of an all-out civil war. Therefore, one should not be surprised if the Turkish Grand National Assembly did not prioritize the ratification of the NPT

Weapons Convention of 1972 and signed the Chemical Weapons Convention of 1993 followed by ratification by the Turkish Grand Assembly in April 1997. Turkey recently assumed full member status in the Conference on Disarmament (CD) in Geneva after a long period of attending its meetings with observer status. Its willingness to become a full member can be considered a reflection of the importance attributed by the security elites to disarmament and non-proliferation matters. At the Extension and Review Conference of the NPT held in New York in April/May 1995, Turkey gave its full support to the indefinite and unconditional extension of the Treaty. Turkey also used its influence on the turkic republics of Central Asia and the Caucasus to induce them to do the same. As a country that never sought to acquire weapons of mass destruction, Turkey is striving hard to strengthen the non-proliferation regime and also participates actively in efforts to enhance the IAEA's verification system. Therefore, Turkey pays close attention to the proceedings of the "93+2 Programme" as an attempt to make IAEA safeguards inspections more intrusive. In a broader framework, the abolition of nuclear weapons is viewed as a noble aim, which should stay on the agenda. Nevertheless, the international context seemingly requires the elites to acknowledge that this aim could only be reached in stages. Furthering the START process, the conclusion of the CTBT, and a cut-off in the production of fissile material are all considered to be such stages.

5.1. Attitudes towards a Test Ban

As a member of the Conference on Disarmament, Turkey is "pleased" to have joined the overwhelming majority of nations in the effort to conclude a Comprehensive Test Ban Treaty (CTBT). The complete ban on nuclear testing, the core function of the Treaty, is thought by the Turkish security elites to be an effective measure to control nuclear weapons technology. The international monitoring of this ban that the CTBT provides for is believed to serve as an important confidence-building measure amongst the states that are (and will be)

---

at a time when the country was struggling with anarchy and there was no non-proliferation culture. In addition, the two very small-scale nuclear research and training reactors were probably not considered by policymakers as compelling reasons for speeding up the ratification process or concluding a safeguards agreement with the IAEA.

party to the Treaty. With specific reference to India's position on the CTBT, the Turkish security elites hope that India will review its position and ensure that the Treaty will come into force. This expectation is in full conformity with the Turkish security elites' conviction that consolidation of the CTBT will be an important step towards the eventual elimination of nuclear weapons.

5.2. Attitudes towards a Cut-Off of the Production of Fissile Material

In a period when there are extended discussions in progress regarding the management of tons of excess plutonium and highly enriched uranium left over from weapons dismantling programmes in both the United States and Russia, questioning the significance of a universal cut-off treaty is obvious[42]. Therefore, the Turkish security elites fully support such an eventuality and believe that the entry into force of such a treaty should secure the ratification of the so-called threshold states like India, Pakistan and Israel. A cut-off treaty is accordingly thought to constitute another significant step towards the ultimate goal of eliminating nuclear weapons. With special reference to the obvious danger of further nuclearisation of the Middle East, Israel being a *de facto* nuclear power, any development that would facilitate the acquisition of fissile material by other aspiring states in the region is believed to be counter-productive. Hence a cut-off in the production of fissile material is considered by the Turkish security elites in the context of its merits in contributing to the non-proliferation goal.

5.3. Attitudes towards a Change in NATO Strategy to "No-First-Use"

At the conceptual level, a change in NATO strategy is considered by the Turkish security elites to be a natural consequence of the revolutionary changes that have taken place in the Soviet bloc, to which

---

[42] Ongoing discussions in some scholarly circles involve divergent views about the significance of a cut-off treaty, while India's position is unambiguous after its rejection of the CTBT.

political system the Alliance was conceptually opposed[43]. The original NATO strategic concept changed several times during the Cold War in response to changes and developments in the military balance between the two military blocs[44]. The NATO strategy of the 1990s incorporates the objective of establishing cooperation with the countries of the former WTO[45]. The military structure of the Alliance is therefore undergoing changes commensurate with its new strategic concept[46]. These changes are mostly welcomed by the security elites in Turkey insofar as they reduce the likelihood of war. Nevertheless, it must be remembered that all of NATO's strategic concepts throughout the Cold War, asserted the right of the Alliance to resort to nuclear weapons at any stage of a conflict. To put it simply, the underlying concept of NATO strategies has always been (and still is) a "first-use" strategy, and this is also strongly supported by the Turkish security elites[47]. As stressed elsewhere in this study, NATO countries relied on their nuclear capabilities to offset the superiority of the WTO in conventional weaponry. Because it was envisaged that NATO might not win a war without resorting to nuclear weapons, whereas the

---

[43] Though no specification of the name of any group of countries as adversaries is found in the text of the North Atlantic Treaty. The geographical delimitation that exists in the text, however, identifies the defense commitment of the Alliance.

[44] The so-called "flexible response" strategy of NATO, designed and adopted in the 1960s, was regarded as defining the characteristics of the Alliance. It prioritized conventional responses to conventional aggression, keeping nuclear weapons as a secondary option that could be resorted to during a protracted conflict. The previous NATO strategy had relied on "massive retaliation", according to which the immediate resort to nuclear weapons would be possible in case of an attack on the allied countries.

[45] NATO's new strategic concept places more emphasis on "crisis management" and "conflict prevention", and is mindful of the fact that Central and Eastern Europe are now fertile zones for potential instabilities resulting from the ethnic composition of the states of the region.

[46] Accordingly, smaller and more flexible force units at lower levels of readiness with greater mobility are replacing the previous concept that relied on rather static linear defense.

[47] In order to avoid any confusion or misinterpretation of the terms, it should be made clear that NATO's "first use" strategy by no means implies "pre-emptive use", which means the use of nuclear weapons before any aggression occurs. Rather, first-use implies that NATO may be the first to use nuclear weapons, during an aggression, in view of the fact that no other option might provide a better way of defending NATO territory against an aggressor. Telephone conversation with Turkish ambassador Omer Ersun, Ottawa, Canada, April 22, 1997.

WTO might, with its conventional superiority. In contrast to this argument, the Soviet Union declared in 1982, as part of a peace offensive, that it would not be the first to resort to nuclear weapons and initiated a "no-first-use" strategy. The Turkish security elites considered the Soviet "no-first-use" pledge to be a mere propaganda tool at the time it was initiated.

However, the tide has turned with the disintegration of the Soviet Union and the dissolution of the WTO. As NATO survived and is moving towards enlargement, Russia is undergoing drastic changes. The imbalance in conventional weapons systems is now more strongly in favour of NATO (even excluding the potential contribution of the prospective members) than it was in the WTO's favour during the Cold War[48]. Therefore, the Russian military elites felt compelled to revise their decade-old "no-first-use" strategy, and to declare instead, in 1993, that Russia would again reserve its legitimate right to resort to nuclear weapons in case of aggression by a nuclear-weapon state or an ally of a nuclear-weapon state, regardless of the weapons used by the aggressor. This change in Russian policy was concomitant with the declaration of the so-called "near abroad" doctrine. The implication of this is that in the case of aggression, given its now inferior position in conventional forces, a feasible alternative for Russia would be to resort to tactical nuclear weapons. This could in theory lead to an exchange of strategic nuclear forces, that is an all-out nuclear war[49].

---

[48] Although a clear retrospective comparison between the conventional arsenals of the NATO and WTO countries is hardly possible, it was generally estimated that WTO had a "1.5 to 1" or even "2 to 1" superiority over NATO. However, the imbalance between NATO (short of new members) and Russia (short of its loose CIS alliance) is now said to amount to "3 to 1" in neighbour of NATO. In case of NATO enlargement and Russia turning the CIS into a military alliance as a reaction, NATO still seems likely to be better off. Conversations with Turkish military experts and with Dr. Nikolai Sokov from the Center for Nonproliferation Studies of the Monterey Institute of International Studies, February 1997. Dr. Sokov worked with the Soviet Foreign Ministry in the late 1980s and participated in the START I and II negotiations.

[49] Strategic nuclear weapons in the arsenals of the United States and Russia can be targetted in ten minutes. This means that the world is ten minutes away from Cold War contingencies. Conversations with James Goodby when he paid a visit to the Center for Nonproliferation Studies of the Monterey Institute of International Studies, November 1996.

Although simple logic might suggest that NATO, which now has an indisputable superiority in conventional forces, should now adopt the "no-first-use" strategy in order to avoid a catastrophe, things are not so simple. A switch in NATO strategy in that direction may not (and probably will not) bring about a concurrent change in Russian strategy from "first-use" back to "no-first-use". Moreover, the present Russian "first-use" strategy is not only an outcome of Russia's inferiority vis-à-vis NATO's conventional posture, but also a reflection of the Russian military elites' assessment of threats from the south. The cumulative threat posed by nuclear weapons in China and by the nuclear capabilities of India and Pakistan, at whatever level, is apparently no less significant a threat to Russia. In addition to these two principal reasons, the traumatic effects of the dissolution of the Soviet Union and the Warsaw Pact on the state of mind of the Russian security elites should also be taken seriously[50]. Therefore, a "no-first-use" declaration by NATO would be of limited significance in the short term[51]. On the other hand, NATO has its own constraints as far as the threat of proliferation of WMD, especially in the Middle East and the Mediterranean basin, is concerned. It is anticipated that within a decade, "Western European capitals will be within the range of ballistic missiles based in North Africa and the Middle East", and that the "southern members of NATO will be the first to feel the political and military consequences of proliferation trends on Europe's periphery"[52]. Therefore, in June 1996, NATO foreign and defence ministers endorsed a comprehensive approach to counter the military risks posed by such threats[53]. NATO's efforts to adapt itself

---

[50] The Russian elites have lost almost all their confidence in their Western counterparts, especially because of the assurances given to them during the unification of Germany, now proved to be void, as regards the future composition of NATO. Therefore, even if NATO turns to "no-first-use", Russia would probably expect further concrete steps from the West to rebuild confidence. This, however, may be a very long process. Conversations with Nikolai Sokov.

[51] It could, however, contribute to confidence building efforts between the parties. In other words, NATO's switch to a "no-first-use" strategy is considered by the Russians to be a "necessary but not sufficient condition" of improved confidence. Conversations with Nikolai Sokov.

[52] See Ronald D. Asmus, F. Stephen Larrabee & Ian O. Lesser, *"Mediterranean Security: New Challenges, New Tasks"*, in: **NATO Review**, No.3, May 1996, pp.25-31.

[53] This issue is explicitly cited in the Communiqué (§ 29) released after the meeting of the North Atlantic Council in Defense Ministers Session, on 13 June 1996. For full documentation, see **NATO Review**, No.5, September 1996, pp.32-35.

to meet the challenges of the new security environment have produced guidelines for appropriate responses to proliferation. The overarching principles envisaged to guide NATO's defence response are, among others, to "maintain **freedom of action** and demonstration to any potential adversary that the alliance will not be coerced by the threat or use of WMD.[54]"

In view of the fact that a change in NATO strategy to "no-first-use" would not induce an immediate reciprocal change in Russia's current "first-use" strategy, and considering that the proliferation of WMD in the proximity of NATO is likely to constitute a more serious threat in the near future than it does now, the exigency and viability of such a change seems questionable[55]. Therefore, the Turkish security elites do not see any prospect of a switch to a "no-first-use" strategy, at least for the foreseeable future. Although dramatic (and also favourable) changes have taken place in Turkey's security environment, the credibility of the nuclear posture and hence NATO's deterrence policy, including the implicit "first use" strategy of the Alliance, is of the utmost importance for the Turkish security elites.

5.4. Attitudes towards a START III Treaty and the Inclusion of the French, British and Chinese Nuclear Arsenals in International Nuclear Arms Limitation and Reduction Treaties

The START III Treaty, although it is unlikely to be signed in the near future, is likely to set US and Russian strategic nuclear forces at levels at which they will remain for some time. START II still awaits ratification by the Russian Duma. This treaty lays down a level of 3,500 strategic nuclear warheads in the arsenals of the two sides, and it is hoped that this will be further reduced to 2,000 warheads each in the START III Treaty. As for the idea of including the French, British

---

[54] For a fuller discussion, see Ashton B. CARTER & David B. OMAND, *"Countering the Proliferation Risks: Adapting the Alliance to the New Security Environment"*, in: **NATO Review**, No.5, September 1996, pp.10-15 (emphasis added).

[55] It is nonetheless interesting to note that in the post-Cold War era, both NATO and Russia have to pay even more attention to factors beyond each other's intentions and capabilities in defining their new defense and security identities; this may have serious consequences for both parties.

and Chinese nuclear arsenals in international arms limitation and reduction treaties, the Turkish political elites' view is positive. This
would be regarded as a step in the right direction, which would contribute to the eventual goal of the total elimination of nuclear weapons. But the Turkish security elites are well aware of the perspective
of the three medium-sized nuclear-weapon-states, which are concerned
about the huge gap between their respective nuclear stockpiles and
those of the United States and Russia. Therefore, the Turkish elites
do not expect the "smaller" three to make any move to join the "big"
two in arms limitation talks.

5.5. Attitudes towards the transfer of Fissile Material to Civilian Purposes

According to some scholarly work and technical reports, in the
years ahead hundreds of tons of fissile material, mainly in the form
of weapons-grade plutonium (Pu-239) and highly enriched uranium
(U-235), will be considered excess as a result of drastic cuts in the
nuclear arsenals of the United States and Russia – provided the START
treaties are fully implemented[56]. The issue of utmost importance then
will be the fate of these excess fissile materials. Comprehensive studies are underway as to the safest and most feasible ways of managing
the excess plutonium[57]. HEU is much less problematic because it can
be diluted with natural uranium to obtain Low Enriched Uranium
(LEU). It goes without saying that strict controls and the concomitant application of safeguards will be necessary no matter which
methods of disposal are preferred for the excess fissile materials that
will be accumulated over the next two decades. A beneficial side-ef-
fect of the effective transfer of fissile materials from weapons to civilian purposes is that it will facilitate the acquisition of low-enriched
uranium or MOX fuel by less industrialised countries, at cheaper rates

---

[56] For an excellent discussion of these matters and a compilation of useful infor-
mation with regard to the estimated global plutonium and HEU stocks, see
David ALBRIGHT, Frans BERKHOUT & William WALKER, **Plutonium and Highly
Enriched Uranium 1996: Inventories, Capabilities and Policies**, Oxford
University Press for SIPRI, Oxford/New York, 1997.

[57] See, for instance, **Management and Disposition of Excess Weapons Plutonium:
Reactor-Related Options**, National Academy of Sciences, National Academy
Press, Washington, D.C., 1995.

and for a longer period, for the generation of electricity in their civilian nuclear plants. Turkey, as a country which recently invited international companies to make bids for one or two nuclear power plants, is likely to welcome such a transition from military to civilian use of fissile materials.

5.6. Attitudes towards a NWFZ in Central and Eastern Europe

This issue is likely to be the most controversial one between Turkey and the United States within the NATO alliance. Moreover, for reasons that will be explained below, the negative stance of the Turkish security elites towards proposals to establish a nuclear-weapon-free zone in Central and Eastern Europe, as well as the enlargement of NATO, may give rise to a dilemma. The Clinton administration has repeatedly declared that NATO enlargement is a high priority for the US, and Germany also follows this issue closely[58]. The Turkish political and security elites have also made it clear on several occasions that, as a NATO ally, Turkey would not oppose (though not necessarily endorse) the idea of NATO enlargement[59] and hopes that such a process will help consolidate the democracies of the former communist countries as they become integrated into the European system. Russia's reaction to NATO expansion in general, and to the report in particular, was clear: opposition. Russian officials and politicians have flatly rejected the idea and on many occasions stated that they would view NATO expansion as a threat that would necessitate

---

[58] It goes without saying that the enlargement of NATO towards the East will contribute most to Germany's security, as there will be a buffer zone between Germany and its historic adversary, Russia.

[59] It has emerged during the revision of this chapter that the Turkish political and security elites seem to be very uncomfortable with the "unequal" and "unfair" treatment they have received from their West European counterparts with regard to Turkey's full membership of the EU, by comparison with the other prospective members from Eastern Europe. Hence the Turkish political elites, though not all of them, have reportedly made their affirmative vote for NATO expansion conditional on Turkey's full membership not only of the WEU, but also of the EU. Such a development can be seen to have worsened the already strained relations between Turkey and NATO because of the dispute over the issue of allocation of NATO assets to the WEU. This dimension of Turkish-European relations will be discussed later in the chapter. As of April 1997, there seems to be no easy way out of this deadlock.

counter-measures[60]. Russia's unambiguous position compelled the NATO partners to come up with solutions. Hence the proposal to establish a NWFZ in Central and Eastern Europe, tabled by Belarus at the United Nations General Assembly in 1990, gained the endorsement of scholarly circles in the United States but not of the government[61]. Other proposals also followed a similar pattern of thinking and suggested making the region free of tactical nuclear weapons, which would mean a *de facto* NWFZ. In this manner, it is believed that Russia might be persuaded that NATO enlargement was not an anti-Russian move, and that NATO would not threaten Russia's security interests with the deployment of nuclear weapons. It is not yet clear whether Russia would be satisfied with this or would ask for further concessions from the West[62]. Even if nuclear weapons are not to be deployed on the territory of the prospective members of NATO, the imbalance created in conventional weapons systems will still disturb Russia. This may lead Russia to take counter measures. Among the concrete steps likely to be taken could be: the transformation of the Commonwealth of Independent States into a military alliance; the rejection of the START II Treaty; withdrawal from the CFE; and the reconsideration of Russia's military doctrine and foreign policy. All these options and others that might follow would undoubtedly be detrimental to Western security including the security of Turkey.

From the perspective of the Turkish security elites, however, the proposal to establish a NWFZ in Central and Eastern Europe, coupled with the unwillingness of countries in the region to accept nuclear weapons on their soil in the event of their joining NATO as full members, is not thought to be an acceptable development. Among other things, NATO membership as a front-line state brought too many

---

[60] See, for instance, the then foreign Minister Andrei Kozyrev's statement at NATO Council, Noordvijk, 31 May 1995; and *"No Role for Russia in a Security Order that Includes an Expanded NATO"*, (The Russia Council's NATO Report), in: **Transition**, Vol.1, No.23, 15 December 1995, pp.27-33. Cited in Ali L. Karaosmanoglu, *ibid.*, p.8.

[61] See, for example, William C. POTTER & David FISCHER, *"Nuclear Free; Better Than NATO"*, Center for Nonproliferation Studies, Monterey Institute of International Studies, Internet Web Site (http://cns.miis.edu).

[62] Alexei Arbatov, Deputy Chairman of the Defense Committee of the Russian Duma, said during his visit to the Center for Nonproliferation Studies of the Monterey Institute of International Studies in November 1996 that top Russian officials viewed the proposal for a NWFZ in Central and Eastern Europe to be of marginal importance to Russian security considerations.

risks as well as responsibilities to Turkey during the Cold War. The Turkish military did its best to attain the training and readiness levels set by the Alliance, which meant a lot of sacrifices for Turkey in many respects. Moreover, Turkey was the playground of two the superpowers during the Cuban missile crisis. Turkey might have suffered severe consequences as a result of the brinkmanship game played by the Americans and Soviets, had not wiser counsels brought the crisis to an end[63]. Therefore, the Turkish security elites cannot appreciate the political concerns of the prospective members of NATO in that respect. These countries will certainly be in a privileged and more advantageous position than some of the other members. The Turkish elites believe that if Central and East European countries are admitted to NATO with a nuclear-weapon-free status they will on the one hand enjoy the status of being full members, thus getting the full security guarantees of the Alliance, and on the other hand, they will not put themselves at risk by deploying nuclear weapons on their soil.

In view of the uncertainties involving the Russian reaction noted above, Turkey's opposition to a would-be NWFZ in Central and Eastern Europe may have to be revised. It should be acknowledged by the Turkish political and security elites that, if NATO is to expand, the most obvious compromise between Russia and NATO would be the non-deployment of nuclear weapons on the territory of the new members. That is a *de facto* or *de jure* NWFZ in Central and Eastern

---

[63] The Kennedy administration agreed to remove Jupiter missiles from Turkey without consulting its Turkish allies. As stated in a previous footnote, Turkish-American relations were soured in the mid-1960 because of the "Johnson letter". Concomitant with the letter, news leaked, presumably from the Soviet embassy in Ankara, that Kennedy had agreed to a trade-off of the Jupiters during the Cuban crisis without informing the Turks. The removal of the missiles had already served to widen the gap between the right and left in the domain of Turkish domestic politics. The leftists argued that the rightist government had sold the country to the Americans. But with the Johnson letter, coupled with the revelations in the press about the missile trade-off, anti-Americanism and neutralist sentiments grew on the part of liberals and socialists alike. In the military domain, however, things went rather slowly, if not smoothly. In 1970, the Turkish government announced, probably after consultations with the military, that the Military Facilities Agreement of 1954 with the United States was abrogated. From then on the Turkish state was able to use the issue of military bases to its own advantage. For further details, see Nur B. CRISS, "... *The Jupiter Affair...*", *ibid.* See also Jerrold I. SCHECTER & Vyacheslav V. LUCHKOV (eds), **Khruschev Remembers: The Glasnost Tapes,** Little, Brown and Co., Boston, 1990, cited in CRISS, *ibid.*

Europe. This being the essence of the dilemma that Turkey is likely to face, however, the Turkish security elites prefer not to express their opposition out loud at this premature stage so as not to prompt a negative reaction from their foremost ally, the United States. Besides, the practicality and feasibility of a NWFZ in Central and Eastern Europe is still being discussed in political and scholarly circles in the United States, and the official stance of the Clinton administration towards the proposal is yet to be clarified.

6. Conclusion

This chapter has concentrated on the military aspects of nuclear related matters as they pertain to Turkey's foreign relations and its role in world politics. However, civilian aspects of the same issue area and their implications for Turkey's foreign and economic relations should also be considered. It seems that after long deliberations over the last decade, Turkey is finally nearing the end in its attempt to benefit from the peaceful applications of nuclear energy[64]. Therefore, Turkey is likely to become much more closely acquainted with a variety of aspects of running large-scale nuclear utilities. But before this happens, Turkey should not risk another backlash in its initiatives to acquire nuclear facilities as has happened in the past[65].

Turkey made attempts to exploit nuclear energy for peaceful uses in the second half of the 1980s. Serious talks were conducted with

---

[64] To this end, Turkey has requested bids for establishing large-scale nuclear installations. In 1995, the Turkish State Power Board (TEAS) hired the Korean Atomic Energy Research Institute (KAERI) to examine the feasibility of renewing Turkey's project at Akkuyu. A review process was scheduled for completion by mid-1996. A contractor will be selected by 1998, with construction scheduled to begin in late 1998. Atomic Energy of Canada is expected to offer a 680 MW CANDU-6 heavy water reactor, and Siemens of Germany is said to be offering a 1,400 MW pressurized water reactor. See Mark HIBBS, *"Turkey Expected to Request Bids for PWR Project in Coming Weeks"*, in: **Nucleonics Week**, March 21, 1996, pp.1-2. According to the most recent reports in December 1996, the Turkish government plans to accept bids for the nuclear plant to be built either as single unit with a capacity of 1,200 MW or as two equal units each of a capacity of 600 MW. The cost of the plant is estimated to be $1.5 billion.

[65] A study including a survey of Turkey's past attempts to install nuclear power reactors is scheduled to appear in Mustafa KIBAROGLU, *"Turkey's Quest for Nuclear Power"*, in: **The Nonproliferation Review**, Monterey Institute of International Studies, Monterey, CA., Spring/Summer 1997 pp.33-44.

Canadian and German firms to that end, and Turkey also almost wrapped up a comprehensive nuclear cooperation agreement with Argentina. Nevertheless, all of these attempts ended in failure. For instance, the Canadian firm AECL which had formed a consortium with a Turkish firm ENKA, won a nuclear plant contract that was later signed by the Turkish Prime Minister Turgut Ozal. However, the bid was withdrawn in response to pressure from Western countries which were concerned that Turkey might build a nuclear bomb with a plant based on CANDU technology[66]. With Argentina much more elaborate talks were held over the years. However, these efforts never materialised, because the possibility of a transfer of the complete nuclear fuel cycle to Turkey raised serious concerns in the United States and also in Greece, Israel, and India, all of whom in turn fuelled US fears so as to thwart such a development[67]. Putting aside the obvious concerns of Greece[68], the fears of Israel, India and the United States converged on the possibility of a re-transfer of the technology and materials that would be acquired by Turkey, to a third country, namely Pakistan. There had already been speculation about a Turkish-Pakistani connection in the nuclear field. It was asserted that Pakistan used Turkey as a go-between to obtain nuclear know-how and materials, and that the two countries would share the nuclear know-how acquired by Turkey, including know-how in the area of nuclear weapons development. Quite a number of similar unfounded speculations appeared in international media all through the 1980s and 1990s. It was no surprise, however, that the sources of information were either Greece or India in most cases, each being the sworn enemy of one of the parties they were accusing of being engaged in illicit nuclear business[69]. To date, however, no evidence has been found to substantiate these allegations. The Turkish Ministry of Foreign Affairs has always denied these reports,

---

[66] See the Turkish daily, **Tercuman** (Istanbul), November 6, 1987, p.10. Source: CNS Databases, Center for Nonproliferation Studies, Monterey Institute of International Studies, Monterey, CA.

[67] For a detailed account of these matters, see Mustafa KIBAROGLU, **Turkey's Quest for Peaceful Nuclear Power**.

[68] For a Greek viewpoint on this particular issue, see Thanos DOKOS, *"Greece"*, in: Harald MÜLLER (ed), **Nuclear Export Controls in Europe**, European Interuniversity Press (EIP), Brussels, 1995, p.208.

[69] See, for instance, **Delhi Domestic Service**, March 23, 1988; **The Times of India** (Bombay), July 11, 1988, p.18; and, **I Kathimerini** (Athens), December 29, 1991, p.1. CNS Databases.

stated that Turkey fulfills "with great care" its obligations under the NPT, and dismissed suggestions that Turkey would sell material to Pakistan for nuclear arms production[70].

Although unsubstantiated, such allegations have stalled the development of the nuclear industry in Turkey. The US Congress has become very sensitive about the issue and has done its best to obstruct Turkey's initiatives in this area[71]. Alas, Turkey's need for additional electricity generation capacity is very great, and the country suffers from electricity blackouts that have a very serious negative impact on its industrial productivity and other activities[72]. This should not have been the case for a country like Turkey which has always been loyal to its NPT commitments as well as to its IAEA obligations, not to mention its "staunch ally" status in NATO, a good reason to forgo a nuclear adventure. There are many other reasons why Turkey should not be interested in the nuclear option for military purposes, and this option has never been pursued. However, the Turkish political and security elites should seriously consider the possibility that misperceptions may cause great harm to Turkey's interests. Unless Turkey's intentions and capabilities are unequivocally understood in the Western world, similar speculations may surface again and again and may make it impossible for Turkey to derive potential benefits in the nuclear field. In order not to leave any room for gossip, rumours etc., transparency is essential – not only transparency of agreements or contracts, but also of transactions *per se*. One simple way to attain this would be for Turkey to join the Nuclear Suppliers Group and to adopt its guidelines,

---

[70] Foreign Ministry spokesman Ambassador Inal Batu made this statement during a press conference held on October 28, 1987. CNS Databases.

[71] In an article published in *The Washington Post* on June 24, 1992, US Senator John Glenn admits that an amendment to the US Foreign Assistance Act of 1977 proposed by Senator Stuart Symington and himself dealing with the issue of nuclear proliferation especially in regard to Pakistan, should have attempted to stop aid to Turkey because of its alleged involvement in aiding Pakistan in its acquisition of uranium enrichment equipment. CNS Databases.

[72] Although there were major advances in electricity generation capacity in Turkey in the 1980s, many of the projects for exploiting the country's hydroelectric potential were either shelved or abandoned in the early 1990s, mainly because of the difficulties in financing and domestic political unrest. Even if all the hydroelectric potential of the country were used, supply will still fall short of demand in the early 2000s. For a graphic account of this problem see Mustafa KIBAROGLU, **Turkey's Quest for Peaceful Nuclear Power**.

which regulate world-wide nuclear exports including dual use materials. Such a move would certainly dispel the suspicion that Turkey acts as a mediator between the suppliers and Pakistan[73].

---

[73] *Ibid.*

ITALY

M. Cristina ZADRA

1. The Security Situation before and after the End of the Cold War

During the Cold War Italy delegated the task of defending its security interests to the Atlantic Alliance and to the USA, with all the implications that such a choice has for foreign and internal affairs. This did not mean the country was never able to pursue its own policies[1]. The degree of independence Italy enjoyed during those years is still a subject of debate among scholars[2].

Whatever Italy's attitude and policy in the Cold War period, it became clear after 1989 that the rentiers' position[3] on the strategic scene occupied by Italy up until then – whether desirable or not – was no longer possible and that the country was required to redefine its security interests and the policies that would be appropriate in the

---

[1] A typical example of this relative freedom of action has been policy towards Libya, for Italy a major oil supplier, but the same can be said in general with regard to the Mediterranean area, Eastern Europe and some African countries.

[2] Two different views are expressed, for example by Sergio ROMANO, former Italian ambassador to Moscow, in his book **Guida alla politica estera italiana**, Rizzoli, Milano, 1993; and, by Roberto GAJA, former ambassador to Washington, in his book **L'Italia nel mondo bipolare: per una storia della politica estera italiana (1943-1991)**, Il Mulino, Bologna, 1995.

[3] This characterisation of the Italian situation during the Cold War was given by the Istituto per gli Affari Internazionali (IAI) in its 1992 report *"The Dual Crisis"*, in: **International Spectator** No.27, 1993, and was then echoed in many other situations and contexts, becoming common in Italian political jargon.

pursuit of those interests[4]. For many different reasons, the country has not been able to do so.

The end of the East-West confrontation swept away in less than three years the entire political class that had ruled Italy since the end of World War II, leading to a situation of instability whose outcome is still hard to foresee[5]. In this situation it was very difficult for any broad and serious debate on foreign and security policy to emerge.

What discussion there has been rarely goes beyond the limits of diplomatic and expert circles, and is conducted between two main groups: there exists an internationalist tradition which strongly supports the completion of the European Union, including political union. Multilateralism at different levels regional European, transatlantic or global – is regarded as the main principle of any foreign and security policy in a world where state actors are less and less capable of intervening in the globalisation process.

At the opposite end of the spectrum, some urge instead a renationalisation of foreign and security policy, believing that the end of bipolarism and the consequent fragmentation of the international scene offer a window of opportunity to act according to national interests. Terms like geopolitics and geoeconomics are central to the argument that "competition for space and the creation of zones of influence has clearly resumed[6]".

---

[4] As early as 1993 Beniamino Andreatta, Minister for Foreign Affairs during the Ciampi Government (April 1993-May 1994) and at present Minister of Defence, argued that the country should elaborate plans and strategies (see his article *"Una politica estera per l'Italia"*, in: **Il Mulino**, No.42, 1993). Andreatta argued here that simple membership of international organisations was no longer enough, and from now on one had to act and qualify in order to be able to get results.

[5] In April 1993, a first "technical executive" was formed with the aim of giving Parliament time to approve the reform of the electoral system. General elections in spring 1994, conducted for the first time under the first-post-the-post system, resulted in a right-centre government headed by Mr. Berlusconi which was to last only seven months. Another technical executive was to lead the country to new general elections held in spring 1996, which brought to power the Olive tree coalition. Since 1992 Italy has had seven different foreign ministers.

[6] Carlo JEAN, **Geopolitica**, Laterza, Bari, 1995, p.XI. See also Ludovico INCISA DI CAMERANA, **La vittoria dell'Italia nella terza guerra mondiale**, Laterza, Bari, 1996. The debate in this direction also takes place in the specialised journal *Limes*.

These two schools of thought do not correspond to political parties or coalitions, but enjoy support with different nuances and to a greater or lesser extent among both leftists and conservatives.

Common to the two schools are a few key beliefs:

1) There is substantial agreement on NATO's eastward enlargement, although some consider the political/economic aspects more important than the strategic ones. In this second view the inclusion of the four Visegrad countries (Poland, Hungary, the Czech and Slovak republics) plus Romania and Slovenia – a position also held by the Italian government – should be considered a fast way of bringing them into the EU's orbit[7]. Future problems caused by a possible Russian authoritarian turn or military revival cannot be excluded. In this context, most insiders still consider nuclear deterrence a cornerstone of the European security system.

2) European security still relies on a strong American presence on the continent, even if a more incisive role should be played by Europe itself, through the EU/WEU.

3) The Mediterranean area, where local conflicts and/or demographic pressure could give rise to major migratory flows towards Southern Europe, deserves special attention in the near future. There is also some concern about the proliferation of weapons of mass destruction and improved delivery capabilities in the Middle East.

Taking into account points 1, 2 and 3, the Mediterranean basin becomes the key sector of possible cooperation between NATO and the WEU[8]. Italy has also officially proposed the creation of a PfP open to the countries that signed the Barcelona Declaration at the end of 1995, in order to balance the eastern PfP.

---

[7] As to the security aspects, and in particular relations with Russia, it is useful to recall here that in November 1996 Italy and Russia concluded two bilateral agreements for the development of cooperation in the defence sector, the first of this kind between a NATO country and Russia. In spite of this, Italian interests in Russia remain strongly related to economic issues (above all oil supplies).

[8] A basis for such cooperation has been established by the Italian initiative for the constitution in 1996 of Eurofor and Euromarfor, together with France, Spain and Portugal. Both these small joint forces will be "on call" for UN/NATO/WEU missions, basically in the field of crisis management.

For the moment this can only be understood as an attempt to involve the "core" group of European countries in Mediterranean issues. In spite of the diplomatic efforts made in this area in the last few years, it seems that no global vision or strategy has yet been elaborated and practical initiatives pose serious difficulties. The success of the Barcelona process, if any, will depend on Spain rather than Italy. There is still a gap between theories, official statements and reality. If we look at the two main elements of Italian engagement abroad during the 1990s, cooperation in development and peacekeeping missions, possible interpretation is that Italy is still hesitating between the two extremes of becoming a pure "trading state" and following "mini-Gaullist" temptations[9].

Finally the significance of the internal debate is confirmed by the limited attention that political parties paid to foreign and security policy in their programs for the last two electoral campaigns. Inside Parliament only very few sessions have been devoted to the discussion of background issues, while the instruments of foreign and security policy, cooperation in development and defence, have still not yet been reconsidered[10]. Given the lack of political guidance, decisions seem to be taken at a lower level, on a case by case basis and often without any coordination, by many different actors or "centres of authority" within the state.

2. The Role of Nuclear Weapons in National Security Policy

As a consequence of the difficulties Italy is encountering in formulating its foreign and security policy, the role of nuclear weapons in this context has not been the object of any specific deliberations. The idea, now widely shared by many prominent politicians and scholars throughout the world, that nuclear defence is of declining importance in the new international situation, still encounters strong

---

[9] See Marta DASSÙ, *"Geopolitica e interessi nazionali italiani"*, in: **Il sistema Italia**, a cura del CASD, Franco Angeli, Milano, 1997.

[10] The text of a new law on international cooperation is still in preparation, after the almost total demise of bilateral aid for development at the end of the 1980s. The New Defence model has also been under discussion since 1991, and has been neither officially adopted nor rejected.

resistance in the country. Italy still firmly believes in nuclear deterrence as the less risky (and probably less costly) strategy of defence, and its policy in this field is the policy of the nuclear ally. In this respect it is useful to recall that Italy has since the early 1960s been an important deployment site for US nuclear weapons and, despite significant reductions in recent years, remains important in this respect[11]. It is not known whether the (secret) bilateral agreements between Italy and the US that regulate this issue, concluded thirty years ago, have ever been modified. Italy also participates in the study on the MEADS project (the European anti-ballistic missile defence system), but this program seems to have a low priority as a countermeasure to proliferation of arms of mass destruction and its industrial aspects might be considered more important.

Italy agreed with the "Principle and Objectives" issued by the 1995 NPT Review and Extension Conference: complete nuclear disarmament remains a long term goal. In this regard Italy officially favours step by step approach put forward by the major nuclear powers rather than an open discussion in a multilateral forum; the efficacy of this last approach is seriously questioned[12].

Italy did in the end vote in favour of the CTBT on September 17, 1996, as proposed in the form of a UN General Assembly resolution. Consensus on this issue was broad both on the international and the internal level. Italy is also going to support the proposal that negotiations on a cut off of the production of fissile material for nuclear weapons be placed on the CD agenda.

The difficulty of dealing with a delicate issue such as nuclear strategies can be seen in the peculiar Italian attitude towards the advisory opinion requested in November 1994 by the UN General Assembly from the World Court at The Hague, on the legitimacy of the use or threat of use of nuclear weapons according to international law. In

---

[11] According to W. ARKIN & R.S. NORRIS' *Nuclear Notebook* in the December 1995 issue of the **Bulletin of the Atomic Scientist**, the number of US nuclear weapons on Italian territory has declined from a total of 549 warheads in 1985 to 40 tactical B-61 bombs in 1995, deliverable by the Tornado fighter-bombers stationed in Aviano (a US base) and Ghedi Torre. For 1996, Arkin and Norris foresee a further downsizing of the arsenal to 25 bombs.

[12] Official statement of Foreign Affairs Minister, Mr. Lamberto Dini, at the signing ceremony of the CTBT, 24 September 1996.

spite of a motion approved by the Senate on April 6, 1995 asking the government to declare nuclear arms to be illegal in the written statement deposited before the Court in June Italy's government asserted that "the production and possession of nuclear weapons by certain States had to be legitimate, not being prohibited".

A few weeks later, on July 13, 1995 a resolution recommending that the government should take a position before the Court which could lead to condemnation of the use of nuclear weapons was adopted by the Senate, in defiance of the opinion expressed during the discussion by the representative of the government[13].

In the oral statement delivered before the World Court on November 6, 1995, the Italian representative declared that there was in international law no explicit prohibition of the use of nuclear weapons and that the Court was not competent to give a response to the questions posed by the UN General Assembly, because such a response would have a political rather than a juridical character. In the end he urged the Court not to consider the questions because whatever opinion it expressed could hinder negotiations on nuclear disarmament[14].

The position of the Italian Senate was reported to the Court on November 7 by the Ambassador of Malaysia during the oral procedure. Italy voted against a draft resolution brought before the UN First Committee by the Malaysian government on the World Court advisory opinion on November 14[15], as it had done with some other draft resolutions passed a few days before. These included the one passed on November 11, 1996, which calls upon the UNGA to reiterate its request that the Conference on Disarmament begin negotiations on a Convention to ban nuclear weapons[16] and the one calling upon the

---

[13] On that occasion the Under-secretary of the Foreign Affairs Ministry stated that the government believed the text of the motion to be contrary to certain international engagements; see Resoconto stenografico della 194a seduta del Senato, 13 luglio 1995.

[14] Quite surprisingly, Italy claimed that according to art. 42 of the UN Charter, the Security Council could decide to intervene with armed forces, no matter what type, provided they be legitimate. This implied that since nuclear weapons are not prohibited, the UN itself could legally use or threaten to use them.

[15] Resolution A/C.1/51/L.37, then A/RES/51/45M when adopted by the General Assembly.

[16] Resolution A/C.1/51/L.19/Rev. 1.

UNGA to urge nuclear states to stop immediately the qualitative improvement and stockpiling of nuclear warheads and delivery systems and to undertake a step by step reduction of the nuclear threat and phased reductions of nuclear weapons with a view to their total elimination[17]. Italy abstained on the resolution passed on the same day which called upon the UNGA to reaffirm the urgent need to reach an agreement on security arrangements for non-nuclear states[18], but cosponsored a draft resolution in favour of the prohibition of the development of new types of weapons of mass destruction[19].

3. Public Debate on Nuclear Issues

The continuing debate on the constitutional changes intended to reshape the country's governmental system and structures – after the fall of the so-called Prima Repubblica – is obviously at present the main focus of attention of political parties and public opinion. The discussion on the future of the European Union is also a very high priority. Italy's capacity to join the core group of the forthcoming monetary union (EMU) – a goal broadly shared by government and opposition – is placed in seriously question by the country's problems in meeting the economic standards laid down by the Maastricht treaty, while contradictory signals coming from the major European capitals help to confuse the scene. Last but not least comes the question of the reform of the welfare state, a need felt by all political forces and in a way related to the two previous issues.

In such a situation there is not much space left for what are generally felt to be less substantial issues. A public debate on foreign policy has not taken place. For example: the question of the reform of the UN Security Council has seen Italy actively at work trying to prevent any quick fix solution, but this activity was virtually unnoticed by public opinion.

The resumption of French nuclear testing between summer and fall 1995 did attract some interest on the part of the public, resulting in a

---

[17] Resolution A/C.1/51/L.39, then A./RES/51/450.

[18] Resolution A/C.1/51/L.30

[19] Resolution A/C.1/51/L.36

few street demonstrations organised by the Green Party together with Greenpeace and other ecological-pacifist movements. A number of motions were adopted in both chambers of parliament, asking the government to condemn nuclear testing in all international fora and to pursue the rapid conclusion of the CTBT. With this exception, the nuclear issue has not been a topic of discussion. What is more, the context in which the protest against nuclear testing found justification was ecological sensibility and a certain concern for the violation of the human rights of the native population of French Polynesia, rather than security concerns as such.

It should be noted, however, that the protests prompted by French nuclear testing had some effect and obliged the government to take action in accordance with parliamentary provisions. On November 12, 1995 Italy voted in favour of the UN General Assembly resolution condemning French nuclear testing and urging the immediate cessation of the tests.

4. The Attitudes of the Political Elite towards Nuclear Arms, Nuclear Arms Control and Disarmament

A range of concerns is expressed by experts and politicians on nuclear issues, but basically the degree of interest in these matters is very low. Only a few basic questions seem to be considered, and the only substantive issues ever dealt with are: 1) those on which there is a broad consensus at international level; 2) those that do not have direct implications for Italy.

There has been a consensus on the adoption of the Comprehensive Nuclear Test Ban Treaty, but ratification is still pending. A cut-off of the production of fissile material will be part of official policy.

The inclusion of minor nuclear powers arsenals in international negotiations is not considered to be urgent, and priority is given to the further reduction of the American and Russian arsenals. In this context, the beginning of negotiations on a START III treaty is viewed favourably by most Italian experts and also by most political forces. This solution could help Russia solve some of the huge problems concerning its nuclear arsenal, some of which derive from the expected entry into force of START II, while a reduction to a lower level of American and Russian nuclear forces would not diminish security levels.

A nuclear weapons register is not considered as an urgent issue because of its purely symbolic significance. A treaty banning the development and production of new nuclear warheads is not on the agenda. The idea of a convention banning nuclear weapons is strongly rejected by the majority in the government and also by the opposition; this attitude resulted, as mentioned above, in a series of votes against UNGA resolutions. The Green Party and the Partito della Rifondazione Comunista might be in favour, but their delicate positions as, respectively, a member of the government coalition and an outside supporter of the government – and their limited significance on the political scene – do not allow them to go farther.

Tighter controls on the nuclear fuel cycle are in general considered desirable, but costs and benefits have to be weighed up.

There might also be consensus on the establishment of "a kind of" nuclear weapon free zone in Eastern and Central Europe as intended by NATO, in the sense that no nuclear weapons will be deployed on the territories of the Alliance's new members. However, it is not yet clear how this objective will be pursued. Due to the importance of Russia in Italian economic relations, Italy would favour greater transparency and openness in the attitude of NATO towards Russia. A change in NATO strategy to No First Use, however, does not seem to be acceptable.

5. Conclusions

The long transformation process that Italy has undergone in the aftermath of the fall of the Berlin Wall, which is likely to lead to a profound reshaping of the state itself, has not yet come to a conclusion. It is hard in such a context to identify the main guiding principles of Italian foreign policy. Its different components – economic and commercial policy, security, cooperation, development, participation in international fora and activities – does not allow us to discern any particular trend. Only a few (and partial) interpretations have been suggested here of the various questions at stake, but in the end it might be true as already stated by many international analysts that foreign policy remains above all a domestic problem for Italy. As long as this is the case, the nuclear question will remain a non-issue. Italy wants to remain a "passive nuclear country".

AUSTRIA[1]

Stephan KLEMENT

1. Introduction: Austrian National Security after the Cold War

The end of the Cold War and the disappearance of the bipolar political realities in Central Europe have occasioned a complex debate about the future orientation of Austrian security policy. Austrian neutrality, as declared in 1955, was eminently suited to the period of intense political confrontation between the two opposing military and ideological blocs; but developments in Europe since 1989 have prompted a discussion about the purpose of, and continued need for, such neutrality.

Although this discussion is generally not conducted in public, because of the high symbolic value which public opinion attaches to neutral status, the possibility of Austrian accession to a collective defence system – be it NATO, the WEU, or some other common European security and defence organization – is at least being subjected to increasing scrutiny by political and military analysts[2].

As a result of its accession to the EU in 1995, and its participation in the European CFSP, Austria has already begun tentatively to relinquish

[1] The research presented here was supported by the *Fonds zur Förderung der Wissenschaftlichen Forschung in Österreich* (Project No.JO1258-SOZ).
[2] E. REITER, **NATO-Beitritt Österreichs?**, National Defence Academy Series, 6/1995.

both its neutral status and the policy of abstention it pursued during the Cold War. This new stance, which is supported by the majority of political leaders and ideologists, is also slowly being accepted by the general public. Initial steps in this direction had already been made in 1991, on the occasion of the Iraqi occupation of Kuwait, when the Austrian government gave permission for coalition aircraft acting in accordance with UN Security Council resolutions to overfly Austrian territory.

However, the next logical step – namely a frank and open discussion about the new objectives and needs of Austrian security policy and about the possible integration of Austria into a new security and defence network – is still avoided by most politicians. The reason for this appears to be a long-established attitude of celebration of Austrian neutrality that ignores the reasons for, and objectives of, that neutrality. These were originally linked to a situation of confrontation in Central Europe quite unlike the climate of co-operation that has now emerged. Austria declared itself neutral in 1955 in order to bring the Second World War occupation of the country to an end, and in order to avoid partition of the country between East and West.

It has been said that an expansion of NATO or the WEU, if carried out with sufficient restraint and the political skill needed to avoid creating new divisions between neighbouring states and areas of confrontation, could significantly enhance not only Austrian security, but European security as a whole[3]. Hence, a detailed discussion about Austrian accession to a European system of collective defence will probably have to take place over the next few years, and there will probably be a referendum to decide the issue before the end of the century[4].

If accession were to occur, any threats arising from possible political changes in Russia or other regions of the former Soviet Union, or from the possession by rogue states in the Middle East or Mediterranean of ballistic missiles and weapons of mass destruction, could

---

[3] J. GOLDBLAT, *"Controversies over the Planned Enlargement of NATO"*, in: **Security Dialogue**, Vol.27 No.3, 1996, pp.360-3.

[4] **National Security: Trends and Alternatives**, National Defence Academy Series, 2/1995 Vienna.

be met with greater confidence in the capacities of national and collective European defence. Austria would then feel more at ease with regard to its security interests, and the EU would be able to make further progress in implementing the CFSP.

2. Nuclear Weapons and Austrian Security Policy

As a signatory to the NPT, Austria pursues a long-term non-nuclear-weapons policy, with a strong emphasis on the need for meaningful steps towards nuclear disarmament. During the Cold War, the nuclear weapons of the two opposing military blocs were seen as presenting a grave threat to the survival of the Austrian state in case of nuclear conflict. This stance has to be viewed in terms not only of military strategy, but also of the environmental implications of an armed conflict, or of a nuclear-weapons-related accident, in the neighbourhood of the Austrian Republic. Because of these factors, the Austrian approach to nuclear weapons has always been a defensive one, as exemplified in particular by the attempt to ensure that the population is provided with sufficient nuclear shelters.

At least partly as result of this ever-present nuclear danger, a strong anti-nuclear movement, concerned mainly with the civilian use of nuclear power for electricity generation, has emerged in Austria over the last twenty to thirty years. Its activities have ultimately led to the adoption of an official anti-nuclear policy, which focuses more on the peaceful uses of nuclear energy than on its military aspects.

Although most Austrian observers would probably assert that Austria's stance is mainly a reaction to the inadequate safety-standards of Russian-type nuclear power plants in Eastern Europe, and to the undoubted risks that currently exist in the whole nuclear-power sector world-wide, it is probably the experience of endangerment during the Cold War that forms the true background to the current Austrian stance on the nuclear issue. For a long time, the country had to face the threat of nuclear annihilation – or at least serious damage – as a result of a nearby nuclear conflict, without being able to build up any significant defensive capabilities against such a scenario. This powerlessness may have led to attention being direct towards the civilian nuclear issue, where more meaningful action could be considered even within an ideologically split European environment. Austrian politicians have therefore found it easier to try to command public attention by focusing on civilian nuclear risks rather than to discuss the inherent dangers of nuclear armaments and nuclear deterrence.

Given these concerns, and the very emotional and irrational nature of the nuclear debate, the deployment of nuclear weapons on Austrian territory, under the authority of NATO, the WEU, or any other collective security system, seems only a very remote possibility. However, were Austria to accede to NATO, a provision such as that which applied to the former GDR might be considered in regard to the introduction of nuclear weapons onto Austrian territory.

The dilemma here lies in the fact that Austria, as a country likely to become a member of NATO in the near future, rejects the idea of having nuclear weapons deployed within its borders but at the same time would like to enjoy the advantages of being under a nuclear umbrella. It would also like to make use of the NATO nuclear deterrent to protect its borders and its territorial integrity – one particular concern being to deter attacks with weapons of mass destruction delivered by ballistic missile. It is not clear whether this stance will be accepted unconditionally by all NATO members when Austrian accession to NATO is negotiated. There are at least signs of a desire on the part of NATO that specific exceptions be envisaged in regard to the deployment of nuclear weapons in case of crisis or armed conflict.

It must be stressed that the Austrian stance on nuclear deterrence is an extremely complex one: Austria undoubtedly appreciates the value of a deterrent force, but at the same time it is highly critical of the measures needed to create and maintain such a force – measures such as the French nuclear weapon tests of 1995 and 1996. It is not yet clear what position Austria will take when substantive discussions begin on the possibility of a Eurodeterrent within the framework of the CFSP. Austria may have to temper its current overall anti-nuclear policy in order to make possible a compromise acceptable to all members of the EU, notably its two nuclear-weapon states – France and the United Kingdom.

3. Public Opinion and Nuclear Weapons

Austria's anti-nuclear policy also exerts a great influence on public attitudes to nuclear weapons and nuclear disarmament. There has been almost no reasoned public debate about the role which nuclear deterrence may have played in peaceful reconstruction and development in Europe after 1945. Of course, the public is generally very much in favour of further steps towards nuclear disarmament; but unfortunately it adopts this stance without taking into account the importance of maintaining a strategic balance or the need to preserve nuclear deterrence in order to protect Europe against possible attack with weapons of mass destruction.

The lack of public interest in the relationship between security policy and nuclear weapons is very regrettable, as is the fact that policy-makers avoid raising nuclear issues because the Austrian population has a skewed perception of these matters and fails to differentiate between the civilian and military aspects. It should be noted here that in the late 1970s, Austria completed construction of a nuclear power plant, but that this never went into operation because a referendum connected to a vote of confidence in Austria's long-standing chancellor, Bruno Kreisky, revealed that a substantial part of the Austrian population was strongly opposed to nuclear energy. This too clearly marked an important stage in the development of Austria's rather biased and not very objective nuclear policy. Since then, the anti-nuclear movement has continued to grow in size and influence.

Although Austria has long been host to the IAEA, and, from 1997, will accommodate the CTBTO and its provisional technical secretariat, the prevailing public attitude to the IAEA is one of scepticism and condemnation of the role it plays in promoting nuclear energy. In contrast, the activities in which the IAEA inspectorate engages all over the world to prevent the misuse of nuclear materials and technology for military purposes attracts little public interest.

In a general climate such as this, Austrian politicians have little scope for developing new and helpful approaches to nuclear weapons and nuclear disarmament. Authoritative official stances on these issues are therefore the exception rather than the rule.

4. The Official Stance on Nuclear Weapons

The three main official Austrian bodies charged with dealing with nuclear issues are: the Federal Ministry for Foreign Affairs *(Bundesministerium für auswärtige Angelegenheiten)*; the Federal Ministry of Defence *(Bundesministerium für Landesverteidigung)*; and the Federal Chancellery *(Bundeskanzleramt)*[5].

The Austrian Parliament can also help in the formulation of nuclear policy by passing resolutions directed at the government. This was done during the NPT Review and Extension Conference in April 1995[6]: a request was addressed to the government that it should work for an indefinite extension of the NPT, ensure the latter's implementation, press for the negotiation and early signature of a CTBT, and promote further nuclear disarmament by the nuclear-weapon states.

Since these guide-lines are of a very general nature, the responsible Austrian authorities have ample scope for interpretation when implementing them. Of course, there are also specific nuclear issues on which no national position has been adopted, or indeed elaborated. These mostly concern questions that are not judged to have any immediate bearing on Austrian security interests.

There is almost unanimous support for a CTBT, for a fissile material cut-off convention, for a START III initiative, and for the inclusion of the British, Chinese, and French nuclear arsenals in negotiations on arms control and reduction. However, the Ministry for Foreign Affairs has stressed that it would like to see all these results achieved within the multilateral framework of the CD, not in purely bilateral agreements between the nuclear-weapon states.

There is also broad support for the creation of a treaty regime that restricts the further development and production of genuinely new types of nuclear weapons – although in the view of the Ministry of Defence, this ought preferably to be done in a way that takes into

---

[5] The official positions as stated here are derived from interviews conducted with representatives of these bodies in Vienna in summer 1996.

[6] *"Entschließung des Nationalrates vom 27. April 1995 betreffend die 1995 stattfindende Überprüfungskonferenz betreffend den Vertrag über die Nichtverbreitung von Kernwaffen"*, E20-NR/XIX.GP.

account the strategic requirements of a future system of collective European security. One such requirement might be the possession of low-yield nuclear warheads, to counter threats posed by rogue states building production sites for weapons of mass destruction.

With regard to the creation of a nuclear-weapon-free zone in Central Europe, the Ministry of Defence is not convinced that this step would improve Austria's security: it sees the nuclear threat to Europe as stemming mainly from the nuclear weapon systems outside the Central European region, the main danger for this region being that of becoming the battlefield in a nuclear conflict.

According to the Ministry of Defence, the possibility of NATO's changing its current nuclear strategy to one of no first use could be given serious consideration as soon as the CFE treaty was fully implemented. This is a very important and sensitive issue: if Austria joins NATO, its eastern border could form part of NATO's boundary, at least until the latter's further enlargement, and would be very vulnerable to conventional attack. Reliance on the mechanism of nuclear deterrence could prove very useful in such circumstances. By contrast, the Ministry for Foreign Affairs inclines to the view that the NATO strategy of first use will automatically become obsolete in the short or medium term, once the CFE treaty has been implemented. In addition, following the ICJ's advisory opinion[7], it considers that the threat or use of nuclear weapons is permissible, if at all, only in very restricted conditions, where the survival of a state is seriously endangered.

Concerning the need for nuclear deterrence against the proliferation of biological and chemical weapons, the Austrian military is in favour of such a mechanism, whereas the Ministry for Foreign Affairs would prefer to rely solely on the successful implementation of the BWC and CWC. Opinions are similarly divided as regards Austrian participation in the development and deployment of a ballistic missile defence system.

---

[7] International Court of Justice, *"Legality of the Threat or Use of Nuclear Weapons"*, Advisory Opinion to the UN General Assembly, 8 July 1996.

Although the Austrian authorities generally support further reductions in the number of nuclear warheads, there is a serious lack of thought as to how weapons-grade fissile material resulting from the dismantling of nuclear weapons is to be disposed of. Since one of Austria's stated political goals is a nuclear-free Central Europe (free, that is, not only of nuclear weapons, but also of nuclear power plants, reprocessing facilities, and waste-storage sites), initiating a discussion about the disposal of fissile material from nuclear weapons in nuclear reactors is problematic. A common Austrian way of dealing with this problem is to refer to a declaration on the autonomy of Austrian energy policy that was made on the occasion of Austria's accession to the EU – which also entailed its accession to EURATOM. Hence, Austria will accept the transfer of fissile material from nuclear weapons to civilian purposes without giving up its long-term objective of a nuclear-free Central Europe. However, it would prefer that no new nuclear reactors or nuclear industrial complexes were developed or built for the above-mentioned purposes. This is a rather dubious position, since new types of reactors – fast-breeders, for example – will probably be needed if the plutonium from former nuclear warheads is to be used to generate electricity in an economic and reasonable way[8]. Furthermore, new fuel fabrication plants will be required for the production of mixed-oxide (MOX) fuel of the kind that can be burnt in existing reactors.

As regards extension of IAEA safeguards to the whole civilian fuel cycle in nuclear-weapon states, there is no known Austrian objection to this, although the costs of such a measure will undoubtedly prompt a major debate about the fair distribution of the resultant financial burden. The Federal Chancellery believes that strengthening the role of the IAEA in the safeguarding of nuclear material could contribute to the development of a sophisticated verification system of a kind that would certainly be needed in any future convention banning the production of fissile material or nuclear weapons.

There is no precise official Austrian position on the question of a nuclear weapons convention, since, in the current Austrian situation, this possibility still seems too remote for major political consideration.

---

[8] "Opinion: Dismantled N-Weapons will Best be used in Reactors", in: **Plutonium** n° 14, 1996, 1.

However, it can confidently be assumed that a treaty imposing a world-wide ban on the production and possession of nuclear weapons and other nuclear explosive devices would be consonant with Austrian objectives, provided the strategic balance within Europe, and more especially in relation to the rest of the world, could be secured by conventional means. This would most probably entail the provision of robust and reliable verification systems for the CWC and BWC, in order to diminish the need for a nuclear deterrent against any threats posed by weapons of mass destruction.

With regard to potential nuclear threats, Austrian concern here mainly relates to the situation in the former Soviet Union, where the safety of nuclear weapons appears not to be assured. The use of nuclear weapons or fissile material by subnational or terrorist groups is therefore considered a significant security risk, to be met not only by instituting additional safety measures, but also by promoting and encouraging timely and effective steps towards further nuclear disarmament.

Naturally, the threat posed by rogue states with nuclear aspirations is another area that most Austrian military planners believe must be carefully monitored until such time as the NPT verification system is upgraded – e.g. through the implementation of the IAEA '93 + 2' safeguards – to meet the new challenges identified after the revelation of the clandestine Iraqi nuclear programme.

5. Conclusions

Our investigations reveal that Austria's current perception of its security interests is leading it in the direction of an abandonment of neutrality. This process has clearly been fostered by Austria's recent accession to the EU, and by the increased pace of European integration – particularly as regards implementation of the CFSP. In addition, the end of the Cold War has created a new political situation in Europe and throughout the world, allowing for co-operation rather than confrontation in the field of national security. Given these circumstances, discussions about Austrian participation in a system of collective regional security will increase significantly during the next few years; and one can confidently predict that a definitive decision on Austrian accession to NATO, the WEU, or some other European security system will be taken by the end of this century or early in the next.

In the run-up to this accession, a number of important issues will have to be subjected to serious scrutiny and discussion by political leaders and the public. These include all the problems associated with nuclear weapons, nuclear disarmament, and the civilian use of nuclear energy, as well as the complex links between these areas.

In this context, a more realistic view will have to be developed about the use of nuclear energy for peaceful purposes: the Austrian belief in an ever-speedier decline in the use of nuclear power in Europe, and indeed throughout the world, is somewhat speculative, and seems more like wishful thinking than a concrete appraisal of the facts. It is crucial to recognize that the military and civilian aspects of nuclear energy cannot be treated completely separately, because implementing certain measures of nuclear disarmament will, in all likelihood, entail interaction with the civilian nuclear sector. As long as this interaction is not taken into account, there will be no chance of any meaningful policy on nuclear issues.

A new approach in this regard would allow Austria to improve the climate of its relations with the international organizations in Vienna, especially the IAEA. Because of the problematic and extreme nature of Austrian attitudes in the areas concerned, these relations have never been free of tension. Were things to change, Austria could support the IAEA as the future verification organization for a cut-off convention or for ensuring the use of fissile material from dismantled nuclear weapons in nuclear reactors was properly managed according to IAEA safeguards.

With regard to the strategic implications of Austrian accession to a collective defence system, it should be remembered that the principle of nuclear deterrence is still considered an important pillar in NATO planning. Although further steps towards nuclear disarmament are highly desirable, the approach to the elimination of nuclear weapons that is currently being pursued is a step-by-step one that will quite probably not lead to the complete elimination of nuclear weapons within the next few years. A certain reliance on the deterrent effect of nuclear weapons, in whatever form, is therefore likely to be part of a future European security system. Such an effect would be necessary to cope with threats posed by rogue states armed with ballistic missiles and weapons of mass destruction.

Austria would be well-advised to acknowledge this situation and the necessities that flow from it, irrespective of whether it accedes to a system of collective European security or not. It would then have the opportunity to develop robust stances on specific issues relating to nuclear energy and nuclear disarmament, and could participate more actively in the ongoing process of nuclear disarmament itself, thus helping the advance towards the ultimate objective of a complete elimination of nuclear weapons.

HUNGARY

Erzsébet N. Rózsa

1. Hungarian Security during the Cold War

Hungary, has been a non-nuclear weapon state since the beginning of the nuclear era, committed to this status – as a country on the losing side in the Second World War – by the peace treaties[1] that followed. The war ended with Soviet troops "liberating[2]" the country, and as a result of Yalta and the policies of the great powers, Hungary came under the influence of the Soviet Union and became a member of the Warsaw Treaty Organization in 1955. These two facts, namely non-nuclear weapon state status and Soviet domination, determined both the Hungarian security situation and the country's foreign and security policy for approximately 40 years.

On the one hand, this meant full obedience to the Moscow centre, ensured by a Soviet-appointed puppet government and Soviet troops stationed in Hungary. In this structure the foreign policy of a vassal state should rather be interpreted as part of Soviet domestic policy, and for the member states of the alliance practically no room was left for an independent foreign and security policy. Soviet control was so strict that at one stage Soviet nuclear weapons were deployed on

---

[1] "Hungary may not own nor construct any kind of nuclear weapons...", para. 15 of the Hungarian Peace Treaty, signed in Paris on 10th February, 1947, entered into force on 15th September, 1947.

[2] "Liberation" has for more than forty years had very negative associations for Hungarian public opinion.

Hungarian territory with only a very few – if any – Hungarian leaders having knowledge of the fact (figures mentioned in this regard are usually not higher than 3)[3]. The Hungarian Army itself has never had any nuclear or nuclear capable weapons in its possession, except for nine nuclear capable missiles which, however, were never meant to be used or equipped for anything other than conventional purposes. (Even these missiles were later dismantled in accordance with Hungary's commitments to the MTCR.)

On the other hand, in an era when the possibility of a nuclear war could not be ruled out entirely, the Warsaw Treaty provided a security framework within which the Soviet nuclear deterrent force protected all the member states by virtue of the positive guarantees laid down in the treaty[4]. It should also be mentioned here that by signing the Treaty, the countries of the Eastern bloc also undertook to "put effective measures into effect to achieve the general reduction of arms and a ban on atomic and hydrogen weapons, as well as other kinds of weapons of mass destruction.[5]" – an undertaking that was later included in the text of the NPT as well. Soviet domination and bloc policy was evident in all fields of international and nuclear politics (among other arms control agreements, Hungary signed the PTBT in 1963 and the NPT in 1969), and was felt in the sphere of the peaceful

---

[3] Although no official statement was issued on the subject in Hungary at the time, General Chervov, Chief of Staff of the Soviet Army, gave an answer in Bonn, Germany, on October 17th, 1983 to the question of whether the Soviet Union had deployed nuclear weapons outside its own territory: "I will give you a clear answer. Everywhere where Soviet troops are stationed outside the territory of the Soviet Union, their missiles are equipped with tactical nuclear weapons of a 100 km range." Chervov added: "However, I must also state clearly that we have no intermediate range or strategic nuclear weapons outside the territory of our country." (quoted by AFP on October 18th, 1983). This was confirmed and made public only much later, in 1991, when it was fairly extensively covered in the media. Among others, Károly Grósz, an ex-prime minister also acknowledged that there had been nuclear weapons on Hungarian territory, of which he had been informed a couple of days after coming into office. These weapons, however, were later withdrawn – again without any publicity. Mr. Grósz was informed of the withdrawal only later. (Interview with K.GRÓSZ, in: **Népszabadság**, 22nd April, 1991.)

[4] "If any state or group of states in Europe attacks with armed forces one or more states party to the Treaty, all states parties to the Treaty, in accordance with para. 51 of the Statute of the UNO, as a realization of its right of... or collective self-defence, ... with all means that seem necessary, including the use of armed forces, provide direct help to the state or states attacked."

[5] Para. 2, Warsaw Treaty.

uses of nuclear energy as well: the four units of the only Hungarian nuclear power station, Paks was supplied by the Soviet Union (1983-1987) and its nuclear fuel was also supplied from the Soviet Union. This power station's spent fuel, in the spirit of co-operation among the socialist countries, was also sent back to the USSR, in spite of the fact that the Hungarian-Soviet agreement did not include such a clause[6].

2. The Present Security Situation

The end of the Cold War, beside providing space for new democratic movements in Central Europe, brought several fundamental changes for the states of the region in general and for Hungary in particular. Some of these had a direct influence on the security situation of these states.

- All Soviet troops left Hungary by the end of June 1991, which meant that full sovereignty was attained.
- The international structures to which Hungary had belonged in the previous decades – the Warsaw Treaty Organization and the Council for Mutual Economic Assistance – collapsed. This also meant that Hungary found itself in a security vacuum which had to be filled somehow, even though no threat from any other state could be perceived. A new, individual foreign and security policy had to be devised.
- The break-up of these structures and the removal of Soviet control were followed by the resurgence of problems long suppressed in the region, the most acute of which were nationalism (after decades of forced "internationalism") and the minority issue, in which Hungary has been directly involved.
- The great structural changes brought about significant changes in Hungary's geopolitical situation. Three of its five neighbours disintegrated:
  - the Soviet Union, which meant there was an unresolved nuclear weapon problem in the immediate neighbourhood until Ukraine joined the NPT in 1994;

---

[6] Erzsébet N. RÓzsA, *"Hungary"*, in: Harald MÜLLER (ed.), **Nuclear Export Controls in Europe**, European Interuniversity Press (EIP), Brussels, 1995, pp.241-242.

- Czechoslovakia, the break-up of which went smoothly, though an independent Slovakia had a different minority policy towards its Hungarian citizens; and,
- Yugoslavia, where a long civil war broke out directly on Hungary's southern border. This not only posed a threat to Hungarian security, but also set off huge waves of refugees, many of whom belonged to the Hungarian community.

The combined effects of these factors gave an added urgency to the search for a solution to Hungary's security problems. In the political elite, two possibilities were considered. The first was neutrality, which was an attractive alternative as it had some legitimacy in Hungarian history. In 1956, at the beginning of the Revolution, the Imre Nagy led government withdrew from the Warsaw Treaty Organization and declared Hungary's neutrality. It should also be mentioned that this option had well-functioning analogies among "capitalist" countries with which Hungary had maintained a traditionally good relationship: neighbouring Austria and distantly related Finland. In spite of these emotionally relevant facts, by late 1990 the neutrality concept had lost support, partly due to the view that a state can only be neutral between two opposing sides (blocs or powers), and partly due to the realisation that joining the main Western institutions was the only really viable option.

3. Hungarian Security Policy and Nuclear Weapons

The first democratically elected government's programme in 1990 stated clearly that joining Western institutions was a priority. Both that government and the present Hungarian government have made every effort to achieve this goal. Hungary became a member of the Council of Europe in November 1990, concluded a Treaty of Association with the European Community in December 1992 (this entered into force on February 1st, 1994) joined NATO's Partnership for Peace programme in February 1994, and applied for full membership of the European Union on April 1st, 1994. In 1995 Hungary agreed to NATO using one of its military bases in the south of the country, at a village called Taszár, in order to be able to bring to an end the civil war in the former Yugoslavia. Within the framework of IFOR Hungary also sent some technical personnel to ex-Yugoslavia whose main task is to build bridges for the NATO forces.

In the spring of 1993 the Hungarian Parliament approved the National Security Policy and National Defence Principles, which set out the country's national security objectives: full integration into Western institutions and improved relations with neighbouring countries, which implies that in Hungary's unique situation of being surrounded by countries with Hungarian minorities, good-neighbourly relations and respect for minority rights are two interrelated subjects, neither of which can be satisfactorily dealt with without the other. At the same time these documents declared that Hungary does not consider any state to be an enemy, and the role of its armed forces is to defend (only) the territory of the country.

As regards Hungarian behaviour in the field of nuclear disarmament, Hungary has continued the former policy determined by its status as a non-nuclear weapon state in the spirit of the disarmament aspirations expressed in the Warsaw Treaty and Article 6 of the NPT. On the other hand, having realised that the nuclear issue takes a quite different form in the new circumstances and that it has become one of the top concerns of the organisations Hungary intends to join, the country started a relatively active policy in various international fora. Hungary participated in the preparations for the 1995 NPT Review and Extension Conference, provided the chairman of the Second PrepCom Meeting, participated in the Joint Action on Non-Proliferation within the European Union, held consultations in an attempt to convince states not in favour of indefinite extension[7], supported the Canadian Initiative and voted for the indefinite extension of the Treaty. Being a member of the Conference on Disarmament in Geneva, Hungary participated in the discussions on the Comprehensive Test Ban Treaty and acted as co-sponsor of the Australian initiative, which resulted in the CTBT resolution in 1996. Hungary was among the first to sign the treaty.

This policy in the diplomatic field was supplemented by very conscientious activity in the field of the peaceful use of nuclear energy. Hungary has traditionally had good relations with the IAEA, but having been a target country of COCOM, after the end of the Cold War it became imperative to have Hungary removed from the list, an aim which could only be achieved by observing strict conditions. Hungary,

---

[7] The authorities especially mentioned India in this regard, a country with which Hungary has traditionally had good relations.

however, fulfilled these and was taken off the COCOM list of pro-scribed destinations in February 1992.

Given these circumstances, it is clear that Hungarian security policy has not foreseen any role for nuclear weapons. This was stated clearly in the Law on Atomic Energy of 1980, which said that "in our country nuclear energy may be used exclusively for peaceful pur-poses.[8]" However, there has been a slight change in this situation. The new Law on Atomic Energy, which has already passed through the Environmental Protection Committee of the Parliament (this means that it is ready to be placed before Parliament), says that: "The Republic of Hungary, in accordance with its commitments undertaken in international agreements, does not use weapons based on the use of nuclear energy.[9]" Although the difference between the two phrases "in our country" and "Hungary does not use" is only slight, it may be considered a reflection of a debate that has developed, even if only on a limited scale, among the public and the authorities. It must also be noted, that only the Hungarian Socialist Workers' Party (a party not represented in Parliament) protested against this modification of the law, claiming that "it makes it possible for foreign states to use nuclear weapons on Hungarian territory.[10]"

Despite this, it should be emphasised that very little attention is paid to nuclear arms control and disarmament issues in Hungary; neither among the public nor in the political elite are these issues considered particularly important.

4. The Attitude of the Public towards Nuclear Weapons

First of all, it must be stated that there has been a change in public opinion's attitude to nuclear weapons. After the end of the Cold War, if nuclear weapons were mentioned at all in public debates, they were referred to "as one of the general problems facing all of humanity,

---

[8] Preamble of the Law on Atomic Energy.

[9] Para. 3, point (1) of the new Law on Atomic Energy (draft).

[10] *"Veszélyt látnak Paks eladásában"* (They see a danger in selling Paks), in: **Népszava** (Hungarian daily), September 17th, 1996.

not as a regional issue"[11] and the comment was usually added that any actual use of nuclear weapons was unthinkable. Now the public has definite views on one aspect of nuclear weapons, which is the possible deployment of NATO weapons in Central Europe and Hungary. In this regard, the public differentiates clearly between accession to the EU and to NATO. While the necessity of joining the EU has now been accepted by the great majority of Hungarians, a poll conducted in April 1996 by one of the leading public opinion companies, MEDIÁN, showed that 20% of the adult population **fully** supported, and 35% would **rather support** Hungary's joining NATO. 49% said they would certainly participate in a referendum on this issue, and 66% of these people would vote in favour of joining NATO[12]. Regarding the possible concrete consequences of NATO membership, however, reactions were much more negative: 74% would totally oppose the deployment of nuclear weapons in Hungary[13]. As these figures indicate, the Hungarian public is not very keen on accession to NATO, and many people ask why such a step is necessary – even though the government has already launched a communication strategy programme. Moreover, public sentiment is strongly against the deployment of nuclear weapons, so much so that for many people this question may decide their vote for or against accession. Otherwise, the Hungarian public is not really interested in any kind of nuclear weapon issues[14], and the above topic is only discussed in very limited circles, and even then only in connection with NATO.

---

[11] An international project was undertaken by Brown University between 1992-1994 entitled *"Security for Europe"*, in the framework of which the security concepts of the public and specialists in 7 Central European states were studied: Germany, Poland, the Czech Republic and Slovakia, Hungary, Ukraine and Russia. *Final Report of the Security for Europe Project*, p.21.

[12] A poll in November 1995 produced slightly different figures: 49% for, 16% against, 35% did not know. **Magyar Hírlap** (Hungarian daily), November 22nd, 1995.

[13] The research was done on a 1200 person representative sample of the adult population.

[14] This is not only a Hungarian phenomenon. The "Security for Europe" project found that with the exception of Russia and Ukraine, in Central Europe "the public is not much concerned or interested in nuclear weapon issues. There is a public consensus that any actual use of nuclear weapons would be either the result of some kind of accident, or, if deliberate, would be the act of madmen." *Final Report of the Security for Europe Project*, p.20. Some people, when asked about possible NATO deployment of nuclear weapons in Hungary even answered that "we were not asked when the Soviets deployed nukes here, and we will not be asked in this case either, so why bother?"

The question of NATO accession, on the other hand, gave rise to a public debate, especially when in 1995 the Hungarian Socialist Workers' Party started a campaign demanding that a referendum be held on this issue. Even though the necessary number of signatures was collected, the Constitutional Court ruled that due to certain legal problems and interpretations the referendum could not be held. This was a huge relief for the parliamentary parties, who argued that one cannot have a referendum on a question one has not been asked. To pacify emotions, Prime Minister Gyula Horn reaffirmed an earlier promise that "when we come to the point, the public will be asked in a referendum on the subject".

In addition to the Workers' Party, a small group of NGOs has also tried to formulate a position. On May 26th, 1995, when the North Atlantic General Assembly convened in Budapest, the Alba Kör[15] issued a 24-point statement regarding NATO. As a non-violent peace movement, Alba Kör rejected Hungary's accession to NATO and argued that: "If nuclear weapons are deployed in our region, it ceases to be a nuclear weapon free zone, which raises environmental protection problems and also means that Hungary and its population become targets of (other) nuclear weapons.[16]"

On August 5th, 46 NGOs and 11 international organisations[17] came together in front of Parliament to demonstrate for a nuclear weapon-free

---

[15] Alba Kör (Alba Circle) is a fairly visible non-violent peace movement founded in 1990. It has two aims: to establish an independent peace movement above political and religious factions and to provide representation and information for those who refuse military service in the armed forces (still obligatory in Hungary) and therefore perform civil service in the army. To this end Alba Kör operates an information and legal advice office in Budapest. The movement has 600 members and local groups in 4 cities: Budapest, Györ, Szeged and Zalaegerszeg.

[16] The position and Appeal of the Alba Kör regarding the Hungarian NATO accession on the occasion of the Budapest meeting of the North Atlantic Assembly (26-29th May, 1995).

[17] 4-6-0 Peace Group, Foundation for Hungarian Homeopathy, Alba Kör, Alternatives Foundation, Alternative Network, American Friends Service Committee (Quakers), Leftist Alternative Union, Technical University Green Circle, Bush Basic Community, Budapest Autonomous Cooperation, BOCS Foundation, Church and Peace Network, Danube Circle, Elpidia Round Table, Eötvös University Environment Protection Club, Energy Club, Anti-Force Forum, "Consciousness" Circle of Friends, Representative Forum of those persecuted by Fascism, Feminist Network, Ferencváros Workers' Free Time Club, Fix Union, Independent People's Representation Union, Gandhi Union,

Hungary and commemorate the victims of Hiroshima. (This Hiroshima Day demonstration has been organised since 1990 and Alba Kör has always participated in it.)

A representative of Alba Kör[18] has said that the aim of this protest movement is to ensure that there will never be nuclear weapons in Hungary. He added that nuclear questions are supervised and controlled in Hungary by a committee which has no authority in military affairs, and said that civilian control should be established over the military even in nuclear-related questions.

5. *The Attitude of the Political and Security Elites*[19]: *Nuclear Consequences of NATO Enlargement*

As already mentioned, ever since 1990 integration into Western institutions, principally the European Union and NATO, has been a practically unquestioned priority in Hungarian political circles, so much so that it has remained a matter of consensus among the parliamentary parties despite the change of government. (It should be noted that in the first parliamentary period the same parties were present in Parliament as today.[20])

This determines the Hungarian elite's opinion regarding nuclear weapons, which are only relevant as far as they are connected with Hungary's possible accession to NATO. Otherwise neither nuclear weapons nor nuclear deterrence are considered part of Hungarian security.

Göucöl Union, World without War Foundation, Humanist Movement, Air Work Group, Martin Luther King Union, Renewable Energy Club, Nagy Lajos Literature and Art Company, Women for Women Together against Force, PECS Green Circle, REFLEX Environment Protection Union, Gypsy Civil Rights Foundation, Svedlid Energy Union, Awakening of Nature Company, "Act against Hate" initiative, Support Tibet Company, Tisza Club, Green Alternative Foundation, Greenpeace, Green Women.

[18] Tamás Csapody in a telephone interview, September 19th, 1996.

[19] The parliamentary parties, Ministry of Foreign Affairs, Ministry of Defense; the full list of persons interviewed can be found at the end of the chapter.

[20] The only difference is that one of the parties, the Hungarian Democratic Forum (MDF) split into two: one party kept the old name, the other is called Hungarian Democratic People's Party.

At the moment and in the foreseeable future, only two such questions arise: the possible deployment of nuclear weapons on Hungarian territory, and the Central European nuclear weapon free zone.

As regards nuclear weapon deployment, the NATO Study on Enlargement of September 1995 is often quoted. Although the NATO Study states that "there is no *a priori* requirement for the stationing of nuclear weapons on the territory of new members[21]", it also says that "new members will... contribute to the development and implementation of NATO's strategy, including its nuclear components". This latter sentence basically determines Hungarian behaviour, which is not to do anything that might prevent the country from joining NATO. Or, as this is usually expressed: we want to be full members, with all the commitments and all the rights, because "Hungary is not in a position to demand a special status for itself.[22]" (It should be mentioned here that the present Minister of Defence, György Keleti, suggested in the previous parliamentary period and while in opposition that the Hungarian constitution be modified in order to ban the deployment of weapons of mass destruction on Hungarian territory. Now, as a member of the government, he agrees with the government's position.[23]) This position is coupled with a policy of keeping a low profile: as long as we are not asked such a question, we do not have to answer it. We have not yet been asked, therefore we only say that we want to be a member of NATO.

On the other hand, one expert warned that the deployment of nuclear weapons by NATO in Central Europe is always discussed in terms of the relations between NATO, Russia and Central Europe. The rest of the world is never considered, in spite of the fact that once the Central European states join NATO, they become NATO states just like the others in the eyes of the rest of the world: i.e. if a state becomes the target of violent attack, restrictions or even just propaganda or emotions because of its NATO membership, this will be valid for the new Central European members as well after their

---

[21] Section (iv) para. 58.

[22] Zoltán Gál, Speaker of the Parliament at a conference organized by the Hungarian Institute of International Affairs on 6-7th September, 1996.

[23] *"Atomvillanást idéztek a fények"* (The lights reminded one of a nuclear flash), in: **Népszabadság**, August 7th, 1996.

accession, although they might earlier have been unaffected. The implications of this have not yet been studied. And while the nuclear issue is kept in the forefront, no mention is made of other weapons of mass destruction. However, elaborating on these and similar ideas, and thinking of a future which does not end with NATO accession, is rare among the political elite and cannot be detected at all among the public.

Some of those interviewed added that in technical terms, it is irrelevant whether or not nuclear weapons are deployed, and that this is rather an emotional question. They argue that instead of ground-launched weapons, sea-launched or air-launched weapons are being or will be increasingly used, which in turn raises another question: if NATO decides and states that it will not deploy nuclear weapons in Central Europe, does that mean that the infrastructure to service such weapons or platforms for such weapons, e.g. storage sites and the necessary physical protection network, etc., will not be built either?

Attitudes to the question of a nuclear weapon free zone in Central Europe are mostly determined by the position taken on nuclear deployment, and are only of secondary interest. Though a greater part of the political elite would not be happy with the deployment of nuclear weapons on Hungarian territory, they would not advocate a nuclear weapon free zone at this stage. It is also mentioned that Hungary and Central Europe is a *de facto* nuclear weapon free zone at the moment in any case. But there is a widespread belief that the issue has been raised as a "trick" by Russia to prevent Central European integration, and the fact is mentioned that the initiative was raised by Belarus and supported by Ukraine at the 1995 NPT Conference after and parallel to lively discussions with the Russian delegation. The same principle holds true for the nuclear weapon free zone issue as for deployment: nothing should be done to hinder NATO accession. (This, one may assume, is the position of the other Central European states as well, in view of the strong opposition at the 1995 NPT conference to the Belarussian-Ukrainian initiative.)

One expert mentioned the possibility of NATO itself initiating a Central European nuclear weapon free zone, in which case all Hungarian parties would probably gladly consent to the idea[24]. Not offering

---

[24] "No one in his right mind could say no to such a proposition." André Erdõs, Head of the Hungarian delegation to the 1995 NPT Conference, Assistant State Secretary in the Ministry of Foreign Affairs.

an open opinion at the moment, however, might be a good choice in the long run. (This was also the Hungarian policy in 1995, when the Belarussian-Ukrainian initiative was put forward.) As the NATO-Russia dialogue develops, it has already been mentioned that one of the conditions set by Russia would be a statement from NATO on non-deployment.

6. Attitudes towards further Nuclear Disarmament Measures

In spite of the fact that Hungary has participated all along in the CTBT negotiations at the Conference on Disarmament in Geneva and the media have covered the issue fairly well, the CTBT is not a topic that is discussed either among the political elite, which thinks that the issue should be handled in the framework of Hungary's international commitments, or among the public.

All those interviewed agreed that apart from other nuclear weapon-related issues or nuclear arms control and disarmament in general are not considered at all. Hungary is a non-nuclear weapon state, behaves accordingly and fulfills its international commitments. Only a few went further and said that Hungary agrees with the goal of non-proliferation and does its best to support it, but they thought that at the moment nuclear disarmament is unrealistic.

The lack of interest is even more surprising as there were and are some specific issues on which one could expect Hungary to have an opinion. Illegal nuclear trade in materials from the former Soviet Union, although well publicised in the media, has not been discussed in connection with nuclear disarmament at all. It has rather been thought of – if at all – in the framework of physical protection loopholes and the danger such materials pose for mankind and the environment. During the Russian-Ukrainian debate on the withdrawal and/or dismantling of nuclear weapons, Hungary kept a low profile in spite of the fact that Ukraine is a neighbouring country. After the collapse of the Soviet Union and the dissolution of the Warsaw Treaty Organization, Hungary could have participated more in the debate on security guarantees. When asked about this issue, those interviewed usually said that sooner or later Hungary will become a member of NATO, and the country will then be protected by the nuclear umbrella. Until then, it's no point annoying those countries upon which Hungary's chances of integration depend. (Some, however, added that it is also very much in Hungary's interests to see the whole region integrated.) In the same spirit and in spite of the fact that Hungary is one of the main promoters of the 93+2 programme, no view at all was expressed about the desirability of extended safeguards in nuclear states, beyond a vague "it would be nice".

On the whole, Hungarian nuclear behaviour will not change in the near future, even if a new government enters office in 1998. A Hungarian delegation will be present in all international fora, and commitments will be fulfilled to the letter, but nothing will be said or initiated that might hinder Hungary's integration into any Western institutions. Since interest in nuclear arms control and disarmament is very low even among the political elite, Hungarian non-proliferation activities will in practice be determined by the desire for integration. Formulating an official position will to a great extent be the job of a handful of people working in the administration and at the relevant embassies in Vienna, Geneva and New York.

List of persons interviewed:

István SZENT-IVÁNYI, Political Secretary of State, Ministry of Foreign Affairs and member of the Free Democrats' Alliance

André ERDŐS, Assistant Secretary of State, Ministry of Foreign Affairs

Tibor TÓTH, former Ambassador of Hungary to the CD in Geneva, Ministry of Foreign Affairs (formerly in the Ministry of Defence)

Colonel László NAGY, Institute for Strategic and Defence Studies

Tamás CSAPODY, Alba Kör

Imre KÓNYA, Hungarian Democratic People's Party

Vilmos SZABÓ, Hungarian Socialist Party, Foreign Affairs Secretariat

Péter ZWACK, independent MP

Jenő PÓDA, Hungarian Democratic Forum

Béla GYURICZA, Young Democrats' Alliance

Zoltán GÁL, Speaker of the Parliament (answering a question at a conference)

POLAND

Genowefa SMAGALA

1. The Security Situation after the End of the Cold War

After the end of the Cold War, Poland found itself in a completely new strategic environment and was confronted with an urgent need to define a national security policy of its own. September 1989 (when the first non-communist government assumed power) is regarded as marking the start of independent domestic and foreign policy in Poland.

For almost half a century, the Soviet Union exercised technical and political control over the decisions of its satellite states. A system of strict dependence in the defence and security fields was operated through the Warsaw Treaty Organization (WTO). Those sectors that were of relevance to military and defence matters (e.g. transport and particular branches of industry) were controlled by Soviet staff acting as advisers or representatives of the WTO's unified command[1]. The subordinate countries had to carry out predetermined parts of overall strategic tasks. Membership of the Warsaw Pact was supposed to provide security guarantees, but that security was limited to military aspects. Though communist propaganda presented the West as posing the main threat to the Pact, history shows that the latter served the imperial interests of its dominant power[2].

---

[1] For further details, see Janusz PRYSTROM, **The Military-Strategic Emancipation of Poland,** PRIF Report No.25, Frankfurt/M., 1992.

[2] *Ibid.*, p.7.

Since the end of the Cold War, the perception of being subject to a military threat has diminished in Poland, but risks of a non-military kind have begun to loom. The country has quite a homogeneous population; the rights of minorities are respected (the German minority, being the largest, is represented in parliament); and Poland's borders are not in dispute (the western border was recognized in a bilateral agreement with Germany in 1990, and the eastern one, as is often affirmed by the Polish government, is not in contention). The situation at present thus seems stable. However, certain internal events that might jeopardize that stability could still occur in the course of democratization and the transition from a planned to a market economy:

- The failure of reforms may create social tensions which could then be exploited by third parties.
- Social unrest may lead to discrimination against minorities (there are about 800,000 Germans, Silesians, Ukrainians, Belorussians, and Lithuanians in Poland), eliciting a negative response from the countries of origin concerned.

There are also a number of external factors that could present a threat to Polish security:

- An influx of refugees from the Former Soviet Union (FSU) following civil war or some other conflict may threaten Polish stability.
- Because of the continuing ease of access to nuclear materials and nuclear weapons in the FSU, there continues to be the opportunity for nuclear blackmail.
- Ignorance, lack of information, and other factors may give rise to threats to the environment from nuclear and chemical plants.
- The military threat may increase once again, if and when Russian regional dominance is restored.
- The sizeable military presence in the Kaliningrad enclave enhances the dangers.

Perceptions of the threats to Polish security have changed in tandem with the political-cum-military situation in Europe. At present, Poland has no officially identified enemy and faces no officially identified threat to its security.

When Poland first regained its sovereignty, its foreign and security policies were determined by specific factors such as:

- The provisions of the WTO, which was eventually disbanded
  on 1st July 1991.
- The considerable number of Soviet/Russian troops deployed in
  Poland. The withdrawal of Soviet armed forces from Poland was
  completed on 17 September 1993. (In fact, the last Russian
  combat troops left Poland in November 1992, but a contingent
  of 5,000 Russian soldiers provided logistical assistance to troops
  returning from East Germany via Poland.)
- The presence of a neighbouring country which continued, up to
  the end of its existence (December 1991), to assert its "readiness
  for help in the name of the communist ideas[3]".

Krzysztof Skubiszewski, Poland's first non-communist foreign
minister (1989-93), laid the foundations of the country's independent
foreign policy. He involved Poland in regional initiatives such as the
Visegrad Group (a system of co-operation between Poland, Czechoslovakia, and Hungary that began in February 1991) and concluded
important bilateral co-operation-agreements with Poland's two powerful neighbours, Germany and the Soviet Union, with which the
Polish government had decided to pursue a policy of close relations.
Poland subsequently adopted a Westward orientation but sought, in
parallel, to establish and develop partnerships with its Eastern neighbours (friendship treaties were concluded with the Ukraine in May
1992 and with Belarus in July 1992). Generally speaking, this multi-
track foreign policy has the support of the ruling parties, the government, and the president. In contrast, not all political elites favour an
active Eastern policy, but those groups that are against it have little
influence – or indeed have lost it completely – and in 1992 the defence minister, Jan Parys, was dismissed for favouring a one-track
Westward orientation.

On no account does Poland want to be part of a buffer zone or adopt
a policy of neutrality, and this has been affirmed in many official and

---

[3] Jerzy J. MILEWSKI (Head of the National Security Bureau and Secretary of State
of the President's Chancellery), *"And yet reform..."*, in: **Rzeczpospolita**,
27 Aug. 1996.

unofficial statements. In a lecture delivered on 9 January 1991 at the Royal Institute of International Affairs in London, Minister Skubiszewski stressed that: "No one ought to think of Central Europe in terms of 'grey' or 'buffer' zones or a neutral zone... open to rivalry or influence [from] stronger states or powers, [a circumstance that] would apply in particular to Poland, situated as it is between Germany and the Soviet Union.[4]"

The dissolution of the Soviet Union made it possible for its former satellites openly to seek admission to NATO, and in October 1991, following the Moscow coup in August of that year, the Visegrad Group, meeting in Krakow, decided to seek NATO's protection. In the view of the government and the political and security elites of Poland, NATO membership is the only way out of the security vacuum. This stance is based on Poland's historical experience and enjoys broad support within the government and all the political and security elites.

Poland's foreign policy has remained unchanged since 1989, despite changes of government. Moreover, each new government has committed itself to continuity in this area. In a speech to the Royal Institute of International Affairs in London in October 1996, the Polish president, Aleksander Kwasniewski, said that to Poles, security meant, first and foremost, membership of the North Atlantic Alliance[5]. Accordingly, the goal of Polish foreign policy is to support NATO and to participate actively in the creation of a European security system that will ensure peace for all countries, including Russia.

Some security elites, and particularly the Polish one, perceive the East as unstable, unpredictable, and tending to imperialism[6]. Hence Poland keeps a watchful eye on developments in that area and seeks to maintain good relations with its neighbours, notably the Ukraine, whose sovereignty it is keen to bolster: Poland was the first country to raise the possibility of an agreement on security guarantees being negotiated between NATO and the Ukraine, analogous to that negotiated

---

[4] PRYSTROM, **Military-Strategic Emancipation...**, p.10.

[5] *"Poland's Kwasniewski pushes to join EU and NATO"*, in: **NNN News**, 24 Oct. 1996.

[6] *"Raison d'Etat"*, a conversation with former Foreign Minister Krzysztof Skubiszewski on the new non-governmental body "Foreign Policy Council", **TVP1**, 1 Sept. 1996.

between NATO and Russia. A further token of friendship was the creation of a joint Polish-Ukrainian battalion, which became operational in January 1997.

Current Polish defence doctrine, approved by parliament in 1992, embraces operations on national territory and contributions to the strengthening of international peace. It allows for peacekeeping operations by Polish troops under the auspices of organizations such as the UN and NATO.

Poland's defence system has inherited many deficiencies from Warsaw Pact days and cannot provide adequate security for the country. Reforms undertaken by the ministry of defence have ensured civilian control over the army, but the modernization, professionalization, and restructuring of the armed forces are proceeding extremely slowly because of financial constraints. In 1996, military expenditure in Poland stood at 2.43 percent of GDP, and, in spite of a parliamentary resolution of 16 February 1995 which stated that there must be an increase to 3 percent by the end of 1997 if Poland's security was to be assured, the defence budget for 1997 amounted to only 2.4 percent of GDP[7]. The economic situation in Poland will not allow any increase in spending at present, but it is fully understood that the country will have at least to double its spending on military modernization if it wants seriously to be considered as a NATO partner. This was the tenor of a statement by President Kwasniewski at the annual conference of Polish military chiefs in Warsaw in October 1996.

NATO membership is the prime strategic goal currently being pursued by Poland, and is the means whereby the country can assure full security for itself. Hence admission to NATO, and to the EU, have been accorded top priority in Polish foreign and security policy. NATO's response in establishing the North Atlantic Co-operation Council (NACC) and the Partnership for Peace system (PfP) represented the first steps in co-operation, and, as a result of this, Polish troops were sent to join the NATO-led peace forces in Bosnia.

On 9 May 1994, Poland was offered the status of associate partner in the Western European Union. At the press conference following

---

[7] Pawel Nowak, *"Fate of the Armed Forces"*, in: **Rzeczpospolita**, 17 Sept. 1996.

the announcement, the offer was described as "symbolic and concrete" by the then Polish foreign minister, Andrzej Olechowski[8]; the Central-East Europeans, he said, were going to be involved in the decision-making processes and security structure of the European Union.

Poland has submitted the document outlining the provisions for its individual entry to NATO. The main opponent to its attempts to join is Russia, which argues that Polish admission would pose a risk to Russian security. And yet President Yeltsin voiced no objection during his official visit to Warsaw on 25 August 1993, when the subject was discussed with President Lech Walesa. A joint document issued at that time stated that any decision by Poland, as a sovereign country, to seek European integration would not conflict with the interests of other countries, including Russia. As regards any agreement between Russia and NATO, Poland considers that this should not pre-empt the NATO summit decision on the commencement of enlargement and should take account of Poland's strategic security interests.

2. The Role of Nuclear Weapons in National Security Policy

From very early on in the nuclear age, Poland tried to prevent nuclear weapons from becoming part of its national security policy or from being deployed on its territory. In 1957, the Polish foreign minister, Adam Rapacki, put forward a proposal – named the Rapacki Plan – that nuclear weapons be permanently excluded from the territories of a number of Central European states, including Poland[9]. Unfortunately, the proposal failed to win support, and Poland ended up having not only Soviet bases, but also nuclear weapons installed on its territory – weapons about whose deployment the Poles only learned when the Russian troops had left the country[10]. Poland itself renounced the nuclear option under the Non-Proliferation Treaty (NPT), which it signed in 1969. As a consequence, all non-military nuclear installations in Poland have been subject to IAEA safeguards, as stipu-

---

[8] *RFE/RL Research Report*, 3/29, 22 July 1994.

[9] Jan PRAWITZ & James F. LEONARD, **A Zone Free of Weapons of Mass Destruction in the Middle East**, UNIDIR, Geneva, 1996.

[10] See the interview with Andrzej ANANICZ (*"Controversial idea"*) of the non-governmental Euro-Atlantic Society, in: **Rzeczpospolita**, 19 Sept. 1996.

lated in the agreement on full-scope safeguards concluded between Poland and the IAEA in 1972.

For decades, Poland did not have a security policy of its own; as a member of the Warsaw Pact, it came – theoretically, at least – under the Soviet nuclear umbrella. At present, being a non-nuclear-weapon state not participating in any military alliance and not having any nuclear-weapon option in its national security policy, it is *de facto* a nuclear-free area.

3. Public Debate on Nuclear Weapons and Nuclear Disarmament

There is no public debate on nuclear weapons or nuclear disarmament in Poland. The subject of nuclear weapons only came into public view in connection with the Polish application to join NATO and the possibility of nuclear weapons being deployed on Polish territory.

Since 1992, surveys have periodically been carried out by the Polish Public Opinion Research Center into public opinion on NATO membership and the possible deployment of nuclear weapons. A survey of January 1996 showed that the proportion of people supporting NATO membership had increased to 80 percent, but that support would diminish if there were a prospect of nuclear weapons being deployed: in that case, 61 percent of Poles would oppose NATO membership[11]. Calls for a referendum on NATO membership have been rejected as pointless by most members of the political and security elites; they argue that there is no need to spend money organizing a referendum on a matter that is as clear-cut as this and that enjoys growing public support.

4. The Attitude of Political and Security Elites to Nuclear Arms, Arms Control, and Disarmament

As mentioned earlier, the Polish political elites were always averse to nuclear arms and tried, through the Rapacki Plan of 1957, to prevent their deployment in Poland and the surrounding area. However,

[11] **Rzeczpospolita**, 26 Feb. 1996.

because this was the period of the arms race between East and West, there was little hope of such initiatives succeeding.

For decades, nuclear disarmament was a matter for the nuclear-weapons states only, as indicated in Article VI of the NPT. The two superpowers co-operated bilaterally on the arms control and disarmament process. Since the end of the Cold War, this situation has been changing, and other countries have been seeking to influence developments in this area. Poland, with an eye on admission to the Western alliance, is very cautious in giving its opinions on these matters, though it participates actively in the negotiating processes relating to global non-proliferation and disarmament. Because of their concern to avoid sensitive issues in case future integration into the West should be jeopardized, Polish diplomats appear merely to follow Western- or US-approved initiatives on nuclear disarmament. Some Polish security experts consider that such initiatives are still the preserve of the nuclear powers and that only the latter's good will and conviction can bring positive results (e.g. START). Polish diplomats believe they can play a more meaningful role within the framework of the negotiations on conventional forces being conducted by the Organization on Security and Co-operation in Europe (OSCE). They intend to call for further reductions following the implementation of the CFE and CFE1A treaties, which laid down ceilings for five major types of conventional weapons and imposed limits on troop numbers. (Poland implemented both treaties before the stated deadline.)

On nuclear processes in general: in a statement delivered during the general debate at the 1995 NPT conference, the Polish deputy minister of foreign affairs, Eugeniusz Wyzner, called for nuclear arms control and disarmament measures to be strengthened and further nuclear disarmament steps to be taken.

As regards the CTBT (Comprehensive Test Ban Treaty), Poland was actively involved in the relevant negotiations at the Conference on Disarmament and strongly supported the positive completion of the CTBT negotiations. In 1995, the *ad hoc* committee on the negotiation of a universal, multilaterally and effectively verifiable CTBT was chaired by Poland (in the person of Ambassador Ludwik Dembinski). Poland signed the CTBT on the day it was opened for signature (24 September 1996).

Poland also welcomed the agreement on a cut-off mandate reached by the Conference on Disarmament. It regards this new negotiating effort as fully consistent with the obligations laid down in Article VI of the NPT. However, the question of a non-discriminatory, multilateral and internationally verifiable treaty banning the production of fissile material for nuclear weapons and other nuclear explosive devices is still open. Deputy Foreign Minister Wyzner stated, at the Conference on Disarmament, that the CTBT should be followed up with a ban on fissionable materials[12] – a move that is also favoured by the US. Ludwik Dembinski, who served as CD chairman until January 1997, held numerous consultative meetings in an effort to reach consensus on the CD agenda. Poland welcomed the US ratification of START II and believes that there are prospects for further reductions in strategic nuclear arsenals not only by the United States and Russia but by other nuclear powers as well.

The most widely discussed nuclear issue in Poland is a Belorussian proposal for the creation of a nuclear-weapon-free zone (NWFZ) in Central/Eastern Europe, as mooted during the NPT conference and repeated on various occasions after this. The Polish government is not keen on such a move, the official position being as follows:

- Poland is applying to become a member of NATO, with all the rights and duties that entails.
- Poland should not pre-empt dialogue with NATO by making decisions that could hinder membership or preclude security guarantees.
- There is no need to deploy nuclear weapons on Polish territory.
- Poland itself has no interest in having nuclear weapons on its territory.
- Nuclear deployment cannot be excluded *a priori*.
- Poland cannot make such a commitment (i.e. to a NWFZ) unilaterally; it has to be agreed jointly by NATO and Poland.
- Discussion on a NWFZ should be postponed until after the 1997 NATO summit.

---

[12] **NNN News**, 14 Oct. 1996.

Additional arguments against a NWFZ:

- The proposal is too general and inadequately worked out[13].
- The idea of a NWFZ was appropriate to the past, when there was a need to prevent nuclear conflict; the present situation calls for active co-operation between former adversaries – in the NACC, the PfP arrangements, the OSCE, or a specific agreement between NATO and Russia[14].
- Poland has no nuclear weapons on its territory and does not trust the Belorussian avowal of friendly intentions; it suspects a Russian-backed ploy, given that Russia seeks to hinder Poland's integration into NATO[15].
- There is uncertainty about the relationship between the proposal for a NWFZ and the Tashkent Treaty providing nuclear security guarantees to the CIS[16].

5. Conclusions

The efforts made by Poland since the end of the Cold War to bring about democratization and assure the country's sovereignty have been hampered by both external and internal factors. Fortunately, many difficulties have been overcome, and Poland is now pursuing an independent foreign policy.

At present, Poland, being a non-nuclear-weapon state not participating in any military alliance and not having any nuclear option as part of its national security, is *de facto* a nuclear-weapon-free area. However, it rejects the notion of a NWFZ in Central/Eastern Europe as being inappropriate to the current political situation. Given Poland's geopolitical position, neutrality and non-alignment are not acceptable options.

---

[13] See the interview with the Polish deputy foreign minister, Andrzej Towpik, **Rzeczpospolita**, 19 Sept. 1996.

[14] *Ibid.*

[15] Interview with the Polish deputy minister of defence, Andrzej Karkoszka, *ibid.*

[16] Interview with Andrzej Ananicz of the Euro-Atlantic Society, *ibid.*

Top priority in Polish foreign and security policy is accorded to NATO and EU membership, and any sensitive issue that might hinder integration is avoided. Polish diplomats are currently very cautious in giving their opinions on nuclear arms control and disarmament, though they participate actively in negotiations on global non-proliferation and disarmament. Some Polish security experts consider that initiatives on nuclear arms control and disarmament are still the preserve of the nuclear powers and that only the latter's good will and conviction can bring positive results. Comprehensive nuclear disarmament and a ban on nuclear weapons are not conceivable in the near future, since the nuclear powers will not accept them. Because their main aim is to involve Poland in the decision-making processes and security structures of the European Union, Polish diplomats appear merely to follow Western- or US-approved initiatives on nuclear disarmament.

THE CZECH REPUBLIC

Jiří Šedivy

1. Introduction

A public debate concerning the deployment of nuclear weapons (NWs) on the territory of the Czech Republic (and until 1993 Czechoslovakia) is something relatively new in our country. Although Soviet NWs were deployed in Czechoslovakia in 1983 as part of the response to US Pershing II and cruise missiles deployed in Western Europe, the communist regime never officially admitted this[1]. Any public debate even remotely similar to the one that took place in the West was strictly prohibited. Solitary voices of protest came from the circles of anti-regime dissident groups and were immediately and brutally suppressed.

For these reasons, the following survey of the main points in discussions concerning NWs and related questions in the Czech Republic only deals with the 1990s. First, the chapter will outline the Czech perception of the new security environment as reflected in official documents. Then we will focus on the nuclear dimension of NATO enlargement by means of an analysis of three interrelated debates concerning: (i) the Study on NATO Enlargement, (ii) the controversy

---

[1] 39 SS-12 nuclear missiles and 24 mobile launchers were installed in Hranice na Moravě in 1983. Facilities for storage of nuclear ammunition were built as well. Up to the present day, as part of their anti-NATO propaganda, the Communists deny these facts – see M. HACKL, *"Jaderné zbraně v ČR již byly"*, in: **Lidové Noviny** (daily, Prague), 30 September 1995.

surrounding the so-called atomic law, and (iii) public and elite perceptions of and opinion about nuclear questions. As the Czech Republic (CR) has experienced one of the most significant cases of illegal nuclear trafficking, this issue and the responses of the Czech security system to it will be mentioned in conclusion.

2. The CR and the New Security Environment

At the time of the completion of this chapter (February 1997), the CR had only one official document – *The Military Strategy of the Czech Republic* – which dealt in many way with national security policy. One can also find basic quasi-official views in the *White Paper on Defence of the Czech Republic*. However, this document is not a standard white paper (i.e. a document issued by a government and accepted by a parliament); it is better described as an information booklet of the MOD[2].

The author also managed to get hold of an unofficial draft of the *National Defence Strategy* – a MOD document which was discussed but not accepted by the government in late 1996 and passed back to the ministry for revision. These are the sources for the following section.

2.1. The Security Situation

The danger of a massive two-bloc confrontation which could result in a nuclear war has disappeared. In contrast, new lower-level threats have come to the fore. These are multifaceted and thus difficult to analyse and predict, in terms both of their nature and of their potential impact. The possibility of the development of regional crises, conflicts and hostilities between states for economic, political, social, nationalist, ethnic and religious reasons has increased. The number of unstable regions in the world has not declined. The determination to use military means to resolve conflicts has been growing

---

[2] *The Military Strategy of the Czech Republic,* adopted by the Czech Government on 21 December 1994. In *White Paper on Defence of the Czech Republic,* MOD Prague 1995.

in many parts of the world. Some parts of Central and Eastern Europe (namely the former Yugoslavia and the Caucasus) have become unstable.

2.2. Risks and Threats to the Czech Republic

According to the documents mentioned, the CR does not perceive any direct military threat at present. However, the following risks and threats are of relevance to the country:

- Continuing internal political instability in Central and Eastern Europe, in the Balkans, the Near and Middle East, in Asia and in Africa, and unsolved ethnic and territorial issues could lead to the use of Weapons of Mass Destruction (WMD) in settling internal and external problems, to social, nationalist and territorial conflicts followed by the large-scale migration of refugees.
- The propagation of Islamic fundamentalism could give rise to new ethnic conflicts in the Balkans and the Near and Middle East.
- Since the end of the Cold War, economic relations have become an even more determining factor in political relations and a source of risk and potential threat.
- Russia and its effort to restore its political and economic influence in Central Europe may endanger efforts to integrate the CR into western political, security and economic structures.
- There is growing pressure from nationalist and extremist forces for revision of interstate and international treaties, especially those concerning the results of the World War II.
- The absence of any general recognition of universal civilised values brings about increased risks such as organised crime, terrorism, illegal sales and proliferation of arms, highly toxic agents, radioactive materials or drugs, and the illegal acquisition of technologies.

2.3. Disarmament and Arms Control

The *White Paper* regards "the process of disarmament and arms control as one of the basic prerequisites of the global survival of mankind". However, in the list of "the most significant... international treaties and agreements", only the BWC and CWC are mentioned of those treaties which concern WMD. In other words, there is no mention in the document of the NPT, the CTBT or other agreements dealing with NWs in the document.

3. Nuclear Weapons and NATO Enlargement

From the perspective of alliance building, L. Freedman has observed that "there remains a strategic role for nuclear weapons as an indicator of states vital interest". By extending nuclear deterrence "the most important political message" is conveyed – an ally for which a nuclear power is "prepared to run the greatest risk" is identified[3]. At the same time, extending deterrence to non-nuclear allies lessens their motivation to develop or acquire NWs. This was the US strategy during the Cold War (especially vis-à-vis Germany and Japan), and it should remain as an effective means of non-proliferation.

A fully-fledged membership of NATO has been the main strategic goal of the CR's foreign policy since the country was founded in 1993. As the following discussion will show, the Czech political elites in their quest for admission to NATO have tried to present the country as a most reliable future ally which will not hesitate to accept NWs on its territory. In exchange, it is expected that the CR will be covered by the US nuclear umbrella – i.e. the country will gain the status of a vital ally. It also appeared from the discussions concerning our investigation (see below) that a possible nuclear-free status within the Atlantic Alliance is perceived by some respondents as a second-class one.

3.1. The Study on NATO Enlargement

In September 1995 the Atlantic Alliance presented its *Study on NATO Enlargement* to the partner countries (PfP and NACC). Though only one of 82 paragraphs of the 28-page study deals with the consequences of enlargement for the Alliance's nuclear posture and with

---

[3] L. FREEDMAN, *"Whither nuclear strategy?"*, in: K. BOOTH (ed), **New Thinking about Strategy and International Security**, Harper Collins Academics, London, 1991, pp.78, 84.

the role therein of potential new members, the possibility of deploying NWs on Czech territory became perhaps the most discussed item
in the debates following the Study's publication[4]. Although the NATO
enlargement-related question of NWs on Czech territory was mentioned in the media as long ago as March 1995 (during the visit of
the German Defence Minister), it attracted no particular attention at
that time[5]. What can be called a public debate about NWs in the CR
only began with the publication of the NATO enlargement study.

Ignoring the wider context which determines the Alliance's current nuclear posture in Europe (NPT, INF Treaty, The New Strategic
Concept of NATO etc.), the biggest Czech daily wrote that new members will "share responsibility concerning the strategic nuclear forces"
of NATO. The deployment of NWs on Czech territory was presented
as "the most fundamental condition of the enlargement"; the three
parties of the ruling coalition (the Civic-Democratic Party, the Civic-
Democratic Alliance and the Christian Democrats) as well as the biggest opposition party (the Social Democrats) expressed their acceptance of this allegedly *sine qua non* condition. Cautious support was
also expressed by the President[6]. In a TV debate dedicated to this
problem on 1st October 1995 the possibility of NW deployment was
supported by the then Defence Minister.

The government further strengthened its position in these debates:
in a joint *exposé* before the Prague diplomatic corps in October 1995,
the deputy Foreign and Defence Ministers rejected speculation about
a search for some kind of Norwegian status in NATO and declared

---

[4] The main principles stated in paragraph 58 ("Nuclear Forces") of the Study
should be mentioned here: "There is no *a priori* requirement for the stationing
of NW on the territory of new members... NATO's current nuclear posture will,
for the foreseeable future, continue to meet the requirements of an enlarged
Alliance... New Members will... contribute to the development and implementation of NATO's strategy, including its nuclear components... should be eligible
to join the Nuclear Planning Group... Decisions on the modalities of and
specifics of this contribution will be based on consultations, and agreements
among allies." Study on **NATO Enlargement**, September 1995. According to
unspecified "NATO officials", the main purpose of the Study was to reserve the
right to station NWs on the soil of new members. B. CLARK, *"NATO to reserve
right on nuclear weapons"*, in: **The Financial Times**, 28 September 1995.

[5] **Dnes** (daily, Prague), 22 March 1995.

[6] **Dnes**, 28 September 1995, 29 September 1995.

that the CR "supports the concept of nuclear deterrence[7]". According to the advisor to the Foreign Minister, P. Kolář, the CR seeks full and equal NATO membership which includes the obligation "to have NW on our territory and perhaps also foreign troops[8]". In the meantime, the Social Democrats (who gained most from the May/June 1996 general elections and became the second strongest party in parliament) have changed their view: their election manifesto contained a "no-troops-no-nukes" requirement. The current minority government (the same coalition as before the elections) has not changed its unconditional support for fully-fledged membership of NATO[9].

Shortly before the Senate elections which took place in November 1996, about 100 candidates in the Prague and Central Bohemia election districts were asked to answer several questions. One among them touched on the problem of NWs: "Do you support integration in NATO including deployment of NWs in the country?" 41 candidates answered yes, 31 no, and 26 somehow avoided a direct answer. All supporters of unconditional integration were members of right-wing or center-right political parties. Left-wing candidates were almost unanimously against linking the CR's membership of NATO with the deployment of NW. What is also interesting is the profile of those answering ambiguously: there are many independent candidates among them and several left-wing persons; surprisingly enough, almost half of those who gave ambiguous answers are from parties which officially support unconditional integration into NATO. This most probably reflects the influence of public opinion, which has strongly opposed the idea of NWs on the CR's territory (see below)[10]. It is quite natural that political elites competing for votes have to take public opinion into account more than those who are already in power, as the following inquiry shows.

---

[7] **Dnes**, 5 February 1995.

[8] S. MORTKOWITZ, *"Czechs want nothing short of full and equal NATO status"*, in: **The Prague Post**, 20 March 1996.

[9] Cf. **Dnes**, 30 September 1995, 5 February 1996, 31 August 1996.

[10] **Dnes**, 12 November 1996, pp.5-10.

3.2. The Views of the Political Elites

Our investigation of the Czech political elites' views on the nuclear question was conducted in September/October 1996[11]. On the two crucial questions of nuclear deterrence and ballistic missile defence we found that almost all respondents believe in the utility of nuclear deterrence against the proliferation of WMD; the support for ballistic missile defence as a countermeasure to proliferation was quite strong, but less so than in the case of deterrence.

A number of further questions were asked. General support for a comprehensive test ban (on 12 November 1996 the CR became the 132nd signatory of the CTBT) and for a cut-off of the production of fissile materials was identified. A change in NATO strategy to "no-first-use" was rejected by the overwhelming majority of the respondents. Wide support for a START III treaty as well as for the inclusion of French, British and Chinese nuclear arsenals in international nuclear arms limitation and reduction treaties was noted, though the chances of realising the latter were viewed sceptically by some respondents. These doubts are based on a lack of belief that the relevant countries would be willing to weaken their power status vis-à-vis non-NW states. There exists a majority (though a rather sceptical one) which supports the idea of an extension of IAEA safeguards to the whole civilian fuel cycle in nuclear weapon states. The same applies to a treaty banning the development and production of new nuclear warheads[12]. Opinion was divided on the idea of a nuclear-weapon free zone (NWFZ) in Central Europe: it was categorically rejected by some, supported by others. Many respondents noted the fact that a NWFZ effectively exists in the region and/or responded ambiguously. This indicates a certain shift towards acceptance of the idea of a NWFZ in Central Europe. In general, the line dividing those supporting the idea and those rejecting it corresponds with support or rejection of the country's membership in the Atlantic Alliance;

---

[11] Twenty-eight questionnaires were distributed among senior state and military officials and members of parliament. The respondents were asked to write short answers (approx. five lines) to the questions. Eleven of the addressed persons responded. Eight additional interviews were conducted.

[12] On closer examination, the scepticism seems to stem from a certain lack of understanding of what these issues actually involve.

supporters fear that promoting a NWFZ in Central Europe may endanger the CR's position in the process of NATO enlargement.

The general impression we have obtained from the written answers and several additional interviews is that there is no deep knowledge or understanding of the nuclear question among the Czech political elites, and neither is there an official (i.e. governmental) position which would cover coherently all the dimensions of the issues investigated.

3.3. Public Opinion

The public perception of the NATO question contrasts sharply with the overwhelming enthusiasm of the political elites. According to a poll which was conducted shortly after the nuclear debate prompted by the NATO study, only 15% of the population would support NWs in the CR. Of more than 75% opposing it, 55% were "strongly" against this possibility[13]. Public support for the CR's membership of NATO has also declined. Public opinion analysts have estimated that the debate made people think about the darker sides of NATO membership. They were also probably scared by the politicians' readiness to accept NWs on Czech soil[14].

Moreover, on 7 October 1995 the Russian daily *Nezavisimaja gazeta* (referring to "a high officer of the general staff" of the Russian army) stated that since the CR and Poland had expressed their willingness to accept NW, Russian nuclear missiles might be targeted at them. Although this was immediately denied by the Russian Defence Ministry, the information was published and commented on in the Czech media. Henceforth, the notion of the possibility of the CR becoming a target of a nuclear attack entered debates on the nuclear issue[15].

---

[13] Cf. **Dnes**, 30 November 1995, 1 December 1995.

[14] While the percentage of those supporting the CR's membership of NATO was previously relatively stable (over 50% in the period between 1993 and 1995), it dropped to 46% in March 1996. On the other hand, the number of those opposing the CR's membership has been growing (in 1993 it was 26%, in 1994 28%, in early 1995 31% and in November 1995 39%, in March 1996 it reached 54%). Cf. **Lidové Noviny**, 14 December 1993, 9 December 1994, **Dnes**, 24 February 1994, 10 July 1995, 30 November 1995, 21 March 1996, **Respekt**, 30 May 1994.

[15] **Dnes**, 9 October 1995. For a lover of spy stories this approach might recall the method of active information (targeted mis-information in fact), as well as the Soviet efforts to shatter the Euro-American strategic relationship during the Cold War (the late 1970s and early 1980s Euromissile debate).

In March and September 1996 opinion polls connected with the coming elections to the Senate were conducted. Two thousand respondents were asked about, *inter alia*, their willingness to vote for a candidate supporting the following thesis: "Our country should join NATO even at the price of deployment of NWs on our territory if this is required." The results were more or less the same in both March and September: only about 18% of people would vote for such a candidate, over 70% of respondents would not[16].

3.4. The "Atomic Law"

After the Study on NATO Enlargement was published, the public debate about NWs gained further impetus when the so-called atomic law (the Law on peaceful use of nuclear energy and ionising radiation) was submitted to parliament in early 1996. This very complicated and comprehensive bill was designed above all to regulate the complex area of the civilian side of atomic energy and the disposal of fissionable materials. Out of the 70-page proposal, however, the greatest attention was paid to the short paragraph five, which contains the provisions of Article II of the Non-Proliferation Treaty[17]. This paragraph was interpreted as a "trap" which could complicate the CR's NATO membership. Dr. I. Gabal (a frequently-quoted sociologist) concluded that "for us, NWs are an important means in negotiations with both NATO and Russia" *(sic)*. Furthermore, according to Dr. Gabal, if the bill is passed, it will diminish our "capability to confront Russian pressure against NATO enlargement" and "disqualify" our reliability in the eyes of NATO. Deputy Defence Minister P. Necas was quoted as saying "I am against non-nuclear status since I am for fully-fledged membership of NATO.[18]" During a TV debate

---

[16] **Dnes**, 14 October 1996.

[17] Cf. Para. 5 of the bill: "Development, production, import, transfer, possession as well as any other disposal of nuclear weapons or their parts, including trade in them, is forbidden". Quoted in: J. VEIS, *"Atomovy zákon – změna názoru, nebo lajdáctvi?"*, in: **Tyden** (Prague weekly), No.7, 1996, p.23; Art. II, NPT: "Each non-nuclear weapon State Party to the Treaty undertakes not to receive the transfer from any transferor or whatsoever of NW or other nuclear explosive devices directly, or indirectly; not to manufacture or otherwise acquire NW or other nuclear explosives; and not to seek to receive any assistance in the manufacture of NW or other nuclear explosive devices."

[18] Cf. **Dnes**, 5, 6, 8 February 1996, 16 March 1996.

on this topic, Mr. Necas defended the theory that during the Cold War nuclear weapons had prevented World War III.

It should be stressed here that although NATO has never officially or publicly warned the Czechs against the possibility of a legal exclusion of NWs from Czech territory, warnings have been expressed many times during closed negotiations and informal encounters on various levels between the Czech and NATO side.

Up until the 1996 elections, parliament had not managed to pass the bill. In summer 1996 the new government proposed a slightly modified version. The controversial paragraph was amended by a qualifying clause. According to the amendment there may be an exception from the ban on NWs if an international treaty, to which the CR may become a party in the future, demands it[19]. Finally, the bill was passed by an overwhelming majority on 20 December 1996. This was made possible by the deletion of any mention of NWs from the bill, a step which was proposed by the opposition Social Democrats and the strongest member of the government coalition, the Civic-Democratic Party[20].

3.5. Civil Defence and Emergency Planning

In 1980, during the debates about the Euromissiles, M. Howard wrote in *The Times*: "If we were to accept cruise missiles... we should also do what we could to protect our civil population.[21]" Although nobody is going to deploy cruise missiles in the CR, any government as eager to welcome NWs on its territory as the present Czech government should bear this in mind. One should definitely have no illusions about the effectiveness of communist Czechoslovakia's civil defence system. Be that as it may, since 1989 this dimension of the national defence system has been totally neglected. This was demonstrated during an incident which happened in October 1995.

---

[19] **Dnes**, 21 August 1996.

[20] Cf. **Lidové Noviny**, 9 November 1996, 18 December 1996, 21 December 1996; **Dnes**, 21 December 1996.

[21] M. HOWARD, **The Causes of Wars**, (2nd edition), Harvard UP, 1983, p.116.

In a small town in Northern Bohemia, the meter which was a part of the nation-wide civil defence monitoring system began to indicate radioactivity at a level corresponding to a NW blast or a Chernobyl-size accident. Civil defence specialists from a nearby district arrived but they were not able to operate the meters they brought with them. This absurd situation, in which no one knew whether the situation was a real disaster or only a false alarm (and during which members of the local municipality personally circulated written warnings to inform the citizens), lasted for ten hours. Only specialists from a government agency who arrived from Prague were able to conclude that there was no radiation in the air and the alarm could be called off. Paradoxically enough, this total break-down of the civil emergency and defence system and procedures took place against the backdrop of the nuclear debate which had been provoked by the Study on NATO Enlargement three weeks before[22].

4. Illicit Trafficking in Nuclear Materials

The biggest seizure so far of illicitly traded nuclear material was reported by the Czech police in December 1994. A quantity of 2.722 kg of highly enriched uranium (up to 87.7%) in the form of uranium dioxide was seized and three persons were arrested. As the legal and systemic instruments together with the internal and external regulations, procedures and regimes which make up Czech non-proliferation policy have been sufficiently outlined elsewhere[23], let us refer to the lower executive level, so to speak, of the bodies which deal with this issue.

Soon after the CR was founded in 1993, a specialised unit dealing with illicit trafficking, smuggling and manipulation of nuclear materials was established. This unit forms part of the section for the detection of international crime of the Czech criminal police. Besides the above mentioned tasks, the force has been trained to assist during

---

[22] **Dnes**, 18 October 1995.

[23] See J. BERÁNEK, *"Czech Republic: Reform of the Nuclear Export Control System"* and L. CUDOVÁ, *"The Czech Republic and Non-Proliferation Regimes"*, in: H. MÜLLER & J. PRYSTROM (eds), **Central European Countries and Non-Proliferation Regimes**, PRIF and PFIA, Warsaw, 1996.

emergency situations in nuclear facilities (breakdowns, thefts, etc.) and to assist in the transport of nuclear material on the territory of the country.

A system of communication and cooperation between this unit and other relevant internal institutions (the State Office for Nuclear Safety, the army of the CR, the Directorate General of Customs, Civil Defence, nuclear scientists) and external institutions (other countries' counterparts, Interpol, Europol's anti-drug unit, the Council of Europe, Euratom, the IAEA) has been established and is being developed and improved. The unit has also cooperated in improving and amending the domestic legal dimension of the fight against illicit trafficking in nuclear materials: the unit initiated § 186 of the Criminal Code ("Illegal Production and Possession of Nuclear Material", in force since 1st April 1994) and cooperated on the so-called atomic law proposal. In addition, the State Office for Nuclear Safety initiated the development of an airborne radiation monitoring system, and at the end of 1996 a dosimetric detection system was installed at the main border checkpoints and is currently being tested.

The Czech police initiated the first international workshop of police and criminal experts which took place in Prague between 30 September and 4 October 1996. The main results of this unprecedented meeting of experts from 14 states (mostly Central and East European, but also from France, Germany and the US), were improvements in the diagnosis and evaluation of the situation in the field of nuclear crime and the setting-up of a cooperation network[24].

It was agreed in a classified *aide mémoire* issued by the meeting that until the next meeting, which will take place in 1998 in one of the participating countries, the section of the Czech police which organised the first workshop will serve as the informal data base of the cooperative network established at the Prague meeting. In other words, initiatives, recommendations, annual reports, statistics and other news and information in the field will be received and processed in the Czech Republic.

---

[24] **Lidové Noviny**, 4 October 1996.

5. Conclusion

In the case of the Czech Republic, the relationship between the country's would-be NATO membership and the possibility of deployment of NWs on its territory has been identified as the main issue in the nuclear debate. A sharp contrast between the opinion of the governing political elites and the public perception was observed. The cases of illegal trafficking in nuclear materials which have become known have not substantially influenced either public debates or the perception of the nuclear question among the country's political elites. On the other hand, it should be stressed that much more appropriate responses to the new risks have been developed at the lower executive level. There has been a continual bottom-up pressure aiming at the early establishment of an integrated system to deal with the multidimensional and multi-level character of the current proliferation challenge.

The willingness of the Czech governmental elites to accept NWs can be explained by (a) their perception of the necessity of maintaining a sort of residual deterrence (vis-à-vis Russia in this case), (b) their perception of the role of NWs as an indicator of vital interest, and (c) their efforts not to hinder the country's integration into NATO. Nevertheless, not only have the elites been unable to gain Czech public support for NWs as a condition (though a false one) of NATO enlargement, but, eventually, the impact of the nuclear debate has been harmful and counter-productive to the attempt to gain public support for the CR's possible membership of NATO[25].

We may conclude that the Czech discourse on NWs suffers from the lack of experience and limited expertise of both politicians and the public opinion formers (media, national security experts). What

---

[25] The increase in public scepticism towards the CR's would-be membership of NATO has been received with a certain alarm in the Alliance. Thus one can read in the Final Communiqué issued by the December 1996 NAC ministerial meeting in Brussels a message directed at both Russia and the candidate countries: "Enlarging the Alliance will not require a change in NATO's current nuclear posture and, therefore, NATO countries have no intention, no plan and no reason to deploy nuclear weapons on the territory of new members nor any need to change any aspect of NATO's nuclear posture or nuclear policy – and we do not foresee any future need to do so." **Atlantic News**, No.2875 (Annex), Brussels, 12 December 1996, p.2.

is more, the tone of the debate is still marked by a Cold War way of thinking. By way of contrast, the areas where the approach to the nuclear question is issue rather than ideologically driven, and where expertise and systemic approaches are being developed – i.e. the lower executive levels – have almost zero input into these discussions.

Although the CR participates in a number of non-proliferation agencies and regimes[26], nuclear arms control and disarmament is by and large an issue which is discussed neither in public debates (questions concerning this issue area have not been posed in any public opinion poll conducted since the establishment of the CR in 1993), nor in the discourse of political elites. The same goes for governmental documents on foreign and security policy and the international/security parts of the programmes of Czech political parties. These documents, if they mention the issue at all, contain only very general statements which indicate an awareness of the existence of the non-proliferation question without mentioning any sort of developed and/or active position.

---

[26] Besides the IAEA, the CR is a member of the Australia Group, Nuclear Suppliers Group and Zangger Committee. The country has also joined the discussions in the framework of the Wassenaar Arrangement on Export Controls for Conventional Arms and Dual-use Goods and Technologies; see **SIPRI Yearbook 1996**, OUP, 1996, pp.xxii-xxxi, 542.

BULGARIA

Radoslava STEFANOVA

1. Introduction

Bulgaria is a non-nuclear-weapon state (NNWS) whose official policy has consistently upheld the objective of global nuclear disarmament. This specific topic is, however, absent from the rhetoric of policy-makers, although a closely related issue, Bulgaria's expressed desire to join NATO, is currently on the public agenda more than at any time in the past. The issue of nuclear disarmament is therefore relevant not only to Bulgaria's adherence to international treaties and foreign policy declarations, but also to the existing interpretations of paragraphs 45(d) and 58 of the 1995 Study on NATO Enlargement presented by NATO to the countries of East-Central Europe, articles 5 and 6 of the 1949 Washington Treaty, and paragraphs 15, 37, 39, 55, 56, and 57 of the 1991 Strategic Concept, where nuclear deterrence is codified as one of the key principles of the Alliance. This chapter reviews these issues and also provides an overview of the current Bulgarian legislation on the use of nuclear energy and possible loopholes that might facilitate the illegal traffic in weapons-grade fissile material.

2. The Official Foreign Policy Position

Bulgaria joined and ratified the Nuclear Non-Proliferation Treaty (NPT) as a NNWS in 1968 and 1970 respectively. Ever since, policy makers have expressed their support for NPT Article VI, which commits signatories to the objective of the complete elimination of nuclear weapons. Moreover, proposals for the creation of a nuclear-weapon-free zone (NWFZ) in the Balkans have been part of Bulgarian foreign policy initiatives both during the Cold War and after.

At the 1995 NPT Extension and Review Conference Bulgaria advocated the indefinite and unconditional extension of the Treaty, which it deemed "a guarantee for the irreversibility of progress of nuclear disarmament [*sic*].[1]" Bulgaria further reiterated its support for NWFZs and declared itself in favour of a Comprehensive Test Ban Treaty (which it signed in September 1996), which is also regarded as a major step towards the final objective of nuclear disarmament. In addition, Bulgaria has indicated that it will support a Fissile Material Cut-off Convention within the framework of the Conference on Disarmament and the right of the International Atomic Energy Agency (IAEA) to perform special inspections, as reaffirmed at the 1995 NPT Extension and Review Conference, and that it will support any measures aimed at the coordination of international efforts to halt the illicit traffic in fissile material (possibly a new convention)[2].

However, the research and interviews conducted for the purposes of this chapter do not indicate any consideration in Bulgarian policy-making circles of a nuclear weapons ban analogbus to the provisions of the recently ratified Chemical Weapons Convention. Many of the officials interviewed expressed serious doubts as to the rationality of outlawing nuclear weapons, as well as certainty that such intricate (and quite hypothetical) matters were of little relevance in the context of Bulgaria. Almost nobody has attached any importance to the July 1996 decision of the International Court of Justice to declare nuclear weapons illegal unless used under "extreme circumstances", a decision judged to be too legalistic and therefore too open to different interpretations to have any effect in practice. The findings of the Canberra Commission on the Elimination of Nuclear Weapons also attracted little attention, and any general speculations in this direction tend to be treated with scepticism.

---

[1] Statement by Georgi Pirinski, former Minister of Foreign Affairs and Bulgarian representative at the 1995 Extension and Review Conference in New York.

[2] Ministry of Foreign Affairs, a preliminary document outlining Bulgaria's official position on issues related to nuclear weapons non-proliferation and disarmament, March 1995.

It is quite certain, however, that if there is a general movement involving the major world powers and above all the NWS, Bulgaria will actively support all of these.

3. An Assessment of Bulgaria's Official Stance

Bulgaria's foreign policy position regarding the non-proliferation of weapons of mass destruction is undoubtedly commendable from the point of view of global progress towards nuclear disarmament. Bulgaria has upheld the normative framework created by the non-proliferation regime[3], and in this way has contributed to the regime's strengthening and continued relevance. However, in order to evaluate Bulgaria's foreign policy choices it is necessary to understand them as a product of the country's internal decision-making dynamics. It is thus essential to identify and discuss the underlying interests of the political elites and determine whether supporting nuclear disarmament *per se* is considered an indispensable part of Bulgarian security interests.

In order to derive a comprehensive picture of policy makers' predisposition towards nuclear disarmament using the tools identified above, past and present attitudes will be taken into consideration. Bearing in mind the rapidly evolving political situation in Bulgaria, an attempt will be made to predict future developments.

4. Past Ambiguities

Before the fall of the Berlin Wall, Bulgaria's foreign policy was at all times coordinated with the Kremlin. As a member of the Soviet bloc, the country's stance on the nuclear issue was a reflection and continuation of the Soviet strategic interest in nuclear non-proliferation, and thus the question of nuclear disarmament was an inevitable part of the largely propagandistic and provocative rhetoric of the Bulgarian leadership. Bulgaria missed no opportunity to stress its non-nuclear status and aspirations for a Balkan NWFZ, and to contrast these policies with those of Greece and Turkey, its neighbours to the South and NATO member states.

---

[3] Pirinski at the 1995 NPT Extension Conference in New York.

However, after the end of the Cold War, some doubts were cast on Bulgaria's presumed non-nuclear status. As early as 1991 allegations claiming that Russian nuclear warheads had been stationed on Bulgarian territory appeared in the press[4]. On 12 September 1996 all major Bulgarian newspapers reacted to a provocative article in the Russian *Komsomolskaja Pravda* from the previous day to the same effect[5]. Bearing in mind the "special relationship" between Sofia and Moscow during the Cold War, these continued allegations should not be dismissed *a priori* as unfounded. A careful evaluation of the overall strategic situation during the Cold War might be helpful both in deriving a plausible explanation of Bulgaria's real status and in providing a new context in which the concept of nuclear disarmament in the country can be analysed.

According to the former Bulgarian Defence Ministry spokesman, Lt. Gen. Ivan Stefanov, there were at least seven Soviet nuclear warheads on Bulgarian territory in 1987[6]. According to the already cited article in *Komsomolskaja Pravda*, seventy nuclear warheads were stored in a small Soviet-operated base close to Borovets (about two hours from Sofia) where there is currently a Bulgarian surface-to-surface missile base. The article further alleges that the warheads were stationed at the base until 1988, when they were transported back to the (then) USSR and the base closed. According to the author of the Russian article, the information was "in principle" confirmed by the Soviet Defence Minister at the time: Dimitri Yazov. As might be expected, the allegations were rejected both by current officials in the Bulgarian Ministry of Defence, the Presidency, and the Ministry of Foreign Affairs and by people who had decision-making authority at the time of the presumed stationing of the Soviet warheads. Besides

---

[4] Lt. Gen. Ivan Stefanov, former spokesman for the Bulgarian Ministry of Defence declared on July 25, 1991 that seven Soviet SS-23 missiles and two launchers were stationed on Bulgarian territory in February 1987 as a result of an intergovernmental agreement signed in 1986, and that no further deployments were made after December 1987. This gave rise to speculation that more warheads might have been transferred from the (then) Soviet Union to Bulgaria in the course of that year (Bulgarian Telegraph Agency, July 25, 1991, as quoted in **Proliferation News**, August 8, 1991, p.8, and in **Missile Monitor**, Spring 1992, p.14). This allegation was later rejected by the Ministry of Defence.

[5] Elena ARDABATSKAJA, *"The USSR Could Have Carried Out a Nuclear Strike on the West from Sofia"*, in: **Komsomolskaja Pravda**, 11 September 1996, pp.1-2.

[6] See footnote 4.

noting the almost universal coverage that the Russian article provoked in the Bulgarian mass media, two further comments are in order.

First, new evidence has shown that Russia was particularly anxious to redress a growing strategic inferiority in the arms race with the US as early as the Cuban missile crisis in 1962[7]. Therefore, it is not unrealistic to assume that the presence of US nuclear warheads in Turkey under the aegis of NATO might have provoked a counter-deployment in neighbouring Bulgaria under a secret clause of the Warsaw Pact.

Second, even though throughout the Cold War Bulgaria was Russia's most servile ally, it is hard to believe that Soviet strategic weaponry would have been placed in the hands of the Bulgarian Army. Soviet military doctrine excluded transferring nuclear warheads and launchers to any Warsaw Pact ally. Therefore, if there really were Soviet nuclear warheads deployed on Bulgarian territory, this would presuppose the presence of Soviet troops on Bulgarian territory – and officially there were none at any time during the Cold War. In fact, the article in *Komsomolskaja Pravda* maintains that the base was operated exclusively by Soviet personnel wearing Bulgarian army uniforms.

Even though the truth surrounding possible Soviet strategic deployments in Bulgaria during the Cold War might never surface, it has to be noted that past ambiguities on the subject make the topic of nuclear disarmament in Bulgaria all the more relevant, as discussions about possible past precedents provide a context in which the attitudes of present policy-makers should be analysed. In this sense, it is useful to bear in mind the preceding discussion when the Bulgarian

---

[7] James G. BLIGHT & David A. WELCH, **On the Brink: Americans and Soviets Re-examine the Cuban Missile Crisis**, New York, Noonday Press, (2nd ed.), 1990, drawing on remarks by Raymond Garthoff at the Hawk Cay Conference (March 5-8, 1987), p.38. According to Thomas Reeves, by late 1962 the US nuclear superiority over the Soviets stood at a 16:1 (5000 US nuclear warheads vs. about 300 Soviet ones), and the Soviets tried to counterbalance this with strategic deployments in Cuba and possibly elsewhere; see Thomas C. REEVES, **A Question of Character: A Life of John F. Kennedy**, Rocklin, Prima Publishing, 1992, p.365. Richard Ned Lebow also notes a sustained Soviet build-up after the Cuban missile crisis at the Hawk Cay Conference, (LEBOW at the Hawk Cay Conference, in: BLIGHT & WELCH, **On the Brink**, p.106).

position regarding NATO enlargement and nuclear disarmament is presented.

5. Bulgaria's Place in the New Security Order and the Question of Nuclear Disarmament

Attempting to pin down Bulgarian security priorities in the post-Cold War security order has been like aiming at a moving target. Since the beginning of the transition process and particularly since early 1996, Bulgarian politics, including the country's stance on fundamental issues, has made a U-turn. This reflects the extremely dynamic and antagonistic struggles that condition the competition for state power in Bulgaria.

As noted at the outset, issues related to nuclear disarmament have to be derived from existing attitudes towards NATO enlargement, as a debate on disarmament *per se* does not currently exist in Bulgaria. However, before making the plunge into the depths of Bulgarian domestic politics, it should once again be emphasised that there has been an enduring foreign policy consensus in favour of nuclear disarmament and all relevant international initiatives on a global level.

Currently, there are three prevalent positions in Bulgaria on the question of NATO enlargement. These coincide with the party affiliations of the major political actors and their foreign policy priorities.

At the time of writing Bulgaria has just acquired a new government, whose general policy seems to promise a new period in Bulgarian politics. This development has reversed the country's previous stance on the issue of NATO membership. On February 17, 1977 the (then) interim Prime Minister, Stefan Sofiyanski, announced that Bulgaria had chosen to seek NATO membership[8]. Early parliamentary elections on 19 April 1997 brought about a new government, headed by Ivan Kostov, which will continue the new pro-NATO trend. This is a major foreign policy shift compared to the wait-and-see approach of the previous government under the premiership of Jean Videnov.

---

[8] *"Now Bulgaria Wants to Join NATO"*, in: **International Herald Tribune**, February 18, 1997, p.5, as quoted from the Associated Press.

A major political actor whose attitude towards NATO and its strategic concept has become decisive is the Union of Democratic Forces (UDF), which was until recently the largest opposition party in parliament and now holds an absolute majority of seats. The UDF's orientation is strongly pro-Western, and NATO membership is viewed as an indispensable prerequisite of Bulgaria's integration into other Western political and economic structures such as the EU. The new government thus considers NATO membership to be a guarantee of democracy and economic recovery. When NATO's Secretary General, Javier Solana, visited Bulgaria in May 1996 he was given a document outlining the UDF's official position on the question of Bulgaria's desire for NATO membership which has now been wholly incorporated in the policy of the current administration. Even though the document recognises that Russia should not be alienated if NATO is to expand to the East, it emphasises that any such move on the part of Bulgaria should be undertaken as a sovereign act and not be made contingent on third party reactions[9]. Nuclear weapons deployment is not seen as a precondition for NATO membership, and a NWFZ in Eastern Europe is viewed favourably. It should be noted that nuclear disarmament is not discussed at all in UDF circles in the context of NATO enlargement, even though there has been no indication that the UDF's policy-makers are adverse to the idea of disarmament *per se.*

A close affinity is therefore observable between the position of the UDF, the stance of the new government, and that of the recently elected President, Petar Stoyanov, who himself belongs to the UDF. His role in the current Bulgarian foreign policy shift has been fundamental. Elected with a significant majority of the popular vote, Stoyanov incorporated NATO membership for Bulgaria in his campaign rhetoric and placed this goal at the centre of his foreign policy priorities as soon as he entered office in January 1997. As already stated, however, NATO membership is viewed in Bulgaria primarily in terms of affinity with Western models of development, and that is how it has been presented by Stoyanov. Considerations related to NATO's nuclear deployment provision under Article 5 and global commitments to nuclear disarmament have not been discussed at any point.

---

[9] *"The UDF Strongly Supports Bulgaria's Joining NATO"*, in: **Democratzia**, 3 May 1996, p.7.

Fundamentally, Stoyanov's position is consistent with the stance of his predecessor, Zheliu Zhelev, who throughout his five-year term had continuously criticised Videnov's government and in particular its lack of policy towards NATO. Zhelev made numerous public statements calling for an immediate indication of Bulgaria's aspiration to join NATO and blaming the government for its inaction. In a 1995 address defining the priorities of Bulgarian foreign policy, Zhelev emphasised that "NATO is not just a defence alliance but a sharing of democratic values. In this sense, a NATO expansion would only bring democracy and stability closer to Russia.[10]" Even though both the current and the previous presidents have suggested that a "dialogue" should be initiated on the issue of nuclear weapons deployment in the process of Bulgaria's possible adhesion to NATO, neither has yet clarified his position as to what Bulgaria's policy on the subject should be or addressed the issue of nuclear disarmament in the light of NATO's expansion. According to the Constitution, however, the President has more or less ceremonial powers and most decision-making power is vested in the Parliament and therefore in the government. Nevertheless, in view of the UDF's convincing victory in the April 1997 general elections, the pro-NATO trend clearly coincides with the foreign policy priorities of President Stoyanov and will certainly be sustained.

Particularly illustrative of the new policy of the Bulgarian government is the position of the Atlantic Club, an NGO which provides a forum for research and debate on the question of NATO enlargement. Its view is worth examining briefly, since it can be associated in many ways with the UDF, the government, and the President, despite the presence in it of some members of the pro-NATO wing of the BSP (the Bulgarian Socialist Party, which until December 1996 had an absolute majority in parliament and formed the country's previous government). In a personal interview the Atlantic Club's President, Mr. Solomon Passy, declared that the question of NATO nuclear deployments in Bulgaria after the country's eventual admission to NATO as part of its obligations under Article 5 was "irrelevant"[11]. Passy further

---

[10] Zhelju ZHELEV, *"The New Foreign Policy of Bulgaria and NATO"*, an address delivered at the Annual Foreign Policy Lecture Series of the Atlantic Club of Bulgaria, 17 April 1995, p.5.

[11] Interview with the author on September 19, 1996.

linked the campaign for nuclear disarmament to Soviet propaganda from the 1960s and 1970s and dismissed it as archaic, stating that the issue should not currently be on the public agenda and expressing doubts as to the overall usefulness of the concept. However, he did not explicitly declare himself in favour of stationing a NATO nuclear deterrent on Bulgarian territory.

It is also important to briefly examine the position of the BSP, the party which has been in power for much of the period since the beginning of the Bulgarian transition to democracy in 1989. The BSP maintains that Bulgaria's adhesion to NATO would not necessarily serve the country's interests as it will not be viewed favourably by Russia, whose role arguably continues to be significant in Bulgarian economic and political affairs. The general pro-Russian orientation of this party and the influence of some hard-liners inside it made the pre-February 1997 Bulgarian policy towards NATO enlargement conditional on Russian approval, or at least non-rejection. Throughout the duration of the BSP government under the premiership of Jean Videnov, who resigned as a result of public pressure in late December 1996, it was made clear that as long as Russia continues to view NATO enlargement to the East as a threat to its own security Bulgaria will abstain from any direct expression of a desire for membership. In a 1996 statement Videnov did not rule out Bulgarian membership of NATO *a priori* but referred to a parliamentary declaration from 21 December 1993, in which Bulgarian membership of NATO and the West European Union (WEU) was viewed as desirable, as long as it shows a "full respect for Bulgarian national interests" and "[does not generate] feelings of isolation and security deficit in anyone"[12].

As a direct result of the priorities of the BSP, the Bulgarian Foreign Ministry had adopted a policy of enlightened interest regarding NATO membership. Several initiatives were started along these lines, such as the so-called "Intensified Dialogue" which Bulgaria began conducting with NATO on the basis of the "Study on Enlargement". In March 1996 the BSP-led government adopted a document consisting

---

[12] Jean VIDENOV, *"Bulgaria and the Future Security Systems: Regional, Continental and Global"*, an address delivered at the Annual Foreign Policy Lecture Series of the Atlantic Club of Bulgaria, 4 April 1995, p.5.

of 55 paragraphs which was essentially a request for clarification of the "Study" with some commentary and without any commitments. Paragraphs 11 and 12 of the "Intensified Dialogue" emphasised the importance which Bulgaria places on the condition that any changes in the European security system be conducted without alienating Russia. The spirit of these paragraphs has now been completely reversed but it is still worth examining them as priorities of the party that shaped Bulgaria's foreign policy until a year ago. Paragraphs 36, 37, and 38 of the document address the nuclear provisions of the "Study", stating that Bulgaria is clearly against any deployments of strategic weapons if invited to join the Alliance. Throughout the document the Bulgarian government underlines its understanding that NATO's enlargement to the East will be primarily politically motivated, and will not involve changes in the nuclear balance in Europe (paragraphs 28, 29, 41).

However, when asked whether considerations of nuclear disarmament had motivated the stress on the continued non-nuclear status of Bulgaria expressed in the "Intensified Dialogue", the Ministry of Foreign Affairs officially interviewed answered in the negative[13]. The emphasis was primarily on Bulgaria's desire to dissipate Russian anxieties. Nuclear disarmament viewed as a global objective and a contribution to world peace was not at any point considered at the Ministry, and the recent political change is likely to strengthen this trend. Moreover, there is a general reluctance to discuss the topic even in the abstract, and the prevalent attitude is one of careful scepticism. It is doubtful that any significance will be given to the debate *per se,* except in very general rhetorical terms, under the new political circumstances. In a private discussion, the officials in charge of conducting relations with NATO even expressed a belief in the general necessity of maintaining a limited stock of nuclear weapons in the current NWS as part of the global balance of power. However, all of the interviewees were convinced that if Bulgaria were to be invited to join NATO, the non-nuclear status of the country would be maintained.

To the extent to which officials at the Ministry of Defence can comment on the essentially political question of Bulgaria's NATO

---

[13] A series of interviews conducted by the author on 12-13 September 1996.

policy, it can be said that the opinions expressed by both civilian and military officials tend to coincide with those registered at the Ministry of Foreign Affairs[14]. For example, the former Director of the Centre for National Security Studies at the Ministry of Defence, Mr. Nansen Behar, pointed (in the spirit of the "Intensified Dialogue") to the need for more information about the process and to the imperative of gaining Russian approval[15]. Certainly, under present circumstances the Ministry of Defence will place less importance on Russian anxieties and more weight on the new Bulgarian position and expressed desire to join NATO.

For the sake of completeness it should be said that there is dissent within the BSP concerning NATO membership, although undoubtedly the prevalent position is the one adopted by the former government under Videnov. There is reportedly a minority in the party which supports a Bulgarian application for NATO membership[16]. These are predominantly young technocrats with strong but not leading positions in the party, often educated in the West, who see Bulgarian willingness to join NATO as a precondition for the country's overall integration in other Western structures. However, they also consider it crucial that Russia be reassured. Currently, this pro-NATO wing of the BSP is avoiding any speculation about possible nuclear deployments as part of the country's obligations in the event of Bulgaria joining NATO. It can be predicted with certainty that due to the overall pro-Russian orientation of the BSP, the possibility of nuclear weapons being stationed on Bulgarian territory under the Treaty clauses will find no advocates even on the pro-Western wing of the party. It should be underlined again, however, that such a stance does not spring from a general opposition to nuclear weapons *per se*, but from concern about a possible hostile Russian reaction.

---

[14] A series of interviews conducted by the author at the Ministry of Defence on September 16, 1996.

[15] Nansen BEHAR, *"Bulgarian Perception on European Cooperation for Conflict Prevention"*, an address delivered at a conference entitled "Post-Dayton Balkans in Europe: Political, Security, and Economic Aspects of an Emerging Relationship", organized by the Institute of International Relations of Greece on 30-31 August 1991 in Corfu, Greece.

[16] Ivo INDJOV, *"NATO Divided the BSP into Three Camps"*, in: **Sega**, 8-14 February 1996, pp.20-22. Philip BOKOV, *"Neutrality Builds on the Presumption of the Cold War"*, interview in: **Democratzia**, 6 May 1996, p.7.

Finally there are the BSP "hard-liners", whose position is currently defined as one of "active neutrality", i.e. not only opposition to Bulgaria's declared intention of joining NATO, but also opposition to NATO expansion in general. In January 1996 Blagovest Sendov, the former chairman of the Bulgarian Parliament, made such a strong public statement while in Moscow denouncing NATO's expansion to the East as a source of insecurity in Europe that the Russian Ambassador to Bulgaria reacted by saying that this was not necessarily his country's position on the issue.

Finally, it is worth noting that in the face of such contrasting positions on the issue of NATO membership, it is not surprising that the electorate is equally divided. According to the 1996 edition of *Central and Eastern Eurobarometer*, 52 percent of the Bulgarian population are in favour of the country's joining NATO, while 48 percent are against such a move[17]. However, the 1997 elections which indicated a considerable loss of voter support for the BSP and a net rise in UDF popularity might have reversed this trend, although no new opinion polls were conducted on the issue in the immediate pre- or post-election period. In that sense, Javier Solana's conclusion in May 1996 that in Bulgaria there was no public consensus about NATO membership[18] might appear to be a bit out-dated. Again, any electoral division is not stirred by an understanding of the topic and its implications, but is simply a reflection of party loyalties.

To recapitulate the picture of existing attitudes among policy-making circles in Bulgaria, it should be reiterated that the debates outlined above are highly partisan and very superficial. It could even be said that views are held not because of their implications, but in opposition to political rivals. As Georgi Pirinski, Bulgaria's former Foreign Minister, put it, in Bulgaria there is "no serious discussion, but an irresponsible shouting at one another on the topic of NATO[19]". It can be concluded that currently there is any lack of any deeper understanding either of the far-reaching global transformation of security or of the real meaning and purpose of nuclear disarmament. The intense dynamics of Bulgarian decision-making in a situation of profound

---

[17] **Central and Eastern Eurobarometer**, EU Publication, Brussels, March 1996.

[18] As quoted in **Democratzia**, 3 May 1996, pp.1-2.

[19] Quoted in **Democratzia**, 5 June 1995, p.5.

economic and political crisis has made irrelevant all debates which are not directly related to the acquisition or preservation of power by political formations. The lack of consideration of nuclear disarmament within a heated controversy over the country's desire for NATO membership could thus be attributed to the low level of political culture on the part of both politicians and voters.

6. Some Relevant Legal Provisions and their Applications and Implications

In 1995 parliament amended the existing (since 1985) Law on the Use of Nuclear Energy for Peaceful Purposes. *Article 1 (2)* outlaws the use of nuclear energy for the production of weapons of mass destruction; *Article 2 (1)* states that special nuclear material (defined as Pu_{239}, U_{233}, and U_{235}, where the percentage of the latter two is higher than their natural concentration in U_{238}) and nuclear facilities are property of the state, although *(2) inter alia* Bulgarian citizens may own other sources of ionic radiation; *Article 8* states that the physical protection of nuclear materials is the responsibility of their users; *Article 12 (1)* designates the Committee on the Use of Atomic Energy for Peaceful Purposes (CUAEPP) to carry out the state's policy regarding the application of nuclear energy; *Article 23 (3)* states that some activities or sources of nuclear energy might be exempted from registration and licenses under the conditions specified by the regulations on nuclear safety; *Article 28 (1)* states that CUAEPP inspectors can perform inspections on related facilities or material at any time; and *Article 39 (2)* establishes a trifling fine in case access is denied to an inspector.

There are eight nuclear facilities in Bulgaria. These include six nuclear reactors at the Kozlodui Power Station, an away-from-reactor spent fuel storage, and the IRT-2000 Research Reactor near Sofia. According to the 1995 Report of the CUAEPP, there are no facilities for the reprocessing of spent fuel, which is in part stored temporarily in the open in the lack of sufficient storage[20]. Because of lack of funds

---

[20] *Nuclear Safety and Radiation Shield: Report 1995*, Committee on the Use of Nuclear Energy for Peaceful Purposes at the Council of Ministers, Sofia, May 1996, p.37.

the building of a new storage facility was terminated four years ago[21]. The current law allows individuals to own or operate some nuclear facilities. Cases of refusal to allow access to an authorised inspector (and there have been such cases[22]) are penalised by a minuscule fine. Furthermore, the budget allotted to individual facilities is insufficient to provide adequate physical protection of the spent fuel[23].

These facts, combined with the difficult overall situation, make Bulgaria a country where the risk of fissile material smuggling is relatively high. While no major cases involving the theft of or illegal trafficking in significant quantities of HEU or Pu_{239} have been registered yet, there have been indications that there is some activity in the market for illicit fissile materials. In October 1992 a negligible quantity of Pu_{239} was smuggled into Bulgaria with capsules used in equipment for chemical warfare[24]. False or unconfirmed scares followed in 1993 and 1994. In mid-December 1996 a total of 13 metal cylinders containing highly radioactive materials (caesium, uranium, plutonium, and iridium) were found in the possession of unauthorised individuals[25]. The quantity and the composition of the illegally stored materials has not yet been made public.

As a recent publication indicates, the uncontrolled traffic in nuclear materials is a threat to world peace and a serious challenge to the goal of nuclear disarmament[26]. The activity that has been observed in the market for nuclear materials allows us to speculate that extremist groups, rogue states, or desperate individuals might be engaged in manufacturing weapons of mass destruction, which makes the question of the physical protection of nuclear materials a top priority. The topic of nuclear disarmament is thus invariably linked to the existence of a well-organised system of regulations and control of the

---

[21] *Ibid.*, p.38.

[22] Interview by the author with an official from the CUAEPP on 17 September, 1996.

[23] *Ibid.*

[24] *Ibid.*

[25] **PPNN Newsbrief**, No.36, 4th Quarter 1996, p.14; **24 Chasa**, December 15, 1996, p.1; Bulgarian National Radio, transmission on December 15, 1996.

[26] Graham ALLISON, T. OWN, R. COTÉ, Jr., Richard A. FALKENRATH, & Steven E. MILLER, **Avoiding Nuclear Anarchy: Containing the Threat of Loose Russian Nuclear Weapons and Fissile Material**, MIT Press, Cambridge, MA, 1996.

sectors related to civilian uses of nuclear energy. The development and efficiency of such a system are in turn linked to the level of political culture in each country, and to the ability of its decision makers to structure policies with a long-term vision of global security as a cooperative enterprise with shared responsibilities.

7. What Can Be Improved?

On the basis of the preceding discussion, we can conclude that in Bulgaria the topic of nuclear disarmament is primarily a function of the country's internal power struggles and of the political actors' perceptions of NATO enlargement. The low priority of the issue in a political context where it should at least be present (as part of the NATO membership debate) can only be explained by policy makers' superficial knowledge of the subject and by a corresponding hierarchy of values on the part of the majority of the electorate. As already mentioned, topical debates tend to be framed within petty and partisan power struggles. However, it also needs to be emphasised that the foreign policy aspects of these debates are to a large extent a reflection of the prevalent international priorities. It is therefore plausible to assume that a more vigorous campaign for nuclear disarmament abroad would have an impact on Bulgarian domestic political realities. Nuclear disarmament needs to be more actively pursued and presented in a normative light both by the West and by Russia in order to remove the partisan tint of the issue in Bulgaria. In that respect, placing the issue on the active agendas of (particularly European) fora of discussion and policy-making, such as EU membership negotiations, bilateral exchanges, etc. would have an amplified effect in Bulgaria which might reactivate the campaign for the creation of a NWFZ in the Balkans. The involvement of France, Britain, and China in similar initiatives, as well as their commitment to nuclear disarmament through concrete steps, would contribute to a revival of the topic in Bulgaria.

Particularly important is Bulgaria's participation in the Partnership for Peace (PfP), now the Euro-Atlantic Partnership Council (EAPC) initiative, which Bulgaria joined in February 1994. Since 1991 Bulgaria has also been a member of the North Atlantic Cooperation Council (NACC), which provides another important forum for discussion.

Finally, the recently-launched campaign for NATO membership in itself provides an excellent opportunity to accord renewed importance to the issue of nuclear disarmament. It would be helpful to use these initiatives to clarify NATO's position on the new members' responsibilities in a manner less ambiguous than the one found in the 1995 "Study". This would certainly help to place the question of nuclear disarmament on the Bulgarian political agenda.

In conclusion, it should be noted that even though Bulgaria's contribution to the current discussions of the topic of nuclear disarmament on a global level is low, it has the potential to become more influential. Despite the controversies surrounding NATO membership, few policy-makers interviewed for the chapter expressed any belief in the necessity to maintain existing nuclear arsenals *per se*, and none were in favour of stationing nuclear weapons on Bulgarian territory. Thus it is not unrealistic to assume that, circumstances permitting, Bulgaria would support the creation of a Balkan NWFZ and get actively involved in the campaign for nuclear disarmament. A more vigorous international campaign in favour of nuclear disarmament, coupled with real progress in nuclear arms reduction, would provide a context in which Bulgaria could contribute substantively to both regional and world peace and security. It should to be noted, however, that due to the present severe economic situation, which imposes more immediate priorities on the domestic agenda, the issue of nuclear disarmament is unlikely to acquire a significantly higher profile in Bulgarian political life by itself.

SWEDEN[1]

Lars van Dassen[2]

1. Threats and Security in a New Environment

For more than 150 years, Sweden has cherished the principle of neutrality; but as post-Cold War Europe becomes more tightly institutionalized, and co-operative links across the old East-West divide become ever denser, the realization is dawning that neutrality is perhaps an increasingly irrelevant relic. Neutrality dictates that there be

---

[1] This study is based to a large extent on interviews with officials from the Ministry of Foreign Affairs and with leading politicians. The interviews with officials were intended to show how Sweden views the possibilities of nuclear disarmament and how it works to accomplish them in international forums. The interviews with leading politicians aimed to convey the extent of the political debate on nuclear disarmament. Those interviewed were: Ms Maria Leissner, leader of the Folkpartiet or Liberal Party at the time of the interviews; Ms Viola Furubjelke, social-democrat chairperson of the parliamentary Standing Committee on Foreign Affairs; Ms Ewa Zetterberg, the Vänsterpartiet or Left Party member on the same committee; and Ms Helena Nilsson, representing the Centerpartiet or Centre Party on the committee. These parties may be regarded as covering most of the positions in the Swedish debate on security. The Social Democratic Party is the party of government, and is closely supported by the Centre Party. The Liberal Party and Left Party respectively represent the right and left wing of the opposition. For the interviews with politicians, general formulations were used to render terms like "cut-off treaty" or "no-first-use" understandable, and interviewees were asked to what extent these issues had been discussed at committee, parliamentary, and party levels. Where specific topics were new or not immediately recognizable, the interviewees were asked to give intuitive responses.

[2] The author is a Ph.D. student at the Department of Peace and Conflict Research, Uppsala University. His special field is the evolution of nuclear non-proliferation cultures in the Nordic countries. His research is financed and supported by the Swedish Nuclear Power Inspectorate.

something to be neutral about or between; something from which one can distance oneself. And yet, although many now question it[3], there are no immediate indications that Sweden will revise its neutral stance, or join NATO, or seek full membership of the WEU.

Sweden has moved much closer both to NATO and to Russia. The latter clearly does not constitute the same threat as the Soviet Union did before 1989, but the situation there still causes concern: the democratic system is not yet on a firm footing, and civil society and democratic cultures are still in the making. The explicit and implicit threats that Russia occasionally directs at the Baltic states, and the remarks it makes about the unresolved status of the Kaliningrad area, are sources of general concern to Sweden[4]; but the main group that continues to perceive Russia as a real or would-be threat is the military[5]. The prevailing attitude outside the military seems to be that the greatest risk is that of a disintegration or implosion of the Russian Federation. If the worst came to the worst, this could have grave consequences for neighbouring states, but it is not likely that it would lead to hostilities between Russia and Sweden.

The perception that threats have diminished, or at least changed, has led to dramatic reductions in defence spending. Although Sweden was one of only a few countries to increase their defence budgets after the end of the Cold War, the increase was used to introduce new weapons-systems, whilst manpower was reduced by a quarter. The 1995 defence budget, totalling 40 billion Swedish Crowns (5 billion ECUs), will be cut by 10 percent in the next defence plan, covering the period 1997-2001[6]. In contrast to the view within the military, in political circles there is a broad consensus that security is different from military protection, and involves more than that which can be provided by military means alone. Hence the emphasis on a form of Baltic co-operation that includes Russia. Sweden attaches great importance to the Baltic Sea Co-operation project, which so far

---

[3] Kaa ENEBERG, *"Enighet om alliansfrihet"*, in: **Dagens Nyheter**, 13 Aug. 1996.

[4] Kaa ENEBERG, *"Utvecklingen i Ryssland oroar"*, ibid.

[5] Mikael HOLMSTRÖM, *"Rysslands arme'kan snabbt restaureras: ÖB varnar för ett försvagat svenskt försvar"*, in: **Svenska Dagbladet**, 22 Sept. 1996.

[6] Sune OLOFSSON, *"Regeringen krympler krigsorganisationen"*; Mikael HOLMSTRÖM, *"ÖB avfyrar tung kritik mot regeringens budgetförslag"*, ibid., 20 Sept. 1996.

has not addressed any security issues; but it is also involved in the Barents Regional Co-operation scheme, which fosters co-operation between the Finnish, Swedish, Norwegian, and Russian provinces of Arctic Europe. It is widely recognized that a lot more will have to be done to ensure stability and development in and among the states in the Baltic region. The steps taken so far are only a beginning. Sweden has launched a modest initiative in the form of a scheme for bilateral co-operation with Russia on disarmament. A pilot study has been under way since 1994 to assess the risks associated with the storage and destruction of chemical weapons. The second phase of the study will cover the safety-related technologies and environmental risks attendant on the dismantling of chemical weapons, and also the fixing of standards for communication with the local communities living near the dismantling and storage facilities.

Swedish attitudes to security arrangements are inclined to shift rapidly at the present time. This is seen most clearly in the response to the Estonian, Lithuanian, and Latvian aspirations to join NATO. At first Sweden opposed the idea; Prime Minister Göran then said that Sweden would not try to influence other states' security choices; most recently, Sweden has begun to support the Baltic endeavours. This does not imply that Sweden itself has an unequivocal or immediate desire to join NATO: the conservative and liberal parties tend to see NATO as an option to be taken up if and when it evolves into a collective European security system that either has very strong ties with or includes Russia. The other parties cling to the traditional perceptions of neutrality, though that neutrality is not seen as being threatened by deeper involvement in peacekeeping operations – for instance, with NATO – or in the Partnership for Peace. The neutrality/NATO issue has a not insignificant bearing on the approach to nuclear disarmament: there is a broad consensus among the political parties on almost every aspect of this issue; what differs is the perception as to whether that disarmament is best achieved in a world where Sweden is neutral or in one where it is integrated into Western defence structures like NATO and the WEU.

2. Nuclear Weapons and Swedish Security

In 1968, after many years of indecision, Sweden opted to forgo nuclear weapons. Despite this, the role of such weapons in national security is of greater significance than one might suppose. From the 1960s, Sweden was covered by the US nuclear umbrella to a far greater extent than Swedish politicians knew or cared to know.

The question of national security is therefore a tricky one for politicians, but it is recognized that Sweden is still tacitly covered by NATO's nuclear umbrella[7]. There is also a realization that this results not so much from any agreement between Sweden and the US/NATO, but from the fact that Sweden is geostrategically so important to the defence of NATO's northern flank that it too has to be defended. That said, it is also generally recognized that the implicit security guarantee that this constitutes for Sweden is of little relevance now that the East-West conflict is over. The dangers stemming from other nuclear hazards (the decline in Russia's ability to control nuclear weapons, illegal dealing in nuclear materials) cause much more concern that the "classical" nuclear threats. Nevertheless, the question of the nature and extent of the coverage Sweden enjoys under the nuclear umbrella is an extremely interesting one. To begin with, it has proved an issue susceptible to exploitation – as in the Swedish parliamentary debate on the 1997-2001 defence budget. The Liberal Party maintained that the reductions in defence spending could only be viewed as responsible if Sweden's defence was part of a larger alliance, and the country thus enjoyed a guarantee of assistance. If, on the other hand, the government wished seriously to pursue neutrality, this had to be underpinned by adequate military forces[8]. Secondly, the tacit nuclear umbrella could be said to have implications for Sweden's general non-proliferation policies. For several decades, the country has worked to secure an international agreement on negative security guarantees, at the same time rejecting the idea that this need be coupled with an agreement on positive security guarantees – something that is seen as difficult, if not impossible, to square with

---

[7] Commission on Neutrality Policy, *Had There Been a War: Preparations for the Reception of Military Assistance 1949-1969*, SOU 1994, 11 Stockholm, 1994.

[8] *"Nya Kundskper"*, in: **Svenska Dagbladet**, 14 Oct. 1996.

neutrality[9]. Positive security guarantees are not as important an issue on the non-proliferation agenda as negative ones. But as long as Sweden remains implicitly or tacitly under a nuclear umbrella, this at least restricts the degree to which it can insist on excluding an agreement on positive security guarantees on the grounds that it cannot coexist with neutrality.

3. The Debate on Nuclear Disarmament

The debate on nuclear disarmament does not rouse the same emotions or mobilize the same crowds as it did from the 1960s till the 1980s. Within the political system, disarmament issues are mainly treated at the level of parliamentary committees and of parliament itself; they are much less discussed within the individual political parties. As has been mentioned, there are few differences here that could stand in the way of the formulation of generally accepted disarmament proposals. This is also the case with peace groups. These are very numerous and differ mainly in their emphases: the group Lawyers against Nuclear Weapons stresses the importance of Sweden's supporting the case brought before the International Court of Justice by the WHO, in which the latter sought to prove the illegality of nuclear weapons. Physicians against Nuclear Weapons, on the other hand, stresses the health hazards involved in the production, testing, and use of such weapons. There may be differences over how issues should be prioritized, but as the peace groups are well organized and are joined in an umbrella-organization, this hardly stands in the way of the formulation of broadly accepted policies.

If there is little party-political involvement or interest in nuclear disarmament, this is at least partly compensated for by the way in which both the government and the Standing Committee on Foreign Affairs are willing to draw on the expertise and suggestions of peace groups.

---

[9] The official reason for rejecting positive security guarantees is that reliance on foreign assistance conflicts with neutrality. But this is not such a great problem, because if there were a case of threatened or actual use of nuclear weapons against Sweden, neutrality would have failed, and there would then be no obligation to be neutral any more. The real problem is that neutrality is circumvented by Sweden's being covered by a US nuclear umbrella.

The proposals made by the Canberra Commission on the Elimination of Nuclear Weapons had considerable repercussions on the Swedish debate on nuclear weapons. The information issued by peace groups makes extensive and frequent references to the commission's work; and the report which the commission published with the Australian government in August 1996 appeared as the official reference-work on disarmament in the Swedish government statement made at the opening of parliament in October 1996. The aims and suggestions set out in it are frequently cited by the Foreign Minister; and Prime Minister Göran Persson has stated that the commission's proposals chime with, and give substance to, Sweden's own overall goal of general nuclear disarmament[10]. In October 1996, members of parliament from six parties, constituting a vast majority in parliament, recommended that the government support the proposals of the Canberra Commission in the UN General Assembly and at the CD[11].

4. Attitudes to Nuclear Disarmament Issues

The *Comprehensive Test Ban Treaty* has been a high-priority issue for Sweden for several decades. Before negotiations started at the CD in 1994, Sweden canvassed the issue repeatedly, and, in the absence of a negotiating mandate, was very active in the Group of Scientific Experts, which was investigating CTBT verification methods and criteria.

In summer 1993, a moratorium on testing was declared by all nuclear-weapon states except China[12]. Sweden viewed this as an opportunity to launch a test-ban initiative and it therefore submitted a draft treaty to this effect at the CD. A few months later, a negotiating mandate was given to the CD, and Sweden submitted a revised draft.

---

[10] Thomas GÜR, *"Australisk kärnvapenutopi: Perssons melodi"*, in: **Svenska Dagbladet**, 20 Aug. 1996.

[11] Flerpartimotion: Motion till riksdagen av Ewa Zetterberg m. fl. (v): Avskaffande av kärnvapen 1996/97:v614, 7 Oct. 1996.

[12] Britain did not officially declare a moratorium, but the lack of access to US testing facilities constituted a *de facto* British moratorium. However, Britain's non-declaration did make a considerable difference in another respect, since it meant that China could not be isolated or put under pressure as the only NWS carrying out test.

Sweden held the chair of the verification committee in 1994, and the diplomatic activities surrounding the negotiation of the treaty has had repercussions at party and parliamentary levels. In both these circles, there is great satisfaction that the treaty has finally been opened for signature. At the CTBT negotiations, there was a long period during which, on the question of the treaty's scope, Sweden and Germany occupied the maximalist position, proposing that the preparation of nuclear tests should also be banned. This position was abandoned in February 1996, because there was little general support for it and because it was realized that other issues must be dealt with if the time-table of the negotiations was to be met[13].

The historical roots of the proposal for a *cut-off treaty* are as long as those of the CTBT: such a scheme was referred to by the Swedish minister for foreign affairs Torsten Nilsson as early as 1965, in an address to the UN General Assembly. At present, however, the Swed-ish view of what can be achieved in the near future is a modest one. There is a general perception that the CD has reached an impasse after a period of great effort, and that this will also affect the cut-off treaty. It may well be that a decision has been made to start negotiations on a treaty; but without a specific negotiating mandate, the impasse may last for a couple of years. None the less, Sweden is preparing itself for the negotiations by drawing up estimates of the respective verifi-cation costs for a treaty covering only future stocks of military-use fissile material, and for one covering existing stocks as well. Swe-den's position so far is that all existing stocks of military-use fissile materials, not just future production, must be covered[14]. Priority is given to getting the cut-off negotiations started, since the negotiating process itself may open up new opportunities. But it is hoped that any agreement reached will at least partly cover existing stocks of nuclear-weapon material. The cut-off treaty was discussed in the Stand-ing Committee on Foreign Affairs, but not subjected to detailed scru-tiny. At present, it is believed that there are currently too many tech-nical elements to be cleared up and that the negotiations must simply

---

[13] Rebecca JOHNSON, *"A Summary of CTBT Negotiations"*, in: **Disarmament Diplo-macy**, Jan 1996, p.10; ead., *"Geneva Update"*, *ibid.*, June 1996, pp.17-19; ead., *ACRONYM No.9: Comprehensive Test Ban Treaty: The Endgame*, p.12.

[14] Statement of the minister for foreign affairs Mrs Lena Hjelm-Wallén to the Conference on Disarmament, Geneva, 11 Mar. 1997.

be got under way. One detail which it has already been decided would be premature to discuss is the entry into force of a cut-off treaty. As far as verification is concerned, there is a general preference for relying on the IAEA's competencies.

One issue that Sweden has been laying stress on for decades is the need for reliable **negative security guarantees** that go beyond the existing declarations made by the nuclear-weapon states. The prevailing attitude is that states that have forsworn nuclear weapons should be guaranteed protection against the use or threatened use of them, and that this can only be achieved through an international treaty or agreement[15]. This issue is constantly being brought up by Sweden in various arenas, though no concrete proposals have been made in disarmament forums. During the PrepCom meeting in April 1997, South Africa suggested that negotiations be opened on a legally binding treaty on negative security guarantees. Sweden fully supports this proposal, though there is so far no clear indication as to whether negotiations can proceed as part of the PrepCom process or must be conducted in a different forum. Sweden considers that the ruling of the International Court of Justice on the use or threatened use of nuclear weapons is an important moral first step in opening up a thoroughgoing discussion on the subject[16].

It would seem futile for Sweden, whilst outside NATO, to attempt to shift NATO's nuclear strategy towards *no-first-use*. However, this is no bar to the Standing Committee on Foreign Affairs discussing the matter – and they have done so. Similarly, an international no-first-use agreement, treaty, or convention forms part of the government's disarmament agenda, because it is close, in spirit and content, to the Swedish ideas on improving negative security guarantees.

---

[15] Interpellation No.1994/95:123. Svar på interpellation av Ewa Zetterberg (v) om Sveriges agerande i frågan om kärnvapennedrustningen, måndagen d. 15 maj 1995; Minister for Foreign Affairs Mrs Lena Hjelm-Wallén, address at the Olof Palme International Centre, Stockholm, 5 Feb. 1996.

[16] This aspect was discussed by the Standing Committee on Foreign Affairs when the Swedish government was asked to give its opinion on whether the International Court of Justice was competent to deal with the case brought before it by the WHO. The committee told the Swedish government that it should make it clear that the use of nuclear weapons could never have any positive relation to international law: Utrikesutskottets betänkande 1994/95:UU6 Svenska åtgärder på nedrustningsområdet.

Nuclear disarmament in accordance with Article VI of the NPT is considered a most important objective by the Swedish government, and, in this connection, the USA and Russia have been encouraged to start negotiating a *START III Treaty*, and also to **bring the three other nuclear-weapon states into nuclear disarmament agreements**. As regards the Principles and Objectives of the NPT Review and Extension Conference: this course was urged before the CD[17] and in bilateral contacts. French and British disarmament obligations were brought up by Swedish MEPs in the European Parliament, and by the Standing Committee on Foreign Affairs when it presented its views to the EP's Subcommittee on Security and Disarmament. The field of tactical nuclear weapons is emerging as one in which progress on disarmament is needed. The issue was brought to parliament's attention in 1993-4[18]. During a CD session in spring 1996, the minister for foreign affairs, Lena Hjelm-Wallén, suggested that the USA and Russia codify their unilateral declarations and that steps be taken both to remove nuclear weapons from naval vessels and to downsize other tactical nuclear arsenals in service, these measures being embodied in a detailed, legally binding agreement.

The prospects of producing a **nuclear weapons register** are regarded as rather dim. This idea was considered by the foreign ministry and by the Standing Committee on Foreign Affairs[19], but the general view is that it would be unacceptable to the NWS at the present stage. Once a general no-first-use rule has been accepted, it may become conceivable for the NWS to allow scrutiny of the size and location of their nuclear weapons. The same applies to **restricting the qualitative improvement of nuclear weapons**. This matter has received some attention in the Standing Committee on Foreign Affairs, and it has been pointed out that the dangers of continued research stem from the fact that the nuclear taboo can be broken more easily if smaller and more precise nuclear weapons more closely resemble conventional ones. Desirable as it would be for international efforts to be directed against this kind of nuclear weapons research, it is believed that the complicated and sensitive verification measures would prevent such a restriction from becoming a feasible disarmament step.

---

[17] Most recently when the foreign minister addressed the CD on 11 Mar. 1997.

[18] Utrikesutskottets betänkande 1993/94:UU 19, pp.3, 18.

[19] *Ibid.*, pp.3, 17.

The only nuclear disarmament issue that presents Sweden with domestic problems is the **transfer of fissile materials from weapons to civilian purposes**. This touches a major political nerve, since Sweden has in principle decided to phase out its nuclear industry before 2010. It is doubtful whether such a step would be sound or feasible, but so far most politicians remain committed to this deadline.

This means that, as things stand, Sweden could not be counted on if an international agreement were to fix how existing producers of nuclear power should consume the fissile material resulting from the disarmament process. On the other hand, using such material is not a problem for Sweden if there is no resultant obligation to continue to use nuclear energy after 2010. According to the Swedish press, Swedish reactors may very soon start using fuel from dismantled Russian warheads[20]. However, no such fuel has yet arrived or been purchased by Swedish nuclear facilities. The uranium in question originates from the US-Russian agreement to convert military HEU into low-enriched fuel for civilian purposes. Use of it would not be problematic for Sweden, since the uranium would only enter the country after having been turned into LEU. Production of MOX fuel is not involved, and so no new government policy or authorization of possible uses of former Russian EU is called for.

The promotion of nuclear energy is a sensitive issue not only on the domestic front, but also in relation to other states. It is supposedly only because of the problems it would cause the Swedish director-general of the IAEA, Hans Blix, that parliament has not demanded that Sweden's financial contribution to the agency not be used for the promotion of nuclear energy. But the underlying attitude has manifested itself within the framework of the EU Joint Action on KEDO: Sweden was able to support this action because the funding came from the EU and not from the member states.

Proposals to **extend IAEA safeguards** to the civil nuclear industries of NWS are regarded at the political level as an important step towards limiting the scope for transfer to the military sector. Extension

---

[20] Johan SELANDER, *"Ryskt vapenuran omvandlas för civil reaktordrift"*, in: **Svenska Dagbladet**, 17 Sept. 1996.

may also increase the physical protection and nuclear safety which seem to be a by-product of safeguards. However, at the Ministry of Foreign Affairs, this issue is not pushed too hard, as this would draw attention to the existing battles over the budget for IAEA safeguards. The benefits that would accrue from safeguards in NWS might easily be thwarted by the reluctance to fund the agency's budget adequately. Though the argument about safety and physical security is important, the perception is that the flow of fissile material proceeds from the military to the civilian sectors, and not the other way round. According to the Ministry of Foreign Affairs, that makes the matter less urgent. However, one could also maintain that this state of affairs further increases the necessity to control the civilian sector, since safety and physical protection is generally less comprehensive here than in the military sectors.

For many years, Sweden and Finland were eager to establish a *NWFZ* in the Nordic countries. Agreement was never reached because of Danish and Norwegian reluctance to join unless the Kola Peninsula was included in the zone. Until recently, the Nordic Council had a task-group working on this issue. Though in principle the prospects for a Nordic NWFZ are better than ever, the need for it has disappeared. It is therefore not high on anyone's agenda except that of the Nordic peace movements, which continue to work for it and seek to influence parliamentarians and the Nordic Council.

On the other hand, the general idea of NWFZ enjoys considerable support as a means of reducing the significance of nuclear weapons. Jan Prawitz of the National Defence Research Establishment has mooted the idea of a NWFZ from the Baltic to the Black Sea as a bargaining chip that would make NATO expansion palatable to Russia. These ideas have met with a favourable response from the Swedish government, though it is not likely that Sweden will exert any pressure on Eastern and Central European states to accept such a scheme.

The Chemical Weapons Convention represents the first successful attempt to ban a whole category of weapons of mass destruction under international supervision. In Sweden, it has not elicited any corresponding initiative for a **convention on nuclear weapons**: such a scheme is regarded as too utopian at present. On the other hand, the fact that the International Court of Justice has restricted the legal uses of nuclear weapons to situations where the survival of a state is in question is seen as a crucial step in the process of using international law to reduce the preponderance of nuclear weapons in international relations. It is felt that further steps should be considered in this area. Moreover, during the NPT Review and Extension Conference, Sweden proposed that the parties agree to work out a scheme for complete nuclear disarmament within the next ten to fifteen years. No further developments have taken place in this area, except that relevant formulations are careful to stress that the ultimate objective is to agree a scheme for complete nuclear disarmament within ten to fifteen years – rather than that this could or should be achieved within the period mentioned[21].

5. A Need for Deterrence?

Whether Iraq was actually deterred from using weapons of mass destruction during the Gulf War is likely to be a matter of discussion for some time to come; but there is no doubt that deterrence is alive and well – albeit in new guises such as counterproliferation.

As has been mentioned already, Sweden continues to be covered by a US nuclear umbrella because the understanding that grew up about this during the 1960s has persisted unchanged. However, when the relevance of, or need for, continued deterrence is discussed with leading politicians, it becomes obvious that this concept is not viewed positively overall, and no reference is made to the specific coverage of Sweden by a deterrent. Deterrence as a means of defending Sweden is not something that is thought of very explicitly. When asked about the possibility, respondents in all cases referred to rogue states like Saddam Hussein's Iraq, and only the Liberal Party saw a need to retain some form of deterrence in extreme situations such as this; the use or threatened use of the deterrent would then be under international control – for instance, that of the UN Security Council.

---

[21] See e.g. Mrs Lena HJELM-WALLÉN, address at the Olof Palme International Centre, Stockholm, 5 Feb. 1996.

6. Conclusions

In Sweden, disarmament and non-proliferation issues do not occupy the place they did during the Cold War. when they were constantly at the top of the political agenda. From the 1960s to the 1980s, Sweden had a disarmament minister, a deputy disarmament minister, and an ambassador for disarmament; today there is no high-ranking government post in this field.

Much of the old creativeness remains, however: Sweden has used its neutrality to promote various disarmament and non-proliferation proposals, and these activities continue, although Sweden's position now has to be aligned with that of its EU partners in the CFSP process. With the clear exception of the Left Party, and to a lesser extent of the Social Democratic Party, the political parties do not treat disarmament and non-proliferation as high priorities. This reflects the dissipation of East-West tension, and the fact that the nuclear arms race is now thought of as much less of a threat to Sweden's security. Besides this, the focus has shifted to more general security issues, such as co-operation with NATO and the creation of regional structures for the promotion of non-military security.

At parliamentary and committee level, there is still active debate about disarmament issues, with very detailed and thorough assessments of various aspects of disarmament and non-proliferation. Because the political parties play less prominent roles in the formulation of disarmament policies, peace groups have remained active players, exchanging views with, and seeking to influence, the Standing Committee on Foreign Policy and the various public bodies. In spite of the decreased interest in disarmament and non-proliferation, the openness that exists between government bodies, peace groups, and parliamentary committees has helped Sweden retain its high international standing on these issues.

NORWAY

Rolf TAMNES & Astrid FORLAND

1. Introduction

The most original aspect of Norway's nuclear policy has been the country's refusal to accept the deployment of nuclear weapons on Norwegian territory in peacetime, while at the same time remaining an integral partner in NATO. This chapter begins by showing how this policy evolved from the 1950s onwards. It then traces the Norwegian debate about the establishment of a Nordic nuclear weapon free zone, or alternatively a nuclear weapon free zone in Central Europe. Both of these aspects of Norwegian foreign policy have gained a new relevance in post-Cold War Europe.

The chapter goes on to outline Norway's attitude towards the arms control issues which are currently under discussion in various fora. The main focus will be on nuclear issues, but issues related to conventional disarmament, which are perhaps of particular interest to a non-nuclear power, are also touched upon. Furthermore, the chapter will also provide an outline of the Norwegian debate about the expansion of NATO, the only security policy issue which is giving rise to a public debate in Norway at present. However, there are indications that disarmament policy is also turning into a contentious issue. These budding debates suggest the uncertainty felt regarding the future of Europe. In this connection it is also relevant to deal with Norwegian-Russian relations in the post-Cold War situation, and especially to say something about Norwegian threat perceptions in a world in flux.

2. Homespun Nuclear Policy

The NATO Enlargement Study which was published in September 1995 made it clear that new members must accept the full obligations of the Washington Treaty, particularly the military obligations under Article 5. The study emphasised that the French and Spanish options of refusing to join NATO's military command structure were not open to aspirant members. It also specifically stressed that the deployment of nuclear weapons should not be foreclosed as an option. On the other hand, NATO has confirmed that the Alliance has no plans for such a deployment. It seems highly unlikely, therefore, that nuclear weapons will be stationed on the territory of new members.

Against this background, Norway's policy may serve as a possible model for new Alliance members.

During the Cold War, Norwegian security policy was torn between the conflicting approaches of deterrence and reassurance of the Soviet Union, and integration and independence with the Western powers. The most visible expression of this compromise was Norway's bases policy, which banned the peacetime stationing of Allied forces in the country. Secondly, Allied forces were not normally allowed to operate in the north-eastern part of the country in peacetime. Thirdly, the Norwegian authorities came out against the deployment of nuclear weapons in Norway.

Norway's nuclear policy was hammered out in 1957, at a time when NATO strategy was based on the concept of massive retaliation. The Government rejected any suggestion of deploying nuclear weapons on Norwegian soil in peacetime. The major reasons for this were a widespread popular fear of a nuclear Armageddon, and the belief that deployment of such weapons might lead to a worsening of the Cold War climate. Additionally, the US Atomic Energy Act of 1954 required that custody of nuclear charges remained in the hands of the Americans, and the presence of US base security units would have run contrary to Norway's bases policy.

The negative Norwegian attitude to nuclear weapons was reaffirmed as official policy in 1960-61. Norway was now moving directly towards a purely conventional defence. The only option left was that

le disarmament, including some concerned specifically with
ar disarmament *(Nei til atomvåpen, Leger mot atomvåpen)*. In
ion there is a forceful environmental organisation, **Bellona**,
h has been particularly active with regard to the nuclear waste
afety problems in north-western Russia.

til recently, it had also seemed that attitudes to nuclear disar-
ent were fairly uniform among the political parties, at least among
rger political parties which have any prospect of ruling the coun-
should be added that there is a strong tradition in Norway for
cal parties to display a "common front" in matters of importance
ional security. Lately, however, there have been indications that
nsensus is breaking down. A new divide is discernible both over
sue of nuclear disarmament and over NATO's eastward expan-
The differences of opinion seem at least partly to reflect diver-
hreat perceptions (see below). As a small power, Norway's influ-
n the international community is, of course, limited. Nevertheless,
ay has traditionally put great weight on contributing, as far as
le, to efforts in international fora to enhance the process of
hament in the world. In 1996, Norway became a member of the
rence on Disarmament (CD) in Geneva. It will be interesting
whether this will lead to more public debate regarding the
ns taken by Norway in Geneva.

Nuclear Weapons Convention?

re are indications that Norway has been following a
y more radical policy with regard to nuclear disarmament since
rn Jagland succeeded Gro Harlem Brundtland as Prime Minis-
he autumn of 1996. The shift in emphasis first became apparent
ection with the Malaysian resolution on the abolition of nuclear
ns at the United Nations in November 1996. Whereas NATO
es generally voted against this resolution, Norway (and Den-
bstained from the vote. Norway supported the resolution's pro-
or the complete abolition of nuclear weapons. The reason for
y's abstention was the fact that the Government disagreed with
plution's suggestion that this goal should be achieved through
teral disarmament negotiations conducted under the aegis of the

nuclear weapons could be brought into the country along with Allied reinforcements[1].

Later, the Norwegian authorities were at times anxious to play down the nuclear aspects of the Alliance. The most visible expressions of this were Norway's policy towards visiting warships carrying nuclear weapons; the idea of nuclear weapon free zones; and the attitude to NATO's plan for the deployment of Intermediate-range Nuclear Forces (INF).

In October 1975 the then Prime Minister, Trygve Bratteli, stated that "our assumption when foreign warships make port visits has been and is still that nuclear weapons are not carried on board." He expected that the Alliance would recognise this stance. The declaration was vague enough not to give rise to serious misgivings in Washington, as it took into consideration the fact that the nuclear powers would neither confirm nor deny (NCND) that their vessels carried nuclear weapons[2].

The question became much more controversial in the 1980s, when countries such as New Zealand and Denmark challenged the American NCND policy. The Labour Government in Norway was tempted to follow suit, but preferred in the end to stick to the 1975 doctrine, both because of the harsh US reaction to New Zealand's challenge and because of warnings that a similar Norwegian move might create huge problems for the NATO fleet on exercises in the north, and, at worst, endanger US commitments to Norway.

3. The Idea of Nuclear Weapon Free Zones

The idea of a Nordic nuclear weapon free zone was first put forward by the Soviet Union in the late 1950s, and was later promoted

---

[1] Background: Rolf TAMNES, *"Integration and Screening. The Two Faces of Norwegian Alliance Policy, 1945-1986"*, in: **Forsvarsstudier**, Oslo, 1987; Rolf TAMNES, *"Handlefrihet og lojalitet, Norge og atompolitikken i 1950-årene"*, in: T. BERG & H.Ø. PHARO (eds), **Historiker og veileder. Festskrift til Johan Sverdrup**, Oslo, Tiden, 1989; Rolf TAMNES, **The United States and the Cold War in the High North**, Oslo, ad Notam forlag, 1991.

[2] See Johan Jørgen HOLST, *"Atom- og basepolitikken i søkelyset"*, in: A.C. SJAASTAD (ed.), **Norsk Utenrikspolitisk Årbok**, Oslo, 1975.

most vigorously by the Finnish President, Urho Kekkonen. Norway rejected the idea for many years, both because such weapons were not stationed in Norway in peacetime and because the proposals did not imply any restrictions on Soviet nuclear capabilities. In 1980-81, however, the governing Labour Party endorsed the concept in principle, to the great irritation of the Americans. We can assess this as part of a long process which saw Norway becoming gradually more restrictive in nuclear matters. Initially the idea seemed to be a major departure from former positions, but as it was gradually tied to a series of conditions, implementation would necessarily be delayed. One of the reasons for this increasing Norwegian caution was the NATO and US reactions. Most notably, in July 1981 Secretary of State Alexander M. Haig rejected emphatically the idea of a Nordic zone, asserting that it might jeopardise the bilateral ties between the two countries[3].

Another aspect of the zone question was Norway's involvement in the discussion of nuclear weapon free zones in Central Europe. This involvement started with the Polish Rapacki Plan in 1957. At the NATO Heads of Government meeting in Paris in December 1957, Prime Minister Einar Gerhardsen signalled his willingness to discuss disengagement and nuclear weapon free zones in Central Europe in the spirit of the Rapacki Plan. The most challenging aspect of these proposals was that if pursued, they would have delayed the incorporation of atomic weapons into the German armed forces, much to the annoyance of the United States. Although the prospects of establishing such a zone were slim, the Polish plans provided for many years the basis of an interesting bilateral dialogue between Norway and Poland.

At the end of the 1970s the zone question reappeared in a new form, first in the split over neutron weapons and later in NATO's 1979 decision to deploy INF missiles. In the face of fierce popular resistance to this modernisation, the Norwegian Government emphasised the need for arms negotiations prior to deployment. In 1982 and 1983 the Labour Party, now in opposition, formulated an increasingly critical stand towards Western deployment, although, in contrast to the German Social Democrats, it never renounced the NATO decision of 1979.

---

[3] See John C. AUSLAND, **Nordic Security and the Great Powers**, Boulder/London, Westview Press, 1986.

United Nations. The Government did not think this a realistic proposition since it was known that the nuclear powers would not agree to it[5].

The public reaction to the vote revealed conflicting attitudes to the issue in Norway. The Centre Party (former Farmers' Party) and the Christian People's Party both supported Norwegian policy[6]. The two right-wing parties represented in the Storting or national assembly (Høgre and Framstegspartiet) were both critical of Norway's vote. The Conservative Party (Høgre) said it regretted Norway's breaking ranks with the general NATO stance[7]. On the other hand, nongovernmental organisations and individuals expressed disappointment that Norway did not support the resolution as a whole. Norway's vote followed in the wake of a unanimous resolution at the Labour Party's convention supporting the abolition of nuclear weapons. This fact made the powerful Workers' Union (Landsorganisasjonen) especially regretful with regard to Norway's abstention[8]. A professor of law at the University of Oslo, Dr. Ståle Eskeland, has also been an active participant in this discussion. Eskeland's initial intervention in the debate occurred when, in October 1996, he interpreted an advice pronounced by the International Court of Justice in The Hague as stating that the threat to use nuclear weapons, as well as their actual use, were breaches of international law[9]. The Malaysian resolution represented a follow-up on this advice[10], and Eskeland has underlined the importance of starting international negotiations with a view to outlawing nuclear weapons[11].

---

[5] *"Norge enig i målet – uenig i fremgangsmåten"*, in: **NTB-tekst**, Oslo, Document No.96-048092, 14 November 1996.

[6] *"Ros og ris for Norges stemmeavgivning i FN"*, in: **NTB-tekst**, Oslo, Document No.96-048107, 14 November 1996.

[7] *Ibid.*

[8] *"LO: Skuffet over at Norge ikke stemte for resolusjonen i FN"*, in: **NTB-tekst**, Oslo, Document No.96-048100, 14 November 1996.

[9] Eskeland's interpretation of the verdict has met with criticism, however. A former Norwegian official with the NATO Secretariat has pointed out that the Hague Court of Justice had made an exemption for the use of nuclear weapons in extreme situations, see *"Atomvåpen og folkerett: Vanskelig grenseskille jus-politikk"*, in: **NTB-tekst**, Oslo, Document No.97-005702, 10 February 1997.

[10] *"Norge avsto i FNs atomavstemning"*, in: **NTB-tekst**, Oslo, Document No.96-048068, 14 November 1996.

[11] *"Norge enig i målet – uenig i fremgangsmåten"*, in: **NTB-tekst**, Oslo, Document No.96-048092, 14 November 1996.

Norway's readiness to support in principle a treaty prohibiting nuclear weapons did not come as a total surprise. Already in his Statement to the Storting in 1996, Foreign Minister Bjørn Tore Godal declared that in the Government's view "we must now continue our efforts to achieve a world without nuclear weapons.[12]" He went on to underscore the special responsibility of the nuclear powers for the attainment of this goal. He also said that Russia and the United States should take the lead and draw other nuclear powers into the process of strategic disarmament. Since then he has signalled Norwegian support for future negotiations on strategic reductions that will go beyond START II and which should involve all nuclear powers[13]. He has furthermore advocated accelerating the pace of reductions in tactical weapons, underlining that such reductions should be carried out on an equitable and mutually binding basis[14]. The Government has also expressed concern about the potential consequences of advances in weapons technology, and especially about the prospects of biological warfare, and it has emphasised the importance of intensifying arms control efforts in order to keep pace with such advances[15]. Finally, in January 1997, Godal stated that the pace of disarmament should be increased. He deplored the amount of money spent on armaments, and said that it should be put to constructive ends instead[16]. Nevertheless, the Government has also maintained that disarmament can only be achieved through a step-by-step process[17]. The START agreements, the indefinite extension of the NPT, the Chemical Weapons Convention, and the CTBT are considered to be decisive steps in the right direction, and the Government emphasises the importance of effective implementation of these agreements[18].

---

[12] Statement to the Storting on Foreign Policy, 30 January 1996.

[13] Speech at the Nobel Institute, Oslo, 23 March 1996.

[14] Statement to the Storting on Foreign Policy, 30 January 1996.

[15] *Ibid.*

[16] *"Godal vil ruste ned"*, in: **NTB-tekst**, Oslo, Document No.97-000086, 2 January 1997.

[17] Statement by State Secretary Siri Bjerke to the Conference on Disarmament, 12 June 1996.

[18] Speech by Foreign Minister Bjørn Tore Godal at the meeting debating "Nuclear Disarmament", held at the Nobel Institute, Oslo, 23 March 1996.

6. Implementation and Follow-up

The Chemical Weapons Convention requires that all chemical weapons should be demolished within ten years. The implementation of this Convention will be expensive. The Norwegian Government is particularly concerned about the ability of Russia to carry the programme through. Russia probably has over 40,000 tons of chemical agents in its stockpile, and parts of this arsenal are stored in the Barents region. Norway has in principle agreed to participate in an international effort to help Russia dismantle its chemical weapons[19].

In respect to the Comprehensive Test Ban Treaty, which Norway incidentally co-sponsored when it was put to vote at the United Nations in September 1996, the Norwegian Government has emphasised the importance of effective verification. Norway's closeness to the Russian nuclear testing site at Novaya Zemlya means that Norway has long been concerned about nuclear testing, and has since the early 1960s been involved in seismic arrays. Today Norway possesses some of the most advanced seismic array stations in the world, and Norway will make its contribution to developing an international seismic monitoring system to ensure that the parties to the CTBT comply with the stipulations of the treaty. Norway has also for many years participated in the Group of Scientific Experts to further this aim. The Government furthermore considers it essential that the nuclear weapon states comply with a moratorium on nuclear testing during the interim period before the CTBT enters into force[20]. The Government has also expressed concern about the test site installations, and would like to see them demolished. It is satisfied that France has signalled willingness to demolish its test site installations on Mururoa. In the Norwegian view, other nuclear powers should do likewise with regard to their test sites. The Government considers such a step to be a logical follow-up to the CTBT itself. Norway raised this issue at the United Nations General Assembly in 1996[21]. In February 1997 the leader of

---

[19] Speech by the Foreign Minister to the Storting concerning nuclear safety issues ("Om atomsikkerhetsspørsmål"), 29 October 1996.

[20] *Ibid.*; Statement by State Secretary Siri Bjerke to the Conference on Disarmament, 13 June 1996.

[21] Speech by Foreign Minister Bjørn Tore Godal to the Storting concerning nuclear safety issues, 29 October 1996.

Nei til Atomvåpen, Ole Kopreitan, urged the Government to follow up this initiative by putting pressure on the United States in order to dissuade the Americans from conducting so-called subcritical nuclear tests in Nevada. Kopreitan expressed the fear that such testing might undermine the CTBT. Referring to the Norwegian initiative in the United Nations, he suggested that the Government should ask the US Government to abandon any plans for subcritical testing[22].

With regard to the Non-Proliferation Treaty, the Government has stated that it would like to see a process that would have substance and be balanced. For the process to be balanced, it must address the disarmament commitment inherent in the treaty. In order to meet this obligation in the years ahead, Norway considers it necessary for the nuclear powers to halt the qualitative upgrading of their nuclear arsenals and to accept comprehensive nuclear reductions[23].

As a follow-up to the CTBT and the ongoing dismantling of nuclear weapons in Europe, Norway sees the need to tackle the problem of fissile materials. The safe storage and handling of fissile material is considered to be a matter of urgency, and Norway supports a ban on further production of these materials for weapons purposes. Norway takes part actively in international co-operation efforts aimed at preventing the smuggling of and illegal trade in fissile materials. Thus the Norwegian authorities co-operate with the Russian authorities as well as with the authorities in Sweden and Finland to improve the control and physical protection of fissile materials in the north-western region of Russia. In his Statement to the Storting on Foreign Policy in January 1996, the Foreign Minister declared that negotiations on an agreement prohibiting the production of fissile materials for weapons use should be started "as soon as possible". The Government has since made it clear that it thinks such negotiations ought to be the next major item on the agenda of the CD[24]. It has also emphasised that more effective measures are needed for registering, managing and monitoring existing stocks of plutonium. In addition it would like to see a regime that would include the declaration of stockpiles

---

[22] Ole KOPREITAN, *"Undergraver USA prøvestansavtalen?"*, in: **Dagbladet**, Oslo, 19 February 1997.

[23] Statement by State Secretary Siri Bjerke, 13 June 1996.

[24] *Ibid.*

of all weapon-grade materials and other transparency measures[25]. Moreover, Norway is strongly supportive of the ongoing efforts to strengthen the IAEA safeguards regime, for instance by introducing on-site and random inspections in order to prevent the diversion of fissile materials as well as sensitive technology.

7. Conventional Disarmament

Norway is not only concerned about the dangers of nuclear proliferation and nuclear waste. As nuclear weapons are dismantled, the focus is shifting to conventional weapons. Norway was pleased that it proved possible in December 1995, after two years of negotiations, to establish a new forum for export control of conventional weapons and sensitive advanced technology that can be used for military purposes. Norway takes an active part in this forum. Nevertheless, the Government would like to see more efforts being made to achieve conventional disarmament, and Norway is in favour of extending the agenda of the CD to include conventional disarmament.

With regard to conventional disarmament, the CFE agreement occupies a unique position. Although Norway has consistently supported mutual and balanced reductions in forces and material on the European continent, it has also been concerned about the consequences of CFE for the flanks. At the Review Conference for the CFE in 1996 Russia sought to obtain a redefinition of the flank zones which would permit a higher ceiling on military vehicles in parts of these zones[26]. Norway and Turkey's efforts to prevent a renegotiation of the CFE as long as Russia had not fully implemented the agreement were not very successful[27]. The Review Conference allowed Russia to postpone implementation for another three years. The parties also agreed that

---

[25] *Ibid.*; Statement by Foreign Minister Bjørn Tore Godal at the Review and Extension Conference of the Parties to the Treaty on the Non-Proliferation of Nuclear Weapons, New York, 19 April 1995.

[26] *"CFE-avtalen-Nedrustning til bekymring"*, in: **NTB-tekst**, Oslo, Document No.96-016471, 16 April 1996.

[27] *"Flankespørsmålet blokkerer CFE-forhandlingene i Wien"*, in: **NTB-tekst**, Oslo, Document No.96-023476, 31 May 1996; *"Norge tapte på CFE-konferansen i Wien – russerne vant"*, in: **NTB-tekst**, Oslo, Document No.96-023676, 1 June 1996; *"CFE-avtalen – store muligheter og mange fallgruver"*, in: **NTB-tekst**, Oslo, Document No.96-023741, 2 June 1996.

the agreement should be adapted to the new post-Cold War situation in Europe. The Norwegian reaction to the result was to say that Norway understands Russia's need for reinforcements on its southern flank[28]. Nevertheless, Norway will be wary of possible changes to the regime that would permit large transfers of forces or material to the flanks.

With regard to conventional weapons, the Norwegian Government has shown a particular concern about the use of antipersonnel land mines which it considers among the most insidiously destructive weapons commonly used in war. This concern is based on experience from many years of involvement in United Nations peacekeeping and mine clearing missions[29]. Norway has consistently advocated a total ban on the production, transfer and use of antipersonnel mines. In June 1995 the Government declared a moratorium on the production, stockpiling, transfer and use of such mines. By mid-1996 all such mines in Norwegian military stockpiles had been removed and destroyed. The Government is in favour of starting negotiations as soon as possible on a comprehensive ban on antipersonnel mines. It is also putting money and effort into remedying the existing situation. So far Norway has trained more than 1000 mine clearance specialists and 400 mine awareness instructors in various countries. Norway has also just started a pilot mine clearance programme in the former Yugoslavia. Furthermore, Norway has contributed about 1.3 million USD to the UN Trust Fund for Assistance in Mine Clearance. In regard to antipersonnel land mines, Norway is thus doing her best to back up its political views with the maximum practical effort. This is a good example of how Norway has, over a number of years, made consistent efforts to follow political declarations with deeds and financial contributions.

8. NATO Enlargement

The Norwegian Government supports the eastward expansion of NATO. Enlargement is primarily seen as a way of enhancing Euro-

---

[28] *"Frykter ikke russisk styrkeoppbygning på Kola"*, in: **NTB-tekst**, Document No.96-024385, 6 June 1996.

[29] The following is based on a draft speech for a meeting of the Security Council entitled *"De-mining in the context of United Nations peace-keeping"*, dated 15 August 1996.

pean integration and security, and such integration is seen as a means to advance the political and economic stability of the East European countries[30].

When confronted with questions about Russia's hostile reaction to the plans for NATO enlargement, the Norwegian Foreign Minister will invariably answer with a counterquestion: "How can NATO refuse membership to the East European countries when they ask for it?" The Government is of course well aware of Russia's hostile attitude to this issue. The Foreign Minister has attributed this attitude to the Russian fear of isolation, and to the fear of being surrounded by an alliance which the Russians have traditionally regarded as their main enemy[31]. The Government no doubt perceives the avoidance of confrontation with Russia over this issue as a particularly challenging task[32]. The Foreign Minister has indeed stated that "enlargement would be a mistake if it were to result in the development of new dividing lines or the resurrection of old ones.[33]" However, the Government hopes that NATO will be able to persuade the Russians that NATO's role has changed in the post-Cold War world, and that there is consequently no need for Russia to feel threatened[34].

Not all parties share this optimistic attitude. When the issue of NATO expansion was debated in the Storting in February 1997, views differed. The Government enjoyed the support of a solid majority on this issue, but two parties, the Socialist Party and the Centre Party (in addition to the one Communist representative) diverged from the consensus. The socialists were strongly opposed to the eastwards shift of the limit of NATO's Article 5 guarantee. They maintained that the expansion would be a grave mistake since it could provoke Russia to retaliate by introducing dangerous new military measures[35]. At a later stage, the leader of the Socialist Party suggested that Russia should

---

[30] *"Enlargement eastwards of the EU and NATO"*, speech by Foreign Minister Bjørn Tore Godal, Europaforum Conference, Oslo, 28 October 1995.

[31] Bjørn Tore Godal, *"Nye sikkerhetspolitiske utfordringer for de nordiske land"*, Oslo handelsgymnasium, 3 November 1995.

[32] *Ibid.*

[33] *Ibid.*

[34] Per Vassbotn, *"Nå er det NATO"*, in: **Dagbladet**, 14 February 1997.

[35] *Ibid.*

become a "political member" of NATO. By this he meant that Russia should be invited to take part in NATO's decision-making with the exception of decisions pertaining to Article 5[36]. The Centre Party was equivocal. It is on record as supporting enlargement on the condition that this will not create more tension in Europe.

The Government's answer to the critics is to point out that NATO has changed and does not represent a threat to Russia. It also supports all efforts to integrate Russia in European co-operation, and especially to strengthen the special co-operation between NATO and Russia. Partnership for Peace is the key here, but the Government is willing to go further to accommodate the Russians. There can be little doubt, however, that there is considerable apprehension in Norway that the enlargement of NATO could trigger an unfortunate development both inside Russia and in Russia's willingness to co-operate with NATO. The uncertainty created by this situation has a strong influence on Norwegian threat perceptions (see below).

9. Co-operation in the Barents Region

In January 1993 the Barents Co-operation was formally established, thus laying the basis for wide-ranging regional co-operation in the North. It is a joint venture in which Norway, Sweden, Finland and Russia take part. In Norway this is perceived as Norway's most important contribution to the integration of Russia into international co-operative structures and thus to the construction of the new Europe[37].

From the beginning, the overriding goal of the Barents Co-operation was related to security policy in the broadest sense of the word[38]. It had two main aims. The first was to create a network of co-operation between the Nordic countries and Russia, which would serve to normalise relations across the East-West divide. The second was to promote economic and social development in the Barents region itself, i.e.

---

[36] Erik SOLHEIM, *"Russland bør bli 'politisk medlem'"*, in: **Dagbladet**, Oslo, 12 March 1997, p.3.

[37] *"Enlargement eastwards of the EU and NATO"*, speech by Foreign Minister Bjørn Tore Godal, Europaforum Conference, Oslo, 28 October 1995.

[38] Foreign Minister Bjørn Tore Godal, Statement to the Storting on the Barents Co-operation, 24 April 1995.

the northern parts of Norway, Sweden and Finland, and the north-western part of Russia. However, co-operation is not limited to these countries. The European Commission is also taking an active part in this venture. A Regional Council was given responsibility for drawing up an action plan. One such plan is the Barents Region Environmental Action Program, which focuses on radioactive contamination and nuclear safety. This plan reflects the fact that the Kola peninsula is the site of one of the largest concentrations of military installations in the world, and that it also suffers from heavy industrial pollution.

The plan covers four main areas: the safety of nuclear installations, sound management of nuclear waste, problems associated with the dumping of nuclear waste, and arms-related environmental hazards[39]. In regard to arms control, the nuclear submarines in the area pose a particular problem. Russia has about 90 nuclear submarines[40] with nuclear fuel on board waiting to be dismantled. At present, Russia only has the capacity to dismantle two nuclear submarines per year[41]. This means that dealing with these outdated submarines is a huge task. In September 1996 the defence ministries of Norway, Russia and the United States signed an agreement on military environmental co-operation in the Arctic. The aim of the agreement is to contribute to remedying some of the immediate dangers in the Arctic region.

10. Threat Perception

To the extent that the Government has commented in public on threat perceptions, the focus has been on threats to international peace and security in general. In this context, the Foreign Minister has singled out regional conflicts outside Europe as constituting the largest challenge. He has pointed to the dangers inherent in ethnic and religious disputes, territorial disputes, social instability and fundamentalist mentalities. He has advocated that non-proliferation efforts should take into consideration these underlying causes of conflict and ten-

---

[39] *Ibid.*

[40] This figure may be too low. The figure of 155 submarines has also been mentioned; see Hans-Wilhelm STEINFELD, *"Trusselbildets troverdighet"*, in: **Dagbladet**, 19 February 1997.

[41] *Ibid.*

sion, and he has maintained that non-proliferation efforts must include political conflict-solving. He has mentioned confidence-building measures as well as regional arms control measures as answers to such potential conflicts[42].

But even if the Government seems to be de-emphasising potential threats in Europe, there are indications that Norway's proximity to the Russian naval base on the Kola peninsula is causing some anxiety. This is probably not linked to fear of a possible attack on Norway, but to potential dangers that could result from a broader conflict or from a social upheaval in Russia. And it is especially linked to the fact that the importance of the Kola naval base has increased as a result of the dissolution of the Soviet Union. Norwegian concern about developments in the Arctic can also be seen in Norway's attitude to conventional disarmament. In this connection Norway underlines the importance of taking into consideration the changes that have taken place in Europe in the post-Cold War period, and of defining the extension of the flank areas accordingly.

The growing importance of the Kola naval base has also led to a change in Norwegian policy with regard to military exercises. From the early 1950s until the 1990s, Norway did not as a general rule permit Allied military exercises to take place east of the 24th meridian. This policy was usually portrayed as a confidence-building measure directed at the former Soviet Union, but it was modified in 1995 in spite of a strong negative reaction on the part of Russia.

Russia's hostile reaction to NATO's plans for eastward enlargement has further contributed to emphasising the risks inherent in being the neighbour of a superpower in a state of political upheaval. Norwegian commentators have expressed concern that NATO expansion might trigger a Russian arms build-up. Given this situation, representatives of the Norwegian peace movement have proposed linking the enlargement of NATO to a change in the military doctrines of both NATO and Russia. They have argued that NATO expansion would be likely to cause less fear and insecurity if NATO and Russia were simultaneously to start negotiations with a view to relinquishing their

---

[42] Speech by Foreign Minister Bjørn Tore Godal, the Nobel Institute, Oslo, 23 March 1996.

first-use doctrines. They have, furthermore, suggested that NATO might initiate the process by a unilateral declaration to this effect. The idea seems to be that Russia and NATO should, for the time being, maintain a nuclear arsenal to deter other nuclear powers. But in a longer perspective the abandonment of first-use should be followed by negotiations on complete nuclear disarmament involving all nuclear powers[43].

Given Norway's support for the 1996 Malaysian resolution at the United Nations, there is reason to believe that the Jagland Government might in principle endorse such a scenario. At present, however, the Government is still supporting the first-use doctrine, as expressed for instance in the communiqué of the NATO Foreign Ministers' meeting in December 1996. Nevertheless, it would seem that the Government is slightly worried that Russia is placing more emphasis on the role of nuclear weapons in its defence planning in the post-Gorbachev period. The Norwegian Foreign Minister has said that NATO should enter into a dialogue with Russia regarding this issue, with a view to convincing the Russians of the wisdom of treating nuclear weapons as "weapons of last resort[44]", as NATO decided to do in 1990[45]. According to the Foreign Minister, this would imply a de facto no-first-use doctrine[46].

There are reasons to doubt whether the Government would have the necessary support in the Storting if it were to go further than this. Norway's support for the Malaysian resolution encountered strong criticism in several political parties. Godal's statement in January 1997, in which he expressed a wish to accelerate the disarmament process in Europe, also met with criticism from the Conservative Party. Commenting on this statement, Anders C. Sjaastad, a former Defence Minister, declared that Norway's defence capacity was already too weak. Sjaastad thought Godal's statement showed a lack of understanding of the European scene. According to Sjaastad, "our

---

[43] Erik ALFSEN, Bjørn KIRKERUD & Bent NATVIG, *"NATO-utvidelse og atomvåpen"*, in: **Dagbladet**, Oslo, 26 February 1997, p.42.

[44] Speech by Foreign Minister Bjørn Tore Godal, the Nobel Institute, Oslo, 23 March 1996.

[45] Erik ALFSEN, Bjørn KIRKERUD & Bent NATVIG, *"NATO-utvidelse og atomvåpen"*, in: **Dagbladet**, Oslo, 26 February 1997, p.42.

[46] Speech by Foreign Minister Bjørn Tore Godal, the Nobel Institute, Oslo, 23 March 1996.

great neighbour to the east" was in such a fragile position that the whole world held its breath whenever there was any sign of the Russian president's health deteriorating. Against this background, he questioned the Foreign Minister's assessment of the security situation in Europe and the wisdom of further disarmament[47].

11. Conclusion

Over the last year or so there have been signs of a reawakened interest in the question of disarmament among the Norwegian public as well as among the political parties. This recent debate has partly been a reaction to what is perceived as a stronger stance regarding disarmament on the part of the Jagland government. While Government policy is considered to be too radical in conservative quarters, it is thought not to go far enough in left-wing circles and among some peace activists. The debate is also partly a response to NATO's plans for eastward enlargement, and as such it reflects divergent views on the security situation in Europe.

During Mrs. Brundtland's premiership, the Government was on record as supporting a cut-off agreement as well as new strategic and tactical nuclear weapons reductions by all nuclear powers including the smaller ones. It advocated a strengthening of the IAEA safeguards system and extended safeguards in nuclear weapon states. It also advocated measures amounting to a ban on the production of new warheads and the destruction of nuclear test site installations. It underlined the importance of ensuring the implementation of existing disarmament agreements as well as making sure they were followed up. At the CD, the Government prioritised negotiations on a cut-off of fissile materials. At the same time, it argued that conventional disarmament should be negotiated at the CD. In fact it seemed to take a particular interest in conventional disarmament, and was actively pursuing a ban on antipersonnel land mines. When possible, the Government sought to contribute by practical means to advancing disarmament efforts. With regard to the question of deploying nuclear weapons in pos-

---

[47] *"Sjaastad: Norges forsvar like viktig i dag"*, in: **NTB-tekst**, Document No.97-003371, 24 January 1997.

sible new NATO member states in Eastern Europe, the Government advocated a "Norwegian" solution, meaning no deployment of nuclear weapons in peacetime. However, Brundtland's Government did not show any interest in the idea of a nuclear weapon free zone in Central Europe.

The Jagland government has taken the strong Norwegian anti-nuclear stance a step further by supporting a proposal for negotiating a treaty prohibiting nuclear weapons. This support could be interpreted as meaning that Norway is willing to go as far as politically possible in its efforts to promote nuclear disarmament, even as far as putting pressure on its nuclear allies. If the Government decides to pursue this goal actively, it is likely to meet opposition from both military allies and domestic political parties. On the home front, the Government's recent emphasis on disarmament has been criticised on two grounds. One argument points to the importance of maintaining NATO cohesion. The other argument pertains to the Government's risk assessment in regard to the Russian and European scene. The recent debate on disarmament and NATO enlargement shows that Norwegian political parties and the general public hold a diversity of views on the security situation in Europe. The debate furthermore reveals that Norway's willingness to disarm is likely to be at least partly a function of how social, political, and military developments in Russia are judged.

NOTES ON THE CONTRIBUTORS

THANOS DOKOS is Director for Research at the Strategic Studies Division, Hellenic Ministry of National Defence.

ASTRID FORLAND has recently completed her doctoral thesis on the genesis of the International Atomic Energy Agency's safeguard system. She has written extensively on Norwegian university history as well as on the history of Norway's nuclear programme.

VICENTE GARRIDO REBOLLEDO is Professor of International Public Law, European Community Law and Security and Defence Studies in the Political Sciences Faculty at the Complutense University, Madrid. He is also Coordinator of Non-Proliferation Projects at the Peace Research Center (CIP) Madrid and a Lecturer in Strategic Studies at the Spanish Army Staff College. From 1995 to 1997 he was a NATO Research Fellow.

CAMILLE GRAND is a Research Fellow at the Institut des Relations Internationales et Stratégiques (IRIS), Université Paris Nord. He is a Lecturer at the Ecole spéciale militaire (St.-Cyr-Coëtquidan) and an Assistant Lecturer at the Université Paris Nord. He is also the Editor of the quarterly *Relations Internationales et Stratégiques*.

DARRYL HOWLETT is a Senior Research Fellow in the Mountbatten Centre for International Studies, University of Southampton and since 1987 he has been the Information Officer for the Programme for Promoting Nuclear Non-Proliferation (PPNN).

ALEXANDER KELLE is a Research Associate at Peace Research Institute Frankfurt. He obtained his Ph.D. in summer 1996 at Frankfurt University.

MUSTAFA KIBAROGLU is Assistant Professor at the International Relations Department at Bilkent University, Ankara

STEPHAN KLEMENT is currently a Junior Professional Officer at the Safeguards and Non-Proliferation Policy Section, Division of External Relations, IAEA. In 1996/97 he was an Erwin Schrödinger Visiting Research Fellow at the Mountbatten Centre for International Studies, University of Southampton. He holds a Ph.D. degree in Physics and in International Law.

QUENTIN MICHEL is an Assistant at the Public and Administration Law Department of the University of Liège.

HARALD MÜLLER is the Director of Peace Research Institute Frankfurt (PRIF) and Director of PRIF's Nonproliferation Programme. He is Associate Professor at the Technical University Darmstadt and Visiting Professor at the Johns Hopkins University Bologna Center, Italy.

ERZSÉBET N. RÓZSA is a Research Fellow at the Hungarian Institute of International Affairs. She is a guest lecturer at the University of Economics at the Department of International Relations, Budapest, and at the University of Miskolc at the Department of Political Science. She holds a Ph.D. degree in International Relations.

JIRI SEDIVY is the Deputy Director of the Institute of International Relations, Prague. He is also a lecturer at Charles University Prague, Institute of Politology.

JOHN SIMPSON is Director of the Mountbatten Centre at the University of Southampton. He is also Director of the Programme for Promoting Nuclear Non-Proliferation (PPNN). He is a member of the UK Ministerial Panel on Arms Control and Disarmament.

GENOWEFA SMAGALA is a Senior Specialist at the Central Laboratory for Radiological Protection in Warsaw.

RADOSLAVA STEFANOVA is a Bulgarian Research Fellow at the Institute of International Affairs (IAI) in Rome, Italy.

ROLF TAMNES is Director of the Institute for Defence Studies in Oslo. He also holds a professorship at the University of Oslo.

PANAYOTIS TSAKONAS is Special Adviser at the Strategic Studies Division, Hellenic Ministry of National Defence.

LARS VAN DASSEN is a Research Fellow and Ph.D. candidate at the Department of Peace and Conflict Research at Uppsala University, Sweden.

MARIANNE VAN LEEUWEN is acting Deputy Director of Studies at the Netherlands Institute of International Relations "Clingendael" in The Hague.

WILLIAM WALKER is Professor of International Relations at the School of History and International Relations, University of St. Andrews, Scotland.

M. CRISTINA ZADRA was a Research Fellow at the Centro di Studi Politici Internazionali (CeSPI), Roma, until summer 1997. She is now a consultant on defence matters for the Gruppo Verdi – l'Ulivo at the Italian Senate.

MOST USED ABBREVIATIONS

BWC	Biological Weapons Convention
CD	Conference on Disarmament
CFE	Conventional Armed Forces in Europe
CFSP	Common Foreign and Security Policy
CSCE	Conference on Security and Cooperation in Europe
CTBT	Comprehensive Test Ban Treaty
CWC	Chemical Weapons Convention
EPC	European Political Co-operation
EU	European Union
FSU	Former Soviet Union
HEU	Highly Enriched Uranium
IAEA	International Atomic Energy Agency
ICJ	International Court of Justice
INF	Intermediate Nuclear Forces
MOX	Mixed Oxide Fuel
MTCR	Missile Technology Control Regime
NACC	North Atlantic Cooperation Council
NATO	North Atlantic Treaty Organization
NGO(s)	Non-Governmental Organization(s)
NNWS	Non-Nuclear Weapon State(s)
NPT	Nuclear Non-Proliferation Treaty
NSG	Nuclear Suppliers Group
NWFZ	Nuclear-Weapons-Free Zone(s)
NWS	Nuclear Weapon State(s)
OSCE	Organization for Security and Cooperation in Europe
PfP	Partnership for Peace
PTBT	Partial Test Ban Treaty
START	Strategic Arms Reduction Treaty
UN	United Nations
UNGA	United Nations General Assembly
UNSCOM	United Nations Special Committee
WEU	Western European Union
WMD	Weapons of Mass Destruction
WTO	Warsaw Treaty Organization

nuclear weapons could be brought into the country along with Allied reinforcements[1].

Later, the Norwegian authorities were at times anxious to play down the nuclear aspects of the Alliance. The most visible expressions of this were Norway's policy towards visiting warships carrying nuclear weapons; the idea of nuclear weapon free zones; and the attitude to NATO's plan for the deployment of Intermediate-range Nuclear Forces (INF).

In October 1975 the then Prime Minister, Trygve Bratteli, stated that "our assumption when foreign warships make port visits has been and is still that nuclear weapons are not carried on board." He expected that the Alliance would recognise this stance. The declaration was vague enough not to give rise to serious misgivings in Washington, as it took into consideration the fact that the nuclear powers would neither confirm nor deny (NCND) that their vessels carried nuclear weapons[2].

The question became much more controversial in the 1980s, when countries such as New Zealand and Denmark challenged the American NCND policy. The Labour Government in Norway was tempted to follow suit, but preferred in the end to stick to the 1975 doctrine, both because of the harsh US reaction to New Zealand's challenge and because of warnings that a similar Norwegian move might create huge problems for the NATO fleet on exercises in the north, and, at worst, endanger US commitments to Norway.

3. The Idea of Nuclear Weapon Free Zones

The idea of a Nordic nuclear weapon free zone was first put forward by the Soviet Union in the late 1950s, and was later promoted

---

[1] Background: Rolf TAMNES, *"Integration and Screening. The Two Faces of Norwegian Alliance Policy, 1945-1986"*, in: **Forsvarsstudier**, Oslo, 1987; Rolf TAMNES, *"Handlefrihet og lojalitet, Norge og atompolitikken i 1950-årene"*, in: T. BERG & H.Ø. PHARO (eds), **Historiker og veileder. Festskrift til Johan Sverdrup**, Oslo, Tiden, 1989; Rolf TAMNES, **The United States and the Cold War in the High North**, Oslo, ad Notam forlag, 1991.

[2] See Johan Jørgen HOLST, *"Atom- og basepolitikken i søkelyset"*, in: A.C. SJAASTAD (ed.), **Norsk Utenrikspolitisk Årbok**, Oslo, 1975.

most vigorously by the Finnish President, Urho Kekkonen. Norway rejected the idea for many years, both because such weapons were not stationed in Norway in peacetime and because the proposals did not imply any restrictions on Soviet nuclear capabilities. In 1980-81, however, the governing Labour Party endorsed the concept in principle, to the great irritation of the Americans. We can assess this as part of a long process which saw Norway becoming gradually more restrictive in nuclear matters. Initially the idea seemed to be a major departure from former positions, but as it was gradually tied to a series of conditions, implementation would necessarily be delayed. One of the reasons for this increasing Norwegian caution was the NATO and US reactions. Most notably, in July 1981 Secretary of State Alexander M. Haig rejected emphatically the idea of a Nordic zone, asserting that it might jeopardise the bilateral ties between the two countries[3].

Another aspect of the zone question was Norway's involvement in the discussion of nuclear weapon free zones in Central Europe. This involvement started with the Polish Rapacki Plan in 1957. At the NATO Heads of Government meeting in Paris in December 1957, Prime Minister Einar Gerhardsen signalled his willingness to discuss disengagement and nuclear weapon free zones in Central Europe in the spirit of the Rapacki Plan. The most challenging aspect of these proposals was that if pursued, they would have delayed the incorporation of atomic weapons into the German armed forces, much to the annoyance of the United States. Although the prospects of establishing such a zone were slim, the Polish plans provided for many years the basis of an interesting bilateral dialogue between Norway and Poland.

At the end of the 1970s the zone question reappeared in a new form, first in the split over neutron weapons and later in NATO's 1979 decision to deploy INF missiles. In the face of fierce popular resistance to this modernisation, the Norwegian Government emphasised the need for arms negotiations prior to deployment. In 1982 and 1983 the Labour Party, now in opposition, formulated an increasingly critical stand towards Western deployment, although, in contrast to the German Social Democrats, it never renounced the NATO decision of 1979.

---

[3] See John C. AUSLAND, **Nordic Security and the Great Powers**, Boulder/London, Westview Press, 1986.

Norway's bases and nuclear policies were part of a broader system of unilateral confidence building measures. It must be emphasised, though, that these measures did not prevent Norway from preparing for the reception of Allied reinforcements, nor did they preclude the option of using nuclear weapons in the High North in the event of war. Thus, while reinforcement from outside was important in many scenarios for the Central Front, it was the very essence of NATO strategy for the High North.

The evolution of NATO's strategy after the Cold War indicates that the "Norwegian model" is becoming more universal. Most notably, instead of the maintenance of a substantial physical peacetime presence in Eastern Europe, flexible plans for rapid reinforcement seem to have become an interesting alternative. The Norwegian Government is most certainly in favour of such an extension of the "Norwegian model"[4]. However, the Government has not shown any inclination to revive the idea of a nuclear weapon free zone in Central Europe.

4. Arms Control in the late 1990s

Generally speaking, nuclear disarmament issues have not figured highly in the public debate in Norway in the 1990s. The reason may well be that the general public has been content with developments in this field, which to a large extent have focused on the implementation of new arms control measures and the dismantling of existing weapons of mass destruction. This seems to be confirmed by the exception to the rule, namely the reaction to the French nuclear tests which took place as the negotiations on a Comprehensive Test Ban Treaty were drawing to an end in Geneva. The French tests provoked a very strong public reaction, reflected for instance in a sharp decline in the consumption of French wine! It is also worth mentioning that the Norwegian Nobel Committee's choice of Pugwash and Joseph Rotblat for the Nobel Peace prize for 1995 was exceptionally well received by the Norwegian public. Norway has several nongovernmental organisations which put continuous pressure on the government to

---

[4] Speech by Foreign Minister Bjørn Tore Godal, the Nobel Institute, Oslo, 23 March 1996.

pursue disarmament, including some concerned specifically with nuclear disarmament *(Nei til atomvåpen, Leger mot atomvåpen)*. In addition there is a forceful environmental organisation, **Bellona**, which has been particularly active with regard to the nuclear waste and safety problems in north-western Russia.

Until recently, it had also seemed that attitudes to nuclear disarmament were fairly uniform among the political parties, at least among the larger political parties which have any prospect of ruling the country. It should be added that there is a strong tradition in Norway for political parties to display a "common front" in matters of importance to national security. Lately, however, there have been indications that the consensus is breaking down. A new divide is discernible both over the issue of nuclear disarmament and over NATO's eastward expansion. The differences of opinion seem at least partly to reflect divergent threat perceptions (see below). As a small power, Norway's influence in the international community is, of course, limited. Nevertheless, Norway has traditionally put great weight on contributing, as far as possible, to efforts in international fora to enhance the process of disarmament in the world. In 1996, Norway became a member of the Conference on Disarmament (CD) in Geneva. It will be interesting to see whether this will lead to more public debate regarding the positions taken by Norway in Geneva.

5. A Nuclear Weapons Convention?

There are indications that Norway has been following a slightly more radical policy with regard to nuclear disarmament since Torbjørn Jagland succeeded Gro Harlem Brundtland as Prime Minister in the autumn of 1996. The shift in emphasis first became apparent in connection with the Malaysian resolution on the abolition of nuclear weapons at the United Nations in November 1996. Whereas NATO countries generally voted against this resolution, Norway (and Denmark) abstained from the vote. Norway supported the resolution's proposal for the complete abolition of nuclear weapons. The reason for Norway's abstention was the fact that the Government disagreed with the resolution's suggestion that this goal should be achieved through multilateral disarmament negotiations conducted under the aegis of the

C